Marketing Analysis and Forecasting

Made Simple

The Made Simple series
has been created
especially for self-education
but can equally well
be used as
an aid to group study.
However complex the subject,
the reader is taken
step by step,
clearly and methodically
through the course. Each volume
has been prepared by experts,
taking account of
modern educational requirements,
to ensure the most
effective way of
acquiring knowledge.

In the same series

Accounting
Acting and Stagecraft
Additional Mathematics
Administration in Business
Advertising
Anthropology
Applied Economics
Applied Mathematics
Applied Mechanics
Art Appreciation
Art of Speaking
Art of Writing
Biology
Book-keeping
Britain and the European
  Community
British Constitution
Business and Administrative
  Organisation
Business Calculations
Business Economics
Business Law
Business Statistics and Accounting
Calculus
Chemistry
Childcare
Child Development
Commerce
Company Law
Company Practice
Computer Programming
Computers and Microprocessors
Cookery
Cost and Management Accounting
Data Processing
Economic History
Economic and Social Geography
Economics
Effective Communication
Electricity
Electronic Computers
Electronics
English
English Literature
Financial Management
First Aid
French
Geology
German

Housing, Tenancy and Planning
  Law
Human Anatomy
Human Biology
Italian
Journalism
Latin
Law
Management
Marketing
Mathematics
Metalwork
Modelling and Beauty Care
Modern Biology
Modern Electronics
Modern European History
Modern Mathematics
Modern World Affairs
Money and Banking
Music
New Mathematics
Office Administration
Office Practice
Organic Chemistry
Personnel Management
Philosophy
Photography
Physical Geography
Physics
Practical Typewriting
Psychiatry
Psychology
Public Relations
Public Sector Economics
Rapid Reading
Religious Studies
Russian
Salesmanship
Secretarial Practice
Social Services
Sociology
Spanish
Statistics
Technology
Teeline Shorthand
Twentieth-Century British History
Typing
Woodwork

Marketing Analysis and Forecasting

Made Simple

P. Clifton, MA (Oxon),
T. H. Nguyen, MBA (Louvain) and
S. E. Nutt

**MADE SIMPLE
B O O K S**

Made Simple Books
HEINEMANN : London

Printed by Richard Clay (The Chaucer Press) Ltd., Bungay, Suffolk.

British Library Cataloguing in Publication Data
Clifton, P.
    Marketing analysis and forecasting made simple.
    — (Made simple books, ISSN 0265-0541)
    1. Marketing research   2. Sales forecasting
    I. Title   II. Nguyen, T.H.   III. Nutt, S.E.
    IV. Series
    658.8'18   HF5415.2

ISBN 0 434 98583 X

Notes on Authors and Examples

Peter Clifton was Manager, Market Research, at ITT Europe from 1973 to 1978, and his experience of the practicalities of carrying out and training a thirteen-country team in analysis and forecasting prompted him to write this book. After a period in new product development with STC, he now runs Peter Clifton Research in London. He has been in marketing research, strategic studies and new product development for twenty-five years, including nine years in Europe, and has worked in a wide variety of consumer and industrial markets, including food, metals, plastics, brown goods, construction products, terminals and telecommunications.

Hai Nguyen has extensive experience of statistical forecasting and quantitative packages including Box-Jenkins and CUSUM techniques for forecast monitoring. After four years of large company experience in forecasting and market assessment, he was appointed Marketing Director of a high technology new venture corporation for the University of Louvain and the Region Wallonne. He is now a consultant in industrial development to the Mekong Secretariat, a Bangkok-based United Nations Committee, responsible for projects financed by the Belgian Government.

Susan Nutt has over ten years' experience of practical industrial and consumer market research, interviewing and report-writing in a wide variety of markets in the EEC, Iberia and Scandinavia.

Most of the material in this book refers to actual markets in Germany, France and the UK. These have been generalised as 'Unteland', a country whose characteristics resemble those of the three countries without matching them exactly, in order to avoid projection of the personal prejudices of the student and to defend the confidentiality of the original material. Money appears in Unteland dollars ($U).

Acknowledgements

The Authors gratefully acknowledge the help of: Mr Steven Joseph of the Conference Permanente des Chambres de Commerce et d'Industrie de la Communauté Européenne; Mr Horst Rudolf of Compagnon Marktforschung; Mr Jan Standaert of Usson-du-Poitou, 8635 France; Mr Ivan Mentre of ECM Development; Dr Kurt Hammerich of Dr Reimund Muller Marketing und Marktforschung; Mr Andrew McIntosh and Mr Edwin Smith of IFF Research Ltd; Mr V. A. Smith of Acumen Marketing; Mr Clifford Prowse of Frost and Sullivan; Mr P. J. T. Gorle of Metra Consulting; Mr Nigel Spackman of RSGB London; Mr Peter Funck of MM & S, Paris; Mr M. Schillinger of Contest-Census; Mr M. T. Laurnece of Atkins Planning; Mr Donald Osborne of Donald Osborne Research Ltd; Mr Gerard Hermet of Burke Marketing Research; Mr Gordon Heald of Gallup; Mr Ph. Perrot-Desnoix of Perrot-Denoix et Cie; and Mr Roger Gane of AGB Research Ltd, for their advice on how and how not to translate intentions to purchase into forecasts of how much will be bought. The Authors also wish to thank Texas Instruments for permission to quote the t scores; Business International S.A. of 12–14 Chemin Rieu, Geneva, for permission to quote from their market indicators from *Business Europe*; Mr Colin Walpole of BIS Marketing Research Ltd for his permission to use his case study for choosing a market research agency as the basis of an exercise; Mr Christopher J. West of Industrial Market Research Ltd for permission to reproduce the sample size calculator; Mr W. F. Harper of ITTE for advice on questionnaire design and consumer research; ITT for permission to quote from *Facts*; Control Data Corporation for illustrations of computer-based forecasts; and A. D. Little for figures of numbers of businesses in the UK, France and Germany.

Contents

Notes on Authors and Examples   v

Acknowledgements   vi

---

1 Marketing Analysis   1
   Why Marketing Analysis?   1
   What is Marketing Analysis?   2
   Key Concepts   12
   Exercises   13

**2 Applying Marketing Concepts in Analysing a New
   Product's Potential**   14
   Principal Concepts for New Products   14
   Need Satisfied by the Product   15
   Competing Products   19
   Similar Products   20
   Price Thresholds   21
   Speed of Market Penetration   22
   Size of Market and Market Penetration 20 Years on   23
   Videotex as a Completely New Consumer Product   24
   Conclusion   29
   Key Concepts   29
   Exercises   30

3 How the Need for Marketing Research Arises   32
   Forecasting   32
   Why is the Information Required?   33
   Stages of Research   34
   Key Concepts   41
   Exercises   41

4 Organising Marketing Research   43
Product Familiarisation   43
Background Statistics   45
Literature Search   54
Fieldwork   55
Key Concepts   61
Exercises   61

5 The Size and Representativeness of the Sample   63
How Certain Do You Need To Be of the Answer?   63
How Large a Sample Do You Need?   64
Estimating Proportion of Population with an Exclusive
   Characteristic   65
Increasing the Sample   71
Confidence Limits for Random Samples of More than 30   72
Sampling Businesses in Practice   73
Some Practicalities of Consumer Sampling   75
Lack of Statistical Confidence Levels for Industrial and
   Distributor Samples   79
Methods of Deciding on Sample Size Used in Commerce   80
Key Concepts   81
Exercises   82

6 Industrial Marketing Research   84
Groups Likely To Be Interviewed   84
Industry Structure—Drawing up the Sample to Represent
   the Whole Industry   86
List of Contacts   87
Method of Approach and Arranging Interview   88
The Schedule   92
Questionnaire or Aide-Memoire   94
Unstructured Interviewing and Conducting the Interview   95
Telephone Research   101
Postal Questionnaires   102
Key Concepts   106
Exercises   106

**7 Consumer Research—Continuous Research and
Questionnaire Design**   107
Continuous Research for Existing Products   108
The Problem of Significance   110
Own Research on New Products   111
Outside Research on Own Products   112
Discussions   113

Designing a Consumer Questionnaire 114
Going from Intentions to Buy to Forecasting Sales 120
Surveying New Sites for Retail Outlets 122
Summary 123
Key Concepts 124
Exercises 125

8 Export Marketing Research 127
Scope of Desk Research 127
Visits to Export Markets 130
Salespersons as Market Analysts in General 132
Task for Field Research—the Advance Party 133
Exercises 137

**9 Forecasting for an Existing Product—Quantitative
Techniques** 138
Quantitative Demand Analysis 138
Extrapolation from Past Data 140
Moving Average to Highlight Underlying Movement of
a Series 153
Seasonal Adjustment 159
Key Concepts 165
Exercises 166

**10 Forecasting for an Existing Product—the National
Market** 168
Why Bother Forecasting for Total Market or Industry? 168
Using Existing Market-related Information 169
Using Industry Consensus Forecasts 169
Longer-term Industry Forecasts 175
Methods of Forecasting Employed in the Business World 178
Exercises 181

11 Forecasting for an Existing Product—the Company 183
Using Market Share 183
Revising Forecasts—Forecast Monitoring 188
Summary 194
Key Concepts 195
Exercises 195

**12 Presenting the Report—Making Marketing Analysis
Actionable** 197
Personal Presentation of Report Findings 198
General Rules for Written Reports 205

Why Recommendations Are Worthwhile 211
Key Concepts 211
Exercises 211

13 Agency or In-house Research 213
Why Employ an Agency? 213
Finding Agencies 214
How to Get the Best from an Agency 217
Multi-client Surveys and Audits 218
Summary 218
Key Concepts 219
Exercise 219

14 Market Analysis and Business Strategies 225
Packaging Strategy Case Study 226
Common Elements in Strategy/Analysis Interface 238
Exercises 240

Statistical Workshops 241
A. Seasonal Adjustment 241
B. Applying Concepts of Time Series Analysis to Forecasts
of National Car Sales, Using Long-term Data 250

Appendices
1 Some Consultants Not Included in *The International
Research Directory of Market Research Organisations* 269
2 European Libraries and Sources of Information 270
3 Professional Marketing Research Institutions 273
4 Sample Size Calculator 274
5 t Scores 275
6 The Normal Distribution Tables 277
7 Bross Plan B Sequential Analysis Chart 279
8 Simple Checklist for Industrial Interviewing 280
9 Recommended Reading 281

Index 282

1
Marketing Analysis

This book has been written to aid students to acquire the tools of analysis and forecasting used in marketing, and to help those in manufacture and commerce who are interested in directing their work towards the satisfaction of customers' wants. Written by three colleagues with experience in both large and small companies, the book necessarily has a practical bias. This chapter explains marketing analysis, shows how the book is structured, and introduces some of the concepts of marketing by considering what marketing is.

Why Marketing Analysis?

John Wilmshurst has written in *The Fundamentals and Practice of Marketing* (Heinemann 1984) '... all company activity in production, engineering and finance, as well as marketing, must be devoted first to determining what the customer's wants are and then to satisfying those wants while still making a reasonable profit'. Satisfying the customer's wants is the goal of marketing; and a theme of all those who teach and practise marketing today is that marketing is too important to leave to the marketing department alone: with the growing complexity of manufacturing processes and products, and the long chains of distribution, a very large proportion of the workforce can lose that detailed awareness of what the customer wants, in terms of product, price, reliability and delivery, which normally feeds the inventiveness and motivation of the successful competitive company.

Distance from the customer can be due to over-nearness to the product, blotting out any vision of what needs the product serves. In product-dominated companies new products with every kind of enhancement may reach an uninterested customer who finds herself presented with something that has been developed solely because of the technical challenge it presents. Another dangerous distancing can occur where managers, owing to their own high incomes and distance from the ordinary customer, are unaware of price constraints in the market. The distorted views of the market held by people without awareness of customers' needs can be put forward with absolute conviction: the holders of the views have had years of industry experience, after all. So marketing analysis can be needed to provide a correct view of what the customer wants, and how much at a certain price; and the analysis needs to be done in a disciplined, professional and ably presented way in order to win acceptance.

The first task in marketing is to convince the world inside the company about the best way to market to the world outside. It can sometimes be the hardest task. Marketing analysis provides a bridge from the outside to the very centre of an enterprise.

What is Marketing Analysis?

Marketing analysis is the systematic understanding of the existing and potential market for a product or service, the provision of this information to management, and the making of recommendations on how the customers' wants might best be served. Everyone concerned with the production and exchange of goods for profit will have to study or make a marketing analysis at some time, and they will find that all the activities listed in the definition come into play. They are shown below:

ANALYSIS OF THE EXISTING MARKET	Understanding the customers' needs, how they are served now, prices paid, how suppliers compete, the strengths and weaknesses of one's own company with reference to the market, how the product reaches the customer, and other relevant factors.
ANALYSIS OF THE POTENTIAL MARKET	Forecasting future sales and trends as affected by changing customer habits and wealth, changes in technology and other factors.
PRESENTATION	Conveying the analysis to others so that they share the analyst's perception of the market with clarity and conviction.
RECOMMENDATIONS	Making recommendations related to the analysis (but not necessarily solely inspired by it) for marketing activity in the relevant market.

Plan of the Book

Marketing Analysis and Forecasting Made Simple familiarises the reader with marketing analysis at work in its first two chapters, and then follows the logic of analysis, forecasting, presentation and recommendations as the components of marketing analysis:

APPLYING THE CONCEPTS OF MARKETING ANALYSIS	After discussing some key concepts related to a definition of *marketing* (Chapter 1), Chapter 2 outlines how marketing concepts are applied to *Analysing a New Product's Potential*, using examples that include Videotex and the personal computer.
COLLECTING INFORMATION AND ANALYSING IT	Chapters 3 to 7 cover the practicalities of collecting information: *How the Need for Marketing Research Arises; Organising Marketing Research; Sampling;* and *Industrial, Consumer* and *Export Marketing Research.*
ANALYSIS OF THE POTENTIAL MARKET— FORECASTING	Chapters 9 to 11 are concerned with techniques of *Forecasting*. Examples of forecasting methods are laid out in full so that the learner can follow them with a calculator.
PRESENTATION AND RECOMMENDATIONS	Chapter 12, *Presenting the Report*, shows how to get the analysis across to busy entrepreneurs in an actionable form. Chapter 13 considers when it is necessary to go outside for marketing analysis in order to have a presentation that carries conviction, under the heading *Agency or In-House.*
STRATEGY AND DATA	Chapter 14 provides a final example of applying the tools of *Marketing Analysis* to *Business*

Strategies, related to the strategic problem posed by a competitor's launch of a new product. The *Statistical Workshops* and *Appendices* at the end of the book provide the details of how to build up a monthly sales forecast, and some useful addresses for the West European analyst.

Having set out the plan, we can begin to look at the concepts used in marketing analysis by considering what marketing is.

A Definition of Marketing

Marketing is the identification of evolving customer needs and satisfactions, and the offer of a mix of products, prices and promotion to profitably serve them. Each of the components of this definition will now be considered in detail, in order to widen our understanding of marketing concepts.

Identification of Evolving Customer Needs

Identification of customer needs can be extremely simple, as, for example, when a small business's customers tell it exactly what they want. Someone running a dry-cleaning service should be able to find out whether late-night opening is needed by simply asking customers about it and running a trial to see if the cost is justified.

But frequently the customers' needs are more complex than we might at first guess; because the product is complicated; because changes in trends are so slight that we are not sure if they are not just a temporary quirk; or because the reasons people give for choosing a product are no longer important (they say they eat high-fibre bread for health—but they have actually come to like the taste now, making them very loyal).

Complication can be illustrated with beers packed in plastic bottles for the off-licence trade. Should a brewer offer this packaging for one of his products? Marketing research might focus on the weight of the pack and whether it affects the taste of the beer, but until plastic bottles are familiar to the market-place, there may be a reaction of rejection by beer drinkers who are questioned, because of unfamiliarity.

A competitive product analysis showing which beers are already packed in this way, and at what price, will aid our judgement but will not answer all the questions, because the beers which happen to be packed in plastic may mainly be bought because of their price, type, taste and brewer. A look at what is happening in the USA—a *leading market* for consumer trends—would be useful for need identification, too, but not conclusive. A **test market** may be necessary before one can come to a conclusion in this case, as in many others.

Generally identification of customer needs and satisfactions is carried out by:

(*a*) monitoring sales trends in the market,
(*b*) monitoring sales trends in leading markets, often the USA,
(*c*) comparative product analysis,
(*d*) marketing research,
(*e*) test marketing.

Our example from the packaging of beer signals that these methods will *all* be used, and the identification of customer needs will be a continuing activity.

Identifying Customer Needs Leads to Market Segmentation

A better knowledge of customer needs will often lead to important distinctions between types of customer, and to a plan to direct marketing effort towards certain customer groups.

Let us consider the example of a service, introduced in the 1970s, called Videotex (formerly Viewdata) generally, and Prestel in the UK, to illustrate this. In this case we might look at what the product offers and try to match it to potential customers' needs, because the service has been created and we wish to participate in it—but only if it is worth our while. Videotex can transmit pages of information held on a distant computer to any colour television set, using the telephone and a special black box. What need might it satisfy?

The need it might satisfy is that for **information**. Immediately it makes sense, in a marketing analysis, to divide the market up into sectors of greater and smaller potential for information, and to have a look at characteristics of each sector in case they are so different as to suggest a different approach. For this new information product one immediately thinks of the difference between the business sector and the private (residential or home) sector. The characteristics are different—the business sector has a large appetite for hot information and the business machines it buys can be very expensive, while the private sector has buyers who have more occasional information needs, contains the rich as well as the poor, and includes people who are hungry for the latest novelty in consumer goods, no matter how expensive. But even more important, the number of households is far in excess of the number of businesses, and this could mean large volume sales of Videotex terminals and purchases of a high volume of information by subscribers.

Marketing analysis will show these facts in a table. As will be seen in Chapter 12 (p. 197), the businessman needs information to be shown as succinctly as possible. The table is the basis of the display of many facts, and Table 1.1 provides an example.

Table 1.1. Characteristics of Potential Videotex Market Sectors in Unteland

		1989
	Business	*Households*
Relevant linked products or services	Libraries and information officers— Information	Colour television (CTV)
'Park'* of same products/services	30,000 professional librarians	13,500,000 CTVs
Penetration of Videotex possible within 20 years	100%	15%
Tolerance of prices over £200	High	Low
Need for information	High	Medium
Importance of fashion	Medium to low	Medium to high

*Number in existence (analogous to 'car park' for the total number of cars in existence). Also called the stock, the inventory, or the product base.

As will be seen later, this is only a first shot at segmenting the market (dividing it into sectors), but it already suggests directions in the marketing strategy—find an information need common to a large number of households, get the price down, attract richer households first, and use the business sector as the method for building up the volume of sales needed to ensure that mass production brings the price down.

The Customer and the Potential Customer

The customer is someone who buys or might buy something you have to offer, and all the customers together constitute the market. There could be a potential customer in part of the market you do not serve, because you have failed to look at the match of consumer need to what you could offer. A small company specialising in the repair of steeples and chimneys could discover that its skills could be extended to the repair, erection and dismantling of aerial masts, thus enlarging its served market; the customer's need is now more broadly defined as the erection, maintenance and demolition of tall structures (not just chimneys and steeples), and the managing director might produce Table 1.2, after diligent analysis of the market, in order to obtain the finance for new cable winching equipment, which will be required.

Table 1.2. Estimated Expenditure of All Companies on Maintaining, Erecting and Dismantling Tall Structures in West Unteland

	Current served market			*Non-served market*	*Grand total*
	Steeples	*Chimneys*	*Total*	*Masts*	
Demolition	20	60	80	40	120
Maintenance	60	120	180	80	260
Erecting	—	5	5	20	25
	80	185	265	140	$U405

$U'000—1990

By looking at those who share the need of the customers in his currently served market, the managing director has significantly widened the scope and horizon of his company. The discipline of defining a market so that the served and non-served sectors are shown is practised in some companies to remind them what growth should eventually be achieved—today the wealthy buy our product, tomorrow every family in Europe will have what we offer.

Evolving Customer Satisfactions

Customers' wants and satisfactions are never exactly matched, and we can trace the evolution of customers' needs by looking at their satisfaction with existing products. In a segmented market we can often identify leading products serving a segment of the market which has more purchasing power, and the assumption that the products they buy today will be tomorrow's standard products is based on the assumption of steadily rising income in the market-place.

New products can therefore change customers' wants, making the **analysis of competitive products** an essential tool of marketing analysis. The analysis will show how product segmentation matches market segmentation by providing statistics of sales to each segment and showing the percentage of potential buyers actually purchasing the product—its market **penetration** by segment.

A successful new product may itself make customers aware of a need of which they were unconscious before. This sounds like a sinister 'creation of needs', but it need not threaten to spoil the simplicity of life. Take, for example, the progress of local bakers making their own bread on their premises. As they set up bakeries in lower-income areas, mass-produced bread sales will inevitably be affected. A need for bread baked on the premises would be something quite new to potential customers with lower incomes all over the USA and the UK, but they would begin to learn it from their satisfaction with a product new to them—good, fresh-baked bread.

Marketing is the identification of evolving customer needs and satisfactions, and the offer of a mix of products, prices and promotion to serve them at a profit.

Product Mix

There is usually a **group of products** for sale, not just one product, and the total profit made is affected by the mix. In the biscuit business in Holland, for example, it is always possible to sell a cheap type of biscuit called *speculaas*, and the biscuit manufacturer may be forced to do this as well as sell more expensive products when there is a downturn in demand. Although volume may hold steady, the average price per pound of biscuit will fall, and so will profit, if more *speculaas* are produced.

Product mix changes are important in **price competition**—the sales manager may refuse to admit that some new entrant to the market is really competing with the main product he sells, yet the new entrant may well be reducing the chances of selling the standard line because of a lower-priced product. Thinner decorative laminates may not have the life of the standard product, but for less critical applications, like facing a cupboard, they can be substituted without problems. If the sales manager says he is not in the thin laminate market, he is right; but thin laminates are in his market and he needs to take account of the average price across the industry's product mix, and trends in that price and mix, in deciding whether his product mix needs to change.

Prices

Customers pay definite prices for the satisfaction of their wants, and marketing must be concerned with the offer of products at prices that optimise profit. In most markets prices are a 'given', even if they are in evolution; and there will often be a reference price set by an important competitor that defines what other competitors can ask for their products.

In many markets there are particular prices which, once undercut, enlarge the market enormously. The best example is probably still the portable calculator, which, once below $20, found a mass market all over the world. Getting below this threshold price could be relevant to new products looking for a market take-off such as that won by the personal computer or disposable razors.

Advertising, promotion and other factors are relevant to the price charged for a product. A well known, well liked product can have a higher price because so many people will prefer it to something else without the same image. This can even be true of complicated industrial, architectural or engineering systems, where the customer may be enamoured of the supplier's hospitality, place of production, ethos or the intellectual elegance of his solution, all justifying a higher priced product.

Promotion, Advertising and Awareness

In the marketing world we often refer to some company or person 'setting out their stall', that is, setting out merchandise (merchandising) like a market trader in a stall. Someone setting out his stall is showing someone else what he has to offer for sale. Some offers for sale are clear to everyone without any special patter, because the situation is one where everyone knows that goods are on offer—the market stall, or the shop. But in other cases potential customers are sought out specially, because the expense of advertising to the whole world would be unjustified. High income earners, for example, often find themselves solicited to buy many things by post because they have given a signal, somewhere to someone, that they have plenty of money—for example, they may live in an expensive apartment, or may have bought some expensive item from a company that likes to use mail-outs to solicit business.

Although advertising, as such, is not always required, promotion is essential. Promotion defines all the ways in which the customer gets to know you have a product on offer—becomes aware of it—which is why promotion is part of the definition of marketing.

Awareness is achieved with advertising, appearances in trade directories, mentions in newspaper or trade magazine articles, by knocking on doors, by simply having the product on the shelf in the shop (i.e. merchandising) or by other means. See Table 1.3.

Table 1.3. Major Methods of Achieving Customer Awareness

Advertising	Packaging	Public relations	Selling
TV, radio, cinema, directories, posters, mail, company vehicles, publicity material, giveaways	Retail goods, merchandising,* retailing	Press articles, conferences, entertainment of key buyers	Person to person, telephone, direct mail, mail-in (newspapers)

Selling is the exchange of goods or services for money, and implies that the goods or services must be known to the buyer. *Promotion, advertising* and *merchandising** are ways in which the potential buyer becomes aware of the product and so can decide to buy it. Merchandising is sometimes used to cover advertising and price discounts as well as preparing goods at the point of sale in order to make them as attractive as possible to the buyer, including the design of the packaging, special displays, even shop-fitting for a retail chain.

Awareness of a product is a precondition of purchasing it, and in many consumer-goods markets goals for awareness of brands are set for their advertising agencies—called 'targeted brand awareness'. Awareness of existing brands of consumer goods should be measured at least every two years to provide a measure of progress. Questions about awareness are very simple: 'Which brands of margarine do you know?' (unaided brand awareness) and 'Which ones have you heard of?' (aided brand awareness, showing a list). Reputation can be measured fairly well for consumer goods, but requires more ingenuity with commercial services and industrial products, entailing the use of a **market research agency**. The problem is that even buyers are too polite to tell you to your face what they think of you; but if what they really think is detrimental, it can cause you a great deal of trouble to put right. The scapegoat supplier is a reality—like the teacher's pet hate, every error is remembered and every success forgotten.

On the other hand, a good image may permit a higher pricing policy because the buyer reinforces his confidence in his contract with a highly regarded company by paying something he knows is above the average market price.

Let us repeat the important maxim. Marketing is the identification of evolving customer needs and satisfactions, and the offer of a mix of products, prices and promotion to serve them at a profit.

Profitably Serving the Market

The target of marketing activity is to receive sufficient money for products or services sold to remain profitably in business. The goal is to have every product contributing towards an adequate profit, but companies often carry low profit and even loss-makers for long periods because competitive conditions force this upon them as a temporary measure. The competitive situation must define whether marketing a product is worth doing within a given period of time.

A great deal of competition is about price, and the ability of the competitor to fight a price war is relevant to any product. This is true even for the new product like Videotex, which has to compete with a great deal of information provided at a negligible cost. But the competition may impose other constraints: buying of expensive capital goods and systems (including telecommunications) may be intensely nationalistic, to the detriment of non-national producers; and anti-monopoly laws can constitute a constraint on how competition can be conducted. A marketing analysis, presentation, or strategy (particularly a glowingly optimistic one) which does not mention competition and particularly the future evolution of competitors' prices is not worth the paper it is written on. Only a very tired management will let it through.

Distribution. Captive retail outlets (owned by the competitor) may be closed to your company. This has been a feature in the sale of decorating products, automotive products and televisions in the past in the UK, and many foreign companies have found out about these constraints the hard way. **Exclusive dealerships** are sometimes a feature in other countries, excluding prospects for new traders.

Quality/technical superiority. The competitor may have a better product (i.e. identified by the buyer as such, no matter what we feel about our product) and the prospect of our catching up may be remote. This product may sometimes also be protected by a patent.

Advertising and promotional policy. The competitor may have a very high **brand awareness**, which we cannot reach, given our own budget constraints.

In this chapter the idea of exchange of goods to satisfy wants has been introduced, with our main attention directed to what the customer wants. We have seen that the marketing analyst takes a realistic and disciplined view of customers' wants, and what is happening and will happen in the market-place, and presents this with clarity and conviction to his company's management. In later chapters the reader will be introduced to the analyst's boss, a dynamic marketing manager we call the **entrepreneur**—someone who will be using marketing analysis as the foundation of soaring bridges which carry products from the centre of the company to the heart of customer need. There is something of the entrepreneur in most of us, and we have seen that the analyst should himself make recommendations as to how better to serve customer need. Enlarging a company's market share or increasing its served market requires a willingness to tackle the new and make it familiar: which starts with marketing analysis and forecasting.

Key Concepts

Served Market. The total purchases from all sources by potential customers to whom you offer your specific goods or services at the present time. The size of the served market consists of all the purchases of the specific goods or services from all suppliers made in a period of time, usually a calendar year.

Non-served market. The total purchases from all sources by potential customers to whom you do not offer your product or services at the present time.

Available Market. The part of the total (served plus non-served) market which could be served by the company within a specific period (e.g. available market in 1991).

Product mix. The group of products on offer by the business, consisting of low and high priced products, different types of product and so on.

Optimum Product Mix. The best comination of products offered to optimise income while satisfying market demand.

Comparative Product Analysis. The systematic comparison of products now competing in the market-place or likely to do in the future, to show their relative success in matching customer need. It will include the description of the products' characteristics, their prices and shares of the market, other measurements of customer satisfaction, their method of distribution to reach the customer, and other relevant factors, wherever possible broken down by segment of the market.

Promotion. The ways by which customers become aware of a product, including advertising, public relations, selling, and merchandising.

Merchandising. (1) The offer of goods for sale by presenting them in a place where goods are available for purchase, such as the retailers' shelves, in the street market, at the exhibition and other points of sale. (2) The optimising of the offer of goods at the point of sale by improving the packaging, price, display, local advertising, shop-fitting and so on.

Market Segmentation. The division of the market into easily identifiable sectors, differing in their characteristics of frequency of purchase, quality required, income, geographical location, place of purchase, use of product, price awareness, need for the product and other characteristics of behaviour such as influence by fashion, in order to direct marketing efforts towards the most income-maximising product mix, distribution, selling and general marketing policy.

Price Threshold. A price below which demand for a product or service increases dramatically (see also p. 30).

Unprompted Awareness. Measurement of percentage of potential customers who know a supplier or his brand.

Prompted Awareness. Measurement of percentage of potential customers who identify the name of the supplier or his brand from a list of competitive suppliers.

Exercises

---

1. Sunglasses are sold from racks and movable pedestals in drugstores, opticians, sports shops and mass-merchandisers. Provide an analysis of the market of a sunglass manufacturer, Topaz, who specialises in sales at skiing resorts world-wide and to European mass-merchandisers (e.g. Woolworth) and suggest what is his strategy. Use your imagination, plus the following concepts:

(*a*) served market,
(*b*) non-served market,
(*c*) market segments,
(*d*) price,
(*e*) product mix,
(*f*) distribution policy,
(*g*) advertising and promotional policy,
(*h*) competitive suppliers.

What is your guess as to the reasons why this manufacturer concentrates in these sectors? How could it be a profit-maximising policy?

2. The table below shows soup sales to three types of user over a four-year period. Work out the average price for each sector and describe trends in this market by means of percentages. What are the strategic implications?

Sales of Low Calorie Canned Soups in Unteland—1992 to 1995

	1992		1993		1994		1995	
	Litres	*Value ($U)*	*Litres*	*Value ($U)*	*Litres*	*Value ($U)*	*Litres*	*Value ($U)*
Hospitals	4,000	2,000	4,040	2,100	4,080	2,205	4,120	2,315
Restaurants	16,000	8,000	20,000	8,800	25,000	9,680	31,250	10,648
Households	60,000	30,000	61,800	29,400	63,654	28,812	65,564	28,236
	80,000	40,000	85,840	40,300	92,734	40,697	100,934	41,199

2
Applying Marketing Concepts in Analysing a New Product's Potential

This chapter uses the concepts of marketing and applies them to the problem of estimating the potential for a new product, in order to deepen the reader's understanding of these key ideas.

Of course a product may be new to the market-place or to your company, or to both, but it is important to realise that there is nothing completely new in this world. Man's needs are limited, and it is the marketing analyst's task to have a look at what need is satisfied by the new product and note what else is on offer to satisfy that need.

Note that the amount of take-home money that potential users of the new product have for saving and to satisfy their needs—their disposable income—will also be of relevance to the future of the product, because almost everyone will drink champagne if it costs only 10p. a glass. Many a new product can be dismissed because its price is in fact too high. Something that sells well in Switzerland may be too expensive for Spain.

The examples in this chapter—Videotex and the personal computer—were both dramatically new ideas when they first came to the market. The reader may find it difficult in the light of his current knowledge to remember that prospects for both products were once unknown, that huge claims were made for their future, and that many companies insisted in producing products or services lest they miss a market opportunity. That same challenge of the new product will occur in most marketing careers, to cope with the claims and counter-claims and the sheer lack of definition that surrounds the new product.

Principal Concepts for New Products

The main headings under which the analysis of the new product is developed are:

(*a*) the need satisfied by the product,
(*b*) competing products,
(*c*) similar products,
(*d*) price thresholds,
(*e*) speed of market penetration,
(*f*) size of the market 20 years on.

Need Satisfied by the Product

It may seem surprising but some products serve a great many more needs than may at first be apparent, while others seem to serve more needs than they actually do. Take, for example, instant coffee, developed first by Nestlé before the Second World War. For a start, it would be correct to say that it serves the same need as for coffee, but in a convenient form. If you analyse the need for coffee, you may be tempted to say that is satisfies the human need to take in liquid refreshment of a stimulating variety. But coffee drinking is more elaborate than that—it is a social activity as well as a way of refreshing yourself or satisfying your thirst. Because it is a social activity, its place in the shopping basket (i.e. the amount of personal disposable income spent on coffee) is susceptible to change in social convention. This change occurred in Britain in the 1950s, and the market for instant coffee grew at the expense of tea then and in the 1960s.

The naive market analyst might have argued, back in 1950, that the total market for instant coffee was made up of (say) 10 per cent of the existing purchasers of coffee (less than 5 per cent of all hot beverages consumed at the time). The 10 per cent were the ones who conceded that instant coffee could be convenient. If he had gone further, he could have argued that instant coffee fulfilled the need met by hot beverages generally, and planned for some penetration of the tea market. But he would have required some imagination and realisation that social needs were met by coffee to guess at the ultimate penetration by instant coffee of over 50 per cent of total hot drinks consumed. If you had sampled the population, you would have found that most people *preferred* tea in 1950. Their preferences changed slowly as they learned about coffee by tasting it again and again in social contexts: that is, they got to like coffee after being offered it by friends and tasting it in the coffee bars which thrived in the 1950s as overseas holidays abroad took off. In fact, the whole market for beverages, even alcoholic, works in terms of inertia (we prefer the drinks we know) and social dynamism (we like to experiment with new drinks which become chic or which mark a step forward in maturity or status). Babycham becomes a success symbol for the teenager on her first date because it answers one of her needs—the need for status. Later on there will be another drink to try.

Table 2.1. Hierarchies of Needs

I Human	*II Business*
1. PHYSIOLOGICAL Air—food—beverage—clothing Housing—rest—recreation Sex	1. BASIC NEEDS Capital—profit Manpower—sales—growth Expansion
2. SAFETY Security—comfort—guaranteed continuation of No. 1	2. SECURITY Market share Continuation

3. LOVE
Social:
   To self
   Towards family
   In work environment
   To society
	3. REPRESENTATION (IMAGE)
	In company
	To clients
	To competitors

4. ESTEEM
Recognition:
   From work
   From superior
   From family
	4. GOODWILL
	From clients
	From superior
	From company

5. SELF-ACTUALISATION Self-realisation Self-accomplishment Independence	5. ACHIEVEMENT Independence Capital decisions

Based on A. H. Maslow, *Motivation and Personality*, Harper and Row, 1970.

Table 2.1 is based on A. H. Maslow's *Motivation and Personality* (Harper and Row, 2nd Edition, 1970), showing the hierarchical of human beings—hierarchical because, having satisfied the first needs, man can go on to the next needs. If he is starving, all his energies go into feeding himself. But as each need is satisfied, man goes on to higher needs, and these use up a great deal of his time and income. Some of the needs high on the list cost money— concert-going, for instance, or playing squash—but other activities satisfying higher needs, such as studying for fun, praying or walking, cost nothing at all.

The list of needs given in Table 2.1 provides a useful aide-memoire when looking at new products. If you are comparing a personal computer with television, for example, you will find that the latter has a much broader base in human needs than the former (Table 2.2). The television provides a one-way link with society and is even part of our security system, giving information about the weather and strikes. Television serials and films provide an escape from reality by allowing us to identify with self-achieving persons and so relate to the highest of human needs. Note that although TV satisfies the higher needs, it is not necessarily very expensive in comparison with some other consumer goods.

Table 2.2. Needs Satisfied by Two Products—for Home Use Only

General Category of need	Television—some motivations for purchase	Personal computer—some motivations for purchase
Physiological	—	Managing family accounts (weak)
Safety	Advice on strikes, weather	—
Love	Window on society	—
Esteem	Unimportant in Europe now	New middle-class status symbol
Self-actualisation	Entertainment—projection of self (passive)	Fun, games—mastery of a new skill

Analysing the needs satisfied by a product will remind you of the total universe of things which compete with it. The telephone in the home is an important part of our security system, because we can contact the police and fire services through it. But this need can also be satisfied by public call-boxes and through using the telephones of neighbours, so public call-boxes in fact compete with private telephones for the low-income families who have yet to install a phone. The need for contact with loved ones can be met simply by visiting them (in small communities) and so another condition of the telephone's growth in household penetration is that the migration of families to new workplaces should begin.

Hierarchies of Needs are Not Rankings for Purchases

The higher the need in the advanced economy, the more money the user may be willing to spend on it. Education, which covers higher needs much more than it is concerned with basic ones, is every expensive. Cars, which satisfy higher needs in the life of urban man (no matter how essential they are in a rural environment), can take up more of the family budget than food. As we have seen, some higher needs can be satisfied without any money—for example, taking a walk. But until the basic needs are met, the higher needs cannot flourish.

In another sense, identifying the physical needs satisfied by a product can remind you that there is more than one market available. Manufactured oxygen serves the same physical need in all humans, but there are more than two different market segments: in hospitals for medical purposes, and in the processing industry for certain chemicals. The needs served by the same product can thus be different. The telephone used in industry and commerce is mainly a tool for organising the satisfaction of our basic needs for food, clothing and shelter (i.e. creating wealth more efficiently), whereas, as we shall see, the use of the phone in the home belongs to higher needs.

An Analysis of Needs—The First and Second Telephone

Before looking in depth at the variety of needs served by a product, the analyst should make a brief statement of what needs a product serves. For example, keeping a pet dog might serve a need for companionship and security; bottled water serves the basic human need for water, but provides the security of a low mineral content. These banal statements are worth making to ensure everyone in the marketing team is on the same wavelength. For a telephone, generally, it is the need to communicate at a distance. The telephone serves all the needs served by human speech, permitting rapid communication for some human purpose. It is a tool that sets up meetings and serves other activities. The box below summarises some of the needs met by the telephone in the home.

Needs Met by the Residential Telephone

Safety—Contact with police, fire service, family
Love—Contact with loved ones
Esteem—Sign of presence in community in
advanced nations, sign of
status in less advanced

That each of these needs is satisfied by the telephone is provable from two directions—commonsense consideration of some of the reasons why people have phones, and published results of research. The research goes on in order to find ways of expanding the market. It sometimes happens that this research is valuable in showing uses of a product that were not realised to be important before.

Consider, however, the needs met by having a telephone extension in the home. What need is being met? Careful thought is required. The second telephone does of course do all the wonderful things that the first telephone does for the householder. But when you 'buy' (possibly rent) a new telephone, what need are you trying to satisfy? Yes, it is the same as the need for the first phone. But in addition, and importantly, the second phone is put in for *convenience*—to save the need to run around the house. See second box.

Reasons Cited for Installing Second Phone in USA Research		
Saving steps	32%	
Convenience	15%	i.e. CONVENIENCE
Needed in bedroom	13%	
Children's use	9%	

Thus, although the need for the second telephone satisfies the same multiple needs satisfied by the first phone, the motivation for buying it is nevertheless very different, based on another, comparatively trivial need. Knowing what is the need satisfied by the product, we shall not be tempted to project a gigantic growth and market penetration for the second telephone. The need to walk smaller distances is perceived as just another need by those who have adequate incomes, but the largest part of the population have more pressing needs to satisfy with their limited incomes just now, and we should be right in expecting washing machines to achieve a more rapid household penetration than second telephones.

Generally, products which offer convenience are based on basic human needs but vulnerable to competition from products that are still required to satisfy basic needs. Convenience products are often therefore marketed in terms of status as well as convenience in order to bring them under the umbrella of a basic need.

Competing Products

Even the completely new product will generally be competing with other products available now. Competing products are those that can be substituted for each other: with coffee, other hot beverages; whisky with gin, brandy and other spirits; and so on. Even the second telephone could be competing with the provision of plugs (also called jacks) in a house, allowing the telephone subscriber to move his main telephone subset from room to room. If there are no competing products, then prospects could be very good; but it is necessary to take the competing products very seriously indeed, as will be shown with the example of Videotex below. In the end, everything competes for the customer's money.

Similar Products

A problem arises with a new product like a personal computer, which has no real competing products, to decide just how big a market it might provide. An analysis of needs shows this product to be fairly elevated in the hierarchy of needs for most people—it belongs to the satisfaction of the need to understand and order things, which was seen to be at the top of human needs. For a segment of the population, however, the personal computer could be used as a means of teaching themselves and their children about programming and thus enabling them to get the software jobs that earn so much (and thus satisfy *all* the needs listed). So the market analyst looks for similar products to help her or him to gauge future demand. A similar product is one which, while not yet competing, shows characteristics that may enlighten our appreciation of a new product by possible parallels in needs served, market segment addressed, price or other characteristics.

The personal computer can be seen, in this light, as an educational aid, and, at prices of over £200, a rather expensive one. A similar product might be an encyclopaedia as purchased by parents for their children. Indeed, it could be that the personal computer will compete with encyclopaedias. What can we find out about encyclopaedias? How many are sold in a year, and how many to parents for their children?

Finding some facts about the encyclopaedia market requires only a few telephone calls. The analyst telephones the marketing directors of the main suppliers of encyclopaedias and explains that he is trying to estimate what demand for personal computers in the home might be. The marketing director of the encyclopaedia company will take the point at once that here is another educational product which will be marginally competitive, and he will probably be willing to help with some facts and figures. The analyst learns from him what is the life of an encyclopaedia (less than 12 years), the fact that the market is fairly flat (not growing rapidly), and (the key fact) how many are sold per year. This sort of information is confidential, so it cannot be reproduced exactly here. However, an important reference point for the future of the personal computer as sold for the home will have been obtained. One of the champions of the product may have been claiming future sales of millions per year, like those for television sets, but cross-reference to encyclopaedias has made it clear that figures in tens to hundreds of thousands would be much more appropriate. See Table 2.3.

Table 2.3. Do Personal Computers Sold for Home Use Resemble Encylopaedias?

Pro	Contra
Sold to those with higher education	Encylopaedias serve non-utilitarian purposes
Broadly similar price ticket	Personal computer serves numerate educational segment only
Educational motivation	

There can never be agreement about similar products. If the analyst shows the potential similarity between a dishwasher as reducing burdensome work in the home and a personal computer as reducing the task of keeping the family accounts in order and providing a list of names, addresses and phone numbers, there will be a cry of disagreement. The personal computer may fulfil those needs, of course, the denier will agree: but it does so much else! If we look on the personal computer as similar to such labour-saving devices as dishwashers, we shall have reached an important conclusion: it saves so little of a week's work that if the personal computer is to depend on the work it can achieve, alone, its household penetration will be below even that of the comparatively low penetration of the dishwasher.

Price Thresholds

A price threshold is a price at which sales will be possible in large enough volume to interest the potential supplier. As a product goes down in price, more and more people buy it and the number of suppliers also increases. In practice, the threshold price of most interest is one at which a consumer product becomes a mass consumer product, something that happened to calculators when they fell below $20 on the international market.

Price thresholds often require little research: a few phone calls to sales managers or retailers in the appropriate markets is quite enough. There is an important price threshold of $100 for Videotex (Presetel) added to TV sets, at which the number of sets purchased would start to increase rapidly. But, as we shall see, this would still not be enough to create a mass consumer market similar to that for colour television.

Price thresholds are vitally important to engineers busy creating new products. They have reference to the purchasing power of the consumer, so that bicycles costing over $300 are not of interest in an undeveloped country but could have a reasonable market share in

Holland. When the sales manager says, 'The housewife is not going to pay £20 for a new sort of window-cleaner', listen to him. Knowledge about price thresholds is commercial commonsense.

Not every product has reached its appropriate price threshold for market penetration. The degree of penetration of telephones in the home in Western Europe, generally available for over 40 years, was overtaken by colour television in less than 14 years from its launch. The television delivers over two hours' entertainment per person over five years old, per day, in the UK at a cost of one third of that for having a phone used for less than seven minutes per day. This reminds us that even if a product is seen as a basic tool of life—like the phone—it will still not achieve its total potential for 100 per cent household penetration until it drops below the threshold price.

Speed of Market Penetration

The rate at which a new product is purchased and installed by the customers in their homes, offices, factories or institutions is the speed of market penetration. It is useful to have a look at some rates of penetration achieved by products which are suggested as similar to the new product investigated. Figure 10.5 (p. 177) shows the fastest rate of market penetration among consumer durables was achieved by colour television. Telephone extensions or even dishwashers do not penetrate the market at such a speed. Could a personal computer penetrate the consumer market at the same rate as a CTV or even a dishwasher? As mentioned above, one test applied by researchers to the personal computer was whether it could save as much time in the household as does the dishwasher. The reason why this particular research suggested a low penetration was its stress on labour-saving rather than on games and fun. In fact, the market analyst might well decide that the consumer market for personal computers should not be considered in terms of all households but rather of no more than 4 per cent of all households, comprising those with high income and higher education. If this number, say 800,000 households, could easily be envisaged as satisfying their need for a personal computer within ten years, then the speed of market penetration could be described as fairly rapid. Looked at another way, the **market window** will be open for only ten years, so that if you want to sell in this market, you had better get your new product launched soon.

Notice how the ideas are all related. The speed of market penetration of dishwashers in Germany is more rapid than in the UK because the UK market has a price threshold lower than in Germany, and the supplier cannot yet get that low. That price threshold is based on how much money the British have in their pockets. They do not perceive any great need for dishwashers because the alternative of washing and drying the dishes is not so unattractive as parting with a large sum of money that can be used for something else, such as a colour television or a car, which will not be purchasable if a dishwasher is bought.

Size of Market and Market Penetration 20 Years on

The **total potential** for the new product needs to be considered. One might use the phrase the **ultimate market:** for example, ultimately 98 per cent of households will own at least one car. The problem with the ultimate market is that we can be bamboozled by its sheer size, however, and need to make so many assumptions with regard to increases in wealth or changes in society that a sceptic will find it difficult to believe our forecast. Focusing on 20 years is better, because it is a timespan that we can understand.

Applying the concept of the size of the market 20 years on to the personal computer, we may decide that the best penetration we could achieve would be the 4 per cent of households with higher education plus another 15 per cent of households buying a personal computer for its television games capability. This figure is reached after talking to two or three entrepreneurs in the television games business, discussing threshold prices for television games and double-checking with our technical experts as to the likely **price evolution** (price in real terms) of the personal computer. Using this data, we reckon that as many as 19 per cent of households might buy a personal computer in 20 years' time. This figure will disappoint those in the organisation who would like every household to have a personal computer, and produce raised eyebrows among some sceptics who are weak on imagination. But it will be a useful figure, keeping a rein on some of the crazier forecasts that may be offered.

One of the reasons why the analyst makes a forecast is to restrain naïve over-optimism on the part of some entrepreneurs. Examples of such optimism are legion, and the usual tactic is precisely one of saying, 'Here is the national market for roofing materials. If we obtain 1 per cent of it, it will represent 600 tons of our material'. The fact that our material costs twice as much as copper and that copper roofs are less than 0.01 per cent of all roofs laid by year might make the naïve forecaster think twice about how much penetration can be achieved in 20 years' time.

Is Size of Market 20 Years on Relevant?

This is one point at which the authors of this book have to signal their disagreement with each other. One of us feels that, with the lifetime of products declining, a timespan of three to five years is quite adequate, and the other believes that 20 years represents the outside limit of forecasting. But it is useful to look at what other products have achieved in the 20-year timespan. The focus of any company will be below five years, but the analyst may find a look at 20-year performance levels useful to get a grip on the far horizon of development. For some forecasters, at least, a look at the horizon can save some stumbling steps in the short distance as the company rushes to a forecast destination that is not there.

The most remarkable case of reaching **saturation** faster than anyone imagined is the Citizens' Band Radio market in the USA in the 1970s. Growth rates of over 20 per cent per annum in three consecutive years were suddenly halted and sales actually declined after 1975. None of the short-term statistical projection methods would have signalled this halt, nor did the industry's consensus about the future. A look further ahead—maybe not 20 years but ten years at least—at the likely ultimate penetration would have been instructive as the market took off. Many products take over 20 years to achieve complete penetration, and this includes photocopiers, transistor radios, electric irons, telephones and hairdriers. However, as one author insists, these figures all derive from past experience, and new technologies may make the life of products much shorter.

Videotex as a Completely New Consumer Product

Videotex is known in Britain as Prestel, and is a service by which information stored in page form on a computer can be accessed by telephone and shown on the screen of a colour television in the home. The summary below provides a very brief picture of how the concepts already developed are applied to this service and the special Videotex terminals needed to use it, applied in Unteland, in order to forecast its potential.

Need Satisfied by Videotex

Videotex serves the need for information required rapidly at any time in the home, particularly information which changes frequently and for which there is a special need to keep up-to-date. The Unteland telephone administration conducted research in 1986 about the sort of information that a sample of the public thought might usefully be shown on Videotex, and we can use their research to list the major items with potential. See Table 2.4.

Table 2.4. Ranking of Top Ten Types of
Information Suitable for Showing in Videotex
Format

Road/weather reports	1
What's on, cinema, theatre	2
Mail-order goods	3
Tourist information	4
Restaurants and cafés	5
Bus/rail timetables	6
Weather information	7
News bulletins	8
Stock market reports	9
Shopping information	10

Competitive Products Satisfying Similar Needs to Videotex

Major information sources include newspapers, television news,
radio, telephone information services and the Yellow Pages, all of
them (except newspapers) already in homes with telephones and TVs.
We need to look at growth rates in these media, where available, and
then examine price trends. See Table 2.5.

Table 2.5. Trends in Usage of Major Information Sources—Unteland

Source	Measure	Reference	Years	Sales /	Usage	% Change (pa)
Daily and Sunday newspapers	Circulation in '000s	1970	1978	14,694	14,193	−0.4
				23,491	18,882	−2.7
TV news audiences	Millions	1970	1978	31	29	Decline
Selected telephone information services (weather, etc.)	Million calls	1971	1976	365.6	503.4	+5.5

We see from Table 2.5 that these growth rates are not of the type to
excite an entrepreneur, who likes to have growth at over 10 per cent
per annum. However, we learn from an advertising agency contact
that Yellow Pages did achieve a growth of this magnitude, and
listening times to the radio are claimed by the independents to have
clocked up a good growth rate. Telephone information from the
telephone administration (excluding the speaking clock), tells us that

the average telephone subscriber uses the information services about two minutes per month—not a large figure.

The characteristic we note about most of these competing information sources is that information is not only very cheap, it is usually virtually free. Thus we note from Table 2.6 that the single information medium which has increased in price, the newspaper, is the only one that has fallen back in usage.

Table 2.6. Price Characteristics and Trends—Competing Products

Product/services	Characteristics
Daily and Sunday newspapers	Price rising in real terms: 1981 = 100 1986 = 123 (daily) 128 (Sunday)
TV News	Virtually free
Telephone information	Virtually free—over 80 per cent of calls are made from business premises
Yellow Pages	Free
Radio news	Free

Thus we note from Table 2.6 that the single information medium which has increased in price, the newspaper, is the only one that has fallen back in usage.

Similar Products to Videotex

Videotex is attached to a TV set, so it might be natural to assume that it will take off at the same rate as television. Television, however, is a product which satisfies the high level need for entertainment (associated with self-actualisation), a need which must be very significant when we consider how high average viewing times are per week and what a large proportion of programmes are non-informational. Because we perceive that the Videotex product answers a need related to obtaining information, we can compare it to purchases of encyclopaedias just as we did for the personal computer. This is because Videotex promises to cost as much as an encylopaedia to the first buyers. It may be better, however, to regard the Videotex product as very much a luxury—it will add say $U600 to the cost of the product. A similar product might then be a sauna, which we find has a household penetration of less than 2 per cent after being on the market for over ten years. Arguments about these perceptions will be fierce, but worthwhile. Either way, the Videotex product looks as if it will not have a large household penetration.

Videotex Competition with Existing Information Sources

This is the nub of the analysis. Unless Videotex has something extra to offer, it has no hope against competing sources of information. Table 2.7 summaries the analysis we make of competition between Videotex and other information sources. What we notice is that Videotex keeps having a low ranking as an information source versus other media.

Table 2.7. Videotex Parameters of Competition with Existing Product/Services

	Ranking			
Parameters	*First*	*Second*	*Third*	*Last*
Price	Radio, TV	Phone call	Newspaper	Videotex
Convenience				
Portability	Newspaper			Videotex
General accessibility	Phone	Newspaper		Videotex
Speed				
Special Events, road/weather, What's on	Phone	Newspaper, Videotex		Radio, TV
Restaurants, pubs	Yellow Pages	Newspaper		Videotex
Where to buy	Yellow Pages	Newspaper		Videotex
Real estate info.	Newspaper	Phone	Videotex	
Amount of information available	Reference books	Videotex	All others	

Videotex's prospects are best sold in terms of its ability to put a reference library in the living room. But if we look at what is available on each page of Videotex, we find that the medium only offers as much as a fact-card, an index card, a cigarette card or a paragraph in Whitaker's almanack. Videotex takes at least 60 seconds to reach the first piece of information, and it is very difficult to scan with the speed with which one looks at the small ads, for example.

Price Thresholds for Videotex

Table 2.8 sets out the forecast penetration at different prices. These forecasts represent the views of professional marketers about the possible potential at different prices, and are the result of interviewing a group for their views and averaging them.

Table 2.8. Forecast Penetration at Differing Incremental Prices—
Videotex Terminals in the Residential Market in Unteland

Purchase price ($U)	F/C average monthly access cost ($U)	Comment	Household penetration (%)
800		Launch price	Less than 0.01
600	45*		0.05
400			0.1
200			0.5
100	20	Price reductions	1.0
50			3.0
Nil	3**	Standard equipment in all TV sets	4.0

*12 pages per day. ** 4 pages per day, smaller users included.

Ultimate Market for Videotex (20 years on)

In the consumer market the ultimate penetration achievable is judged
to be 4 per cent after 20 years. This represents the total number of
households that might elect to be subscribers to a Videotex system
after a period of 20 years, at an optimum price. The figure is judged to
be as low as 4 per cent because competitive information sources—the
telephone, radio, newspapers and TV—will remain superior to
Videotex in terms of cost and convenience. Even if Videotex modems
(the components that take digital signals and convert them to coloured
letters on the TV screen) become standard in the CTV, the need to
have an engineer make the telephone connection (at some cost) will
also act as a deterrent. However, Videotex should be able to establish a
corner in the market in higher income/educational level households,
particularly if linkage to computer programs becomes possible and
speech is added to make the medium more user-friendly. Growing
familiarity with computers in secondary schools will also overcome
user reluctance in the same sector of households.

Judgements that the ultimate market is 100 per cent, based on
analogies with television, are rejected. Perception of the desire to
purchase and public interest in television was high from the moment
that the system was established, but this is not true for Videotex.

Forecast Sales of Videotex

Finally we look at all our evidence and make our forecast. For this it is
useful to use semi-logarithmic paper as shown in Fig. 10.5. We set out

the total market to be penetrated and then compare it with some graphs of other markets and the rate of penetration. The semi-logarithmic paper shows the growth rate by the steepness of the slope of the lines drawn on it and we notice a typical fast, medium and very slow phase of growth. On top of this we have replacement demand, which we will ignore here as we expect the life of the product to be nine years and we are forecasting to 1995. Products with an average life of nine years do of course have a percentage replaced after six and seven years, but for the purposes of simplifying our analysis we shall ignore it here. The forecasts are as given in Table 2.9.

Table 2.9. Forecast Penetration of Videotex Domestic Market in Unteland

	1989	1990	1991	1992	1993	1994	1995
Price ($U)	700	500	400	300	180	140	100
% Penetration	0.03	0.07	0.15	0.3	0.5	0.8	1
Park at Y/E ('000)	6	14	31	61	102	163	204
Sales in year to new customers ('000 units)	6	8	17	30	41	61	41
Replacement sales	0	0	0	0	0	0	0
TOTAL SALES	6	8	17	30	41	61	41

Thus we reach the conclusion that Videotex does not represent another product with a potential growth like that of colour television.

Conclusion

The forecast for a completely new product can be very wrong. Those presented above for Videotex in Europe have so far been generally over-optimistic, but this view is only available with hindsight. With new products the important thing is not to be exactly right but to be wrong in the right direction with regard to the truth. A red flag warns of danger and no one accuses it of being over-dramatic if it prompts the correct reaction. Often, as has been explained, a forecast is lower than others suggest, but sometimes it will be about products with startlingly high demand. The response to such a signal should be even stronger in a healthy company.

Key Concepts

Competing Products. Products that can be substituted for each other by the buyer, either partially or completely.

Similar Products. Products that may display parallels in sales to products yet to be launched, either because of their price ticket, the needs they serve, the market segment they address, or other characteristics. Two luxury products, characterised by a high price, may be similar products as defined, even though serving very different needs (e.g. private flying, jacuzzi pools), because their price tickets guarantee low penetration.

Price Threshold. A price at which demand for a product becomes so large that its total sales will be large enough in volume to interest many potential suppliers, and the market will be capable of large penetration.

Market Penetration. The percentage of households, offices, factories or other institutions with a particular product purchased and installed.

Rate of Market Penetration. The speed at which a new product advances from zero to ultimate penetration of the households, etc., which constitute its market.

Market Window. The length of time it is possible to launch a new product. The market window closes generally because the market has enough suppliers, leading suppliers have learnt how to produce more cheaply than a newcomer (so that price competition is not possible), and technical innovation has ended.

Exercises

1. Using only the information available to you and your group of friends and family, make a forecast for the following products as if they were absolutely new:

(*a*) electric-powered car,
(*b*) ready-pasted wallpaper,
(*c*) pocket calculators,
(*d*) Sinclair ZX91 personal computer.

Use as many of the concepts in this chapter as possible.

2. You are approached by a manufacturer of a revolutionary product capable of causing excitation of the air (fanning) by a simple black box with no moving parts. The product does not directly cool the air, is remarkably quiet, and is capable of handling any space up to 30 cubic metres in size. For industrial applications individual units can be placed in different places to cover the complete area. The system costs half as much to run as a normal fan, has no installation costs (it plugs into the electricity supply) but is ten times as expensive to buy as a conventional fan.

List the main facts you would require to know to investigate its potential, together with the main sources of such information.

3. State briefly the needs satisfied by the following products and which products compete with them:

(*a*) indoor plants in offices,
(*b*) air transport,
(*c*) horses,
(*d*) pumps,

(*e*) fertiliser,
(*f*) water,
(*g*) car parks,
(*h*) television.

3
How the Need for Marketing Research Arises

Research into products which are new to your company is often required because of a desire to **diversify**, although in some companies (especially packaging) the newness of the particular product may be related to an application rather than to changes in the nature of the company's output. In other cases the company has an existing business based on a certain technology and finds that there is an opportunity for exploiting its technology in a completely new market. Texas Instruments' launch of 'Speak and Spell', a spelling toy for children, is an example of the latter case. The toy market was unknown to TI, yet they developed a completely new product (despite forecasts of very doubtful demand) because the product could exploit their know-how in speech-processing (the ability to generate speech with electronic chips). The market research carried out was designed to forecast how many they might sell, and then went on to examine how the product might best be presented, and at what price. TI have published some of their research on the product, and if they had heeded it, they might never have launched 'Speak and Spell'. The views of 'experts'—educational psychologists and even teachers—were that children would not necessarily receive useful instruction from the toy. But children in fact enjoyed playing with it, *and* their parents bought it for them. Concentration on the final specifying group—parents and children—was more useful than asking experts for their opinions.

Forecasting

In every case the marketing analyst will be asked to make a forecast of how many products can be sold or how much money can be earned by a new service—this is the target of the exercise. Sometimes the analyst is asked to have a look at the total market and limit his attention to the market in general; in other cases he may actually be asked to look at the prospects for his company with a new product. In either case, a forecast of future sales and profit will be generated.

There is no way of avoiding personality bias in making the final judgement. The qualities that make for a good marketing analyst and which keep him credible in his job will be a rare mixture of shrewdness, imagination, openness to the facts about the market, an ability to state his perceptions clearly and a good 'filter' to sort out what is relevant, what is changing and capable of change, and what is actually untrue.

Two Problems in Reaching the Forecast—Self-protection and Inertia

The existing suppliers to a market, if approached, have an interest in protecting their own sales, which may lead them to lie, if they think it necessary. The picture the researcher will receive is of a market overfull of existing competitors, with fierce price-wars, low margins and imminent bankruptcy for fringe operators. All this should be discounted by the analyst. He will even discover that some potential customers will give the same story, because they too are interested in protecting themselves from change. Relations between themselves and existing suppliers will probably be very good. Why complicate life?

Inertia rules outside in the market, but inertia inside a company may also be strong. 'What on earth can our company do in the toy market?' someone in Texas Instruments might well have asked. As the analyst looks at the person who poses this question inside his company he should say to himself, 'Well, it won't be you who will be doing it, anyway'. In some cases it may be appropriate for the analyst to point out gaps in the skills of his company when addressing a new market, with recommendations that appropriate personnel be recruited. But to decide that a new market cannot be taken on at even the lowest level of test-marketing or supply to existing companies in the market simply because of the novelty of the new and the conservatism of the old is like committing commercial suicide.

Why is the Information Required?

A request for information about a market may reach the marketing analyst from any level in a company, and the amount of work necessary to produce the information can be enormously variable. For example, a request for information about how many language schools there are in Western Europe is a question you could answer by checking the Yellow Pages (classified telephone directories) for London, Bradford, Paris, Nantes, Stuttgart, Frankfurt, Brussels, Milan and Florence and making an estimate for Europe based on the sample and the number of cities with populations of over 100,000. With some telephone calls to the marketing managers of such international language schools as Berlitz, it will be possible to make a good estimate of the total number in Western Europe, broken down by country, and the work could be done in less than a day.

However, if we enquire about why this request is being made, the task may become more simple or more difficult. If the managing director's daughter wants to be a language instructor and her father wants to use the information to warn her off Greece, rather less than 60 minutes' work might satisfy him. If, on the other hand, the request comes because the company has a language laboratory package using instantaneous computerised translation of single words, the task may be much more complicated. Which educational establishments use language laboratories? What is the cost of a language laboratory? Indeed, the first question the researcher may have to answer is 'What is a language laboratory?' Others may include 'What price are universities and language schools willing to pay for such a product?' and 'What advantages must the product show in order to be able to mount a credible sales campaign?' Questions of this order of complexity demand research among potential customers—what is called **field research**.

This chapter will show the steps in tackling a piece of research that requires more than a day or two of casual enquiries. These steps must be followed if you wish to carry out your work in the most efficient manner possible, i.e. if you wish to offer a continuing service which aids your enterprise in identifying opportunities and offering profitable products and services to the market.

Stages of Research

The stages of research are the following:

(*a*) Briefing—problem definition.
(*b*) Desk research and the market hypothesis.
(*c*) Stating the problem—the remit or terms of reference:

   background,
   objectives,
   methods,
   timing and personnel.

(*d*) Desk research.
(*e*) Field research.
(*f*) Report writing.

Briefing—Problem Definition

Briefing can be a long business and should be as long as possible. The person requesting information from the analyst has normally reached a decision to request help because of his successful marketing professionalism and/or because he has been prevented by senior management from developing his concept further without testing the market-place, and in either case he will be full of expertise, jargon and fears about the competence of the researcher. The market analyst cannot be the master of every type of product and market.

The briefing meeting is critical because the analyst must convince the person briefing him that he understands enough about the technology or features of the product in question to be able to research the market adequately. For this reason it is wise to find out as much as possible about the market and product to be offered even before the briefing meeting. It can avoid some of the dangers of being badly briefed because of fears of confessing ignorance.

Table 3.1. Worst Scenario for a Briefing Meeting

Function	Target	Action	Result
Analyst	To understand the problem	Ask questions until he understands	Convinces briefer he is incapable of research
Briefer	To ensure his product is researched well	Ask questions to probe competence of analyst	Convinces himself the analyst is incapable of research

The **scenario** in Table 3.1 (a scenario is one of a series of alternative outcomes or occurrences, usually arranged to show the best, the worst and something in between) has seldom occurred in my experience within a company and is rare even with market research agencies who are being briefed. Nevertheless, it is the analyst's and researcher's nightmare. If you really want to know what you are researching, detailed questions on the product must be asked; it is essential to know what the problem really is. In a not untypical case an analyst was asked to investigate the probability that manufacture of a certain type of packaging could be made by the existing customer in his own plant instead of buying from the company. After five hours of discussion it emerged that the real motive of desire to undertake research was in order to make a case for opening a new factory in a more central location vis-à-vis all the customers. This changed the research requirement considerably.

Briefing Part-time Researchers

Much research is carried out by part-timers or consumer researchers who have an initial ignorance of the product to be investigated. It may be necessary, for example, to make hundreds of telephone interviews with plumbers about taps (American faucets) with plastic instead of metal handles, and the best way of doing this might be by using the spare time of the secretaries in the company to obtain rapid interviews. Women interviewers will get better results (in terms of successfully completed interviews) than men, and the sheer number of interviews required might compel this approach in the face of time and cost constraints. The interviewers must know what they are talking about, must know to whom they want to talk and must be motivated to get the answer to the question by a careful explanation of how their input will aid the company's strategy. Usually two or more hours will be needed to show the product to the interviewers, to discuss why the information is needed, to explain how to carry out a telephone interview, and to answer all the queries that will arise. Refreshments will be needed and the creation of an atmosphere of competition between interviewers to add some extra spice will be desirable. This can be achieved by having a final **debriefing** meeting after research is completed with a prize for the best interviewer, at the same time as the results of the research are presented to the interviewers.

Hands On the Product

An essential part of the briefing is to show what the product looks like, preferably by letting everyone touch and use it when this is possible. You can talk about modems, teleprinters, disposable bottles, thin laminates, FKD furniture, half-scalp hairpieces, speaker independent word recognisers, wood stoves or anything else, but if the researcher is not absolutely clear about what the existing product is, what the future product would offer as an improvement, who buys the product and what the benefit is in knowing the answer, there is little point in giving him or her a questionnaire.

Sometimes the promoter of the product wants to keep it all hazy because he believes the idea is explosively new and could easily be stolen. Fight this as hard as you can: for example, 'Do you *seriously* believe that ten minutes talk about a 3 cm. diameter coloured chocolate drop is going to send other chocolate manufacturers pell-mell towards producing a similar product?' The extent to which future competitors monitor developments in the market-place can be easily overestimated by the entrepreneur. The second question to pose to him is, 'Is your new product idea fully defined?' Only if you know exactly how clear the existing idea is, can you hope to get the answers to make the concept even more clear and market-adapted. The best plan is to persuade the entrepreneur to take you on a tour of outlets where competing products are already in use, letting him comment on the improvements he hopes the new product might offer.

Desk Research and Market Hypothesis

After as thorough a briefing as possible, the analyst must go away and get together as much information as possible in the next two or three weeks in order to make a proposal for the complete research required to solve the problem. Desk research entails searching for market statistics, books and articles on the market in question: finding out who the major suppliers are, requesting sales literature for their relevant products, reading trade journals, obtaining data on advertising levels where relevant, sometimes getting financial information on particular suppliers (annual company data); in short, getting everything together which is available in printed form on the market in question and the products which are relevant.

This data, rough as it is, can be presented as a working document that is called a **market hypothesis** in some companies. The market hypothesis will show all sorts of data on the size of the market, its rate of growth, and features of demand and supply, and will be laid out just like a report—but scrappily, with photocopied tables and information inserted under the relevant headings. What will be 'hypothetical' about it is that it will suggest all sorts of questions, which will be laid out as such at the end of each section. For example, the analyst might write, 'Is the market being upgraded to a higher quality product? Is there room for a new premium offering from our company?' Or he might note, 'Will the number of suppliers, which seems to be decreasing, go on declining in the future?' The market hypothesis raises questions, often additional questions, which should be fed into the terms of reference of the research.

Draft Research Proposal

At the end of the desk research a **proposal** can be prepared to carry out as much market research as is needed to provide the market forecasts needed. This is sometimes called the **draft terms of reference**, but it is important to hang on to the word 'draft', which signals that it is a working document, capable of being changed according to the requirements of the person for whom the work is being done. For the analyst may propose twenty visits to retailers while the entrepreneur will be nervous unless forty retailers are seen, and so on. There are also frequent redefinitions of the questions to be posed, all making it necessary to go to a new draft proposal or **remit**.

The draft proposal usually begins with a statement of the *background* to the task of analysis. This states why the company is interested in the market, and can sometimes make reference to some of the facts discovered during desk research. A complete example, describing research on sunglasses, will be given below. The *objective* of the research is clearly stated, and should be paraphrasable as a question. For example: 'Objectives. To forecast the number of disposable razors that the company will be able to sell in Germany in 1994 at DM 1 and at DM 1.20 per unit'. This could be paraphrased as 'How many disposable razors could we sell at DM 1 and how many at DM 1.20 per unit in 1994?' The draft proposal then goes on to *methods*, outlining whether field research is required and how much. A *completion date* is set, and the personnel who are doing the research and the number of man-days required to do it should normally be set out. Where there are exceptional costs to be borne, like international travel, the arrangements for paying these may need to be detailed. Here is an example.

DRAFT PROPOSAL—ANALYSIS OF THE PROSPECTS FOR FL SALES IN THE EUROPEAN MARKET FOR SUNGLASSES

Background

Futuretime Laboratories have developed a new glass moulding technique that permits the complete moulding of plastic optical quality sunglasses in one piece, including a hinge at the earpieces that will withstand being opened and closed 100,000 times. The glass moulding technique is a spin-off from a R&D project—night-vision new products (NVNP)—for night-vision systems and is ranked as the most likely volume usage of the new technology, which requires high volume usage in order to justify a large capital investment. It is envisaged that the price will remain high even at high volumes and, for this reason, usage for couturier brands such as Givenchy and Dior will be explored in depth. Economies in production will be achieved through the single moulding, but the basic raw material is forecast to remain expensive. Differentiation of components of the sunglasses (gold rims, black earpieces, etc.) will not be possible, as painting costs will remove the economies of one-piece moulding.

Objectives

1. To forecast demand for the FL product incorporated in sunglasses in sixteen European countries (EEC + Scandinavia + Austria + Switzerland + Iberia) in years 1 to 5 of a launch of sales to companies marketing sunglasses.
2. To show the structure of the market for sunglasses, identifying major competitors in the market and the distribution system.
3. To forecast sales of sunglasses of all types in Europe from 1987 to 1992.
4. To identify changes in technology, styling, pricing and sourcing that significantly affect the proposed entry of a new competitor to the market.

Methods

1. Desk research will establish whatever statistics are available for market size in European countries, including import and export data, purchasing patterns for sunglasses, channels of distribution, competitive data and other information, as set out in objectives.
2. Field research will include visits to one buyer of sunglasses for major retail chains in Germany, France and the UK. The nature of the proposed product will not be revealed in any way, but the interviews will be employed for market data, information on suppliers, mark-ups and so on.
3. Field research will include visits to retailers in the UK, Germany and France to establish prices at the point of sale for major brands. The characteristics of the sunglasses will be described, with particular attention to the quality of the nose-piece and eye-glass joining member.
4. Consumer research will be carried out with a random sample of 100 in order to find out the importance of parameters of choice of sunglasses (price, quality, brand name, appearance, etc.), using the services of a market research agency.

Completion Date

A task force will be reporting on the prospects for the Night Vision New Products project on 3 July 1987, and the research must be made available to them by 20 June. The research will require 12 man-days to complete and will be carried out by Dean Sturgeon and Arthur Inkrep. Research will begin on acceptance of these amended proposals.

Date of Proposal: 7th June, 1987

This document incorporates the results of desk research and preliminary explorations already carried out, although it does not spell out the fact. An article on the sunglass industry has been uncovered after looking at many copies of trade magazines and requesting help from a business library (the City Business Library in this case, but it could have been the Bibliothèque de la Chambre de Commerce in Paris). The article shows that certain retail outlets dominate the sale of sunglasses in the UK and are very important elsewhere—their buyers will be very influential in the national market and their methods of assessing sunglasses will set the standard.

The researcher will also have noticed how elaborate sunglasses are, with different materials employed to make the product (glass, plastic, metal). It is essential to mention these facts to management, as, on the face of it, a single-substance plastic product does not sound attractive.

One of the major problems of this piece of research is that the new product cannot be shown or even described to professional and ultimate buyers. The analyst should make a great deal of fuss about this, stressing that theft of a new product idea by someone in a random sample of 100 is unlikely (although the buyers would gossip to existing suppliers). If a good copy of the product or an excellent picture can be employed, you have a chance of finding out what consumer acceptance will be, at little cost. Push hard for this—it can save huge, misguided investments from being made. In this case, of course, there are no mock-ups available, but the analyst will insist that if there proves to be some potential in the market, such research will be carried out as soon as possible.

The sample size will be modified as the analyst discusses prospects with the persons requesting the research. The need to visit some buyers is clear, and the only question is 'How many?' The client for the research may well ask for more retail buyers to be seen in order to be happier about the validity of the findings.

Timing and money will be the great constraints. Sampling can always be extended if there is more time but most work of this type is done rapidly to meet deadlines and is often no worse for that. Timing will be the great issue at the pre-fieldwork meeting in many cases at which, in the worse scenarios, the client will ask for world-wide information on every facet of an undocumented market to be produced in three days. There is only one way to beat these hysterical deadlines and that is to show how the information gathering is broken down day by day. 'You're a professional, you should be able to pull this off your computer databank' is the entrepreneur's taunt. The reply is that information does indeed exist in all sorts of places and the analyst will be able to pick some of it up very fast because of old personal contacts, but a list of all the products sold in retail outlets already requires a sixty-page catalogue of minutely printed items. It is worthwhile having a copy of price-lists of the type produced by *Chemist and Druggist*, *The Grocer*, or a mail-order catalogue just to show the thousands of products that are retailed. A glance at the index of *Kompass*, the industrial directory, or Yellow Pages will show how impossible it is to keep track of everything that is sold. There are, of course, reams of information printed about each and every product. Getting reliable information takes a lot of time—even arranging interviews with buyers will take at least an hour's work with letters and phone calls before the buyer's premises are visited a week or so later.

Always give yourself enough time to complete the work well, and set out a very late date in your draft if you suspect that haggling about the completion date will take place. Arrange an **interim presentation** if a complete report cannot be made available at some crucial time.

Use has been made in this example of your own resources for most of the industrial interviewing and of a market research agency for consumer interviews. There are no rules as to when to use outside services, but in this case you decide that it will be cheaper if you use an agency for the very simple research required. Market research agencies offer a resource, at a price, and their use is further discussed later in the book.

Key Concepts

Scenario. A description of the future, referring to different outcomes depending on chance events or human behaviour. Sales scenarios are often produced to show at what level sales or other important activities may stand in future years, depending on different events. A pessimistic, an optimistic and a central scenario are usually presented. Scenarios are also developed to cover different eventualities with regard to competition, such as amalgamations or failures.

    Terms of Reference. A written document setting out how marketing research will be undertaken and listing objectives, methods, timing and other information as relevant.

    Market Hypothesis. A summary of desk research arranged to highlight probable facts about the market place and show gaps in information, thus indicating the information that it should be planned to obtain by the bulk of field research and further desk research.

    Hands on Product Familiarisation. Being shown a product in use and being allowed to touch it and learn its function, benefits, facets capable of improvement and so on.

Exercises

    1. Write terms of reference showing how you would carry out research on the national market for any one of the items listed below, in order to write a 3,000-word article for a magazine selling to businessmen, with three weeks to complete the task:

(*a*) paperback books,	(*f*) anoraks,
(*b*) stockings,	(*g*) edge-connectors,
(*c*) cars imported from Italy,	(*h*) fishfarms,
(*d*) PVC drainage pipes,	(*i*) steel cladding,
(*e*) tennis balls,	(*j*) scaffolding services.

    2. Invent a new product which you believe will have potential because it offers an improvement on an existing product (it could also be an existing product that you might import). Brief a colleague on the product and receive his proposals for research set out as draft terms of reference. Agree a final research programme.

    3. Business graduates frequently complete their studies by undertaking an industry study. Assuming that the industry is steel or plastics production, estimate the number of interviews required to obtain adequate information, and calculate the total cost of travel, including accommodation.

    4. The sales manager for Polotroat, a metal coating originally marketed in the 1940s, is delighted to report a very significant upturn in sales over the past four years. It has been fashionable to point to Polotroat as a product that has been superseded, but the sales manager believes that the product is finding new uses, and sales are now growing rapidly. She wants the analyst to explore what is happening in the market in order to build on success. As the analyst prepares his market hypothesis, he obtains the data tabled below on national

sales of Polotroat. What does the information suggest about the need for research? Present the information in such a way as to support your conclusions.

National Sales of Polotroat from All Sources ('000 tonnes)

1978	261	1984	230	1990	127
1979	301	1985	231	1991	62
1980	298	1986	159	1992	18
1981	220	1987	68	1993	22
1982	107	1988	74	1994	56
1983	153	1989	130	1995	68

4
Organising Marketing Research

This chapter will provide some guidance on how to organise the work of marketing research, breaking down the task by segments to be tackled one at a time, as follows:

(*a*) product familiarisation,
(*b*) background statistics, mainly desk research
(*c*) literature search,
(*d*) field work.

Particular stress is put on the need to obtain as much personal knowledge of the product to be researched as is possible.

Product Familiarisation

Requests for information about a market often come from persons who know only a little about the market in question. Occasionally, it is true, someone who knows a market intimately will call on a marketing analyst to provide information in order to find out if his own perceptions are correct and if there are any other facts that should be known. It can sometimes happen that a malicious manager will ask for research on a market he knows intimately in order to discredit the marketing analyst's unbriefed findings by pointing out a myriad of trifling errors in the analyst's report. The best weapon against disagreeable findings in a report by an angry recipient (the conclusions and recommendations of which may be correct or incorrect) is for the recipient to rapidly mark up the errors with a red pen, photocopy the annotated report and send the original with its bold red-ink corrections and glosses to the managing director. The more rapidly this is done, the more devastating the effect on the analyst. This sort of thing takes place in industry, but the managers who try to fly in the face of reality by using such ploys always come to grief in the end. The logic of the market is invincible—no one buys a poor product for very long.

The analyst usually starts off knowing very much less about the product than the person who is briefing him. He needs to familiarise himself with the product as thoroughly as possible. If it is something made in the company, it needs to be seen and discussed with the people who sell it. Consider any of the products below and how much you know about them:

(*a*) hot-tops for metal castings,
(*b*) valve sacks,
(*c*) cable television,
(*d*) polycarbonates,
(*e*) systemic insecticides,
(*f*) KD kitchen cabinets.

Yet all these products have partial links with the chemical industry as markets for raw materials and might require investigation by an analyst in a chemical company.

Each market has its own language to be mastered. The analyst may be requested to find out about 'hot tops' and wonder what they are. He will have to find out. Or in the case of kitchen cabinets, someone may refer to 'KD kitchen cabinets'. As has been explained in Chapter 3, it is not always a good idea to admit to the full state of one's ignorance of a market at the start, and it may not always be possible to discover exactly what distinguishes a KD kitchen cabinet from any other sort of cabinet at a briefing meeting. But after the briefing is completed, the analyst will need to find out what KD means as soon as possible.

Factory, Shop and User Visits

The best method of familiarisation is to go to the factory (if your company or your client's company make the product) and look at it being made and packaged. The analyst would rapidly learn that 'KD' means 'knocked down' (i.e. in kit form, ready to be erected by the final user) and that 'FKD' means 'fully knocked down', in contrast to the sometimes partly knocked down status of furniture that is 'KD'. The foreman on the production line will be able to point out all sorts of differences between products in language used in the market-place, which will be understood by the retail buyers of the same product. The analyst will find the time spent talking to persons who make the product to be absolutely invaluable. 'What distinguishes this KD kitchen cabinet from that one?' 'This one is made from blockboard with thin low-pressure laminate; that one is made with plyboard with decorative laminate.' The analyst asks the foreman to explain the terms, thus learning the vocabulary, the reason why some products are cheaper (and nastier) than others, and just what the customer gets for his money.

Usually it is a question of simply looking at the product, feeling it and understanding what it does. Occasionally it may be necessary to have a lesson in the basics of the science behind a product, be it chemistry, electricity or computer science. The analyst might need to find out what the 'bus' is for a personal computer system. If it cannot be seen, at least it must be explained. The analyst must seek out those who can explain the whole process, and a good point to start is within the company itself, in the factory where the goods are produced.

Shop visits for retailed goods are essential and usually inexpensive. Baby food, for example, might require to be researched because of an impending change in packaging affecting the analyst's client. How does baby food look on the shelves of the retailer? Is it competing by the attractiveness of its packaging or is it entirely dependent on the recommendation of the doctor or maternity clinic? There are many steps in finding the answer but if the analyst neglects the obvious step of looking at what is happening in the chemist's, he will be making a big mistake. The analyst should talk to chemists, and ask them about the pattern of buying. 'I'm just investigating the market for dried-milk baby foods—here's my business card. I wonder if you can tell me about your experience? Do mothers swap brands very much?' The chemist will usually be able to provide some interesting information, making the product more familiar to the analyst at this early stage.

Because the research has not started yet, the goal so far is to become familiar with the product—what it looks like, what it costs, who buys it, why they buy it—but only in a very general way. Logically the analyst should talk to some users of the product at this point and even use or consume it himself if the product in question is a consumption good. If you are investigating the market for instant photography, you must get some experience of buying film and taking photos in order to know what you are talking about.

Of course, it is not always possible to get **hands-on experience** in every market, nor is it always necessary. If phenolic resins are used as part of the process of making metal castings, the analyst may, because of time constraints, be unable to visit a user early on, and for the purposes of the research it may be enough for him to know simply that the resin is used in making castings, and direct his attention to the next stage of research, where he has a look at the statistics for castings in general.

Background Statistics

Every market can be seen as part of a larger market, and it is usually worthwhile situating the product to be investigated in the larger market to which it belongs. In an investigation of the prospects for a new roofing tile, information on roofing tile deliveries over the past few years is obviously of value; but trends in construction in general are also of relevance. 'Is it a good idea to launch a new building product in the middle of a construction slump?' is a question which someone is going to pose, and it is the analyst's job to provide the background statistics that show the extent of the depression. He will look for data on size of the **replacement market** (re-roofing is a replacement market) and decide that national figures for maintenance expenditure are of relevance. Table 4.1 shows some commonly used background statistics required for the analysis of different types of market, indicating how important it is to look at the figures and how many years' data is required. The table highlights the need for five years' data to get a reliable feel for trends.

Table 4.1. Background Statistics Required for Market Analysis

Years' Data Needed	Type	When used	Importance
5	Gross National Product, deflated Gross Domestic Product, deflated	Mainly export-related research	Not high: the national GDP is part of most managers' background knowledge
5	Industrial investment, deflated	For investment goods: machinery, machine tools	Important if this is a new market to the company
5	Value of construction, deflated Housing starts Housing completions	Construction products —residential	
5	Value of non-residential construction, deflated	Factory, institutional	Vital for construction products, even if the company is in the industry
5	Service industry statistics Value (inc. deflated) Volume	In all service industries	Essential
5	Industry output statistics Value (inc. deflated) Volume	In all market analysis	Essential

5	Personal disposable income, deflated	For consumer goods	Optional, unless the consumer market is unknown to your company, because it is something that management is aware of
5	Consumption statistics Volume Value (inc. deflated)	For consumer goods	Essential, where the statistics exist
5	Retail statistics Volume Value (inc. deflated)	For consumer goods	Essential, where the statistics exist
5	Net acquisition of financial assets by business sector	Indicator for office equipment of all types	Useful to highlight business cycle effect on demand

GNP and GDP

Gross National Product and Gross Domestic Product are two measures of the national output of goods and services, the first of which includes income from abroad. Generally these measurements are not required in marketing analysis, because the history is well known to management. Occasionally, however, when you discover that the statistics for the product in question show enormous fluctuation in output year on year, it may be worthwhile going back to the GDP figures (the most often used) in order to show the degree to which the fluctuation in growth in the economy in general (measured by GDP) affects the product in question.

To do this the analyst should use **GDP deflated** that is, with the effect of inflation removed. The sources of economic statistics—the most usual one employed in the UK being the *Annual Abstract of Economic Statistics*—provide this information in deflated terms by giving the value of the GDP in pounds of a certain year, thus removing the effect of inflation. A simple way of illustrating the effect of the economy on the product in question is then to show the percentage change year on year in GDP next to the percentage change year on year in the output of the industry, provided that the growth rate for the product is not too high. If the long-term growth rate is high, it may be better to use percentage deviation from trend to show the cyclical nature of demand. See Table 4.2.

Table 4.2. GDP Growth and Cylical Effects on Production of Two Plastics Materials in Unteland

	1990	1991	Actual 1992	1993	1994	Forecast 1995	1996
GDP in constant 1990 $U	3212	3279	3329	3312	3415	3430	3405
Year on year change (%)	+2.6	+2.1	+1.5	−0.5	+3.1	+0.4	−0.7
Low density polyethylene	413	438	457	461	517		
Year on year change (%)	+8.1	+6.0	+4.3	+1.0	+12.0		
Supertherm—tonnes	13.8	15.9	18.9	20.7	24.9		
Year on year change (%)	+33	+15	+19	+10	+20		

Tables like 4.2 will be acceptable in an accountant-dominated company, but in many companies a chart will be preferable (see Fig. 4.1). You will have noticed that, although it is very clear that low density polyethylene is cyclical, Supertherm seems to suffer only minor fluctuations. If we have a good reason for wanting to highlight the vulnerability of Supertherm to recession—and we may have reason to do this because we are forecasting that growth is going to slow down considerably—then we can show this by plotting percentage deviation from trend (Table 4.3). However, you generally need at least eight years' data to show the trend for GDP, i.e. long enough to cover two business cycles. The number of years you use to show the trend for consumption of materials is a question of judgement.

The percentage deviation from trend is calculated by taking the difference between the year's actual consumption and the calculated trend and showing it as a percentage of the trend.

Per cent deviation from trend =

$$\frac{\text{Actual as reported} - \text{trend as calculated}}{\text{Trend as calculated}}$$

for each year.

Logarithms are used for Supertherm because of its high growth rate. But a characteristic of a new product is that its growth rate starts to slow down. The first logarithmic projection at line E in Table 4.5

Fig. 4.1. Actual and forecast Supertherm consumption and real GDP growth in Unteland, 1991–6.

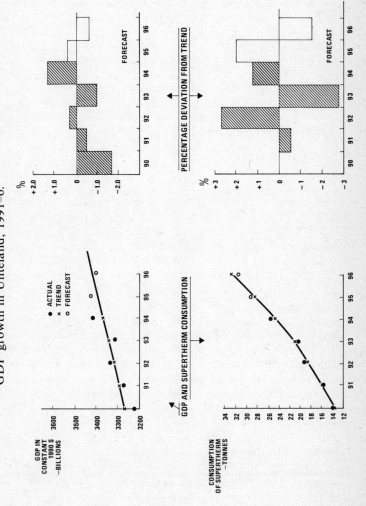

Table 4.3. GDP Growth and Cyclical Effects on Production of Two Plastics Materials in Unteland

	1987	1988	1989	1990	1991	1992	1993	1994
A. GDP in constant 1990 \$U (billions)	3181	3253	3269	3212	3279	3329	3312	3415
B. Trend	3190	3126	3242	3268	3294	3320	3346	3372
C. Difference	−9	+37	+27	−56	−15	+9	−34	+43
Percentage deviation from trend$=\dfrac{A-B}{B}\times100$	−0.3	+1.1	+0.8	−1.7	−0.5	+0.3	−1.0	+1.3
D. Supertherm— tonnes	3.0	6.1	10.4	13.8	15.9	18.9	20.7	24.9
E. Trend (based on logs from 1987)	4.6	6.0	7.9	10.4	13.7	17.9	23.0	30.9
F. Difference (D−E)	−1.6	+0.1	+2.5	+3.4	+2.2	+1.0	−2.3	−6.0
Percentage deviation from trend$=\dfrac{D-E}{E}\times100$	−35	+2	+32	+33	+16	+6	−10	−19
G. Trend (based on Logs from 1990)	—	—	—	13.8	16.0	18.4	21.3	24.6
H. Difference	—	—	—	0	−0.1	+0.5	−0.6	+0.3
Percentage deviation from trend$=\dfrac{D-G}{G}\times100$				0	−0.6	+2.7	−2.8	+1.2

gives far too high a figure for 1994—a growth curve which includes the first two rapidly growing years of a newly launched product will always project too high a growth. So the analyst chooses 1990 as a starting point.

The result is plotted in Fig. 4.1. It shows that Supertherm is already affected by economic cycles—something that the original data did not show clearly.

Industrial Investment and Construction Statistics

Industrial investment, deflated, is a readily available figure which is sometimes of relevance. Construction statistics are only of relevance to construction products. Housing starts 'lead' housing completions by about a year, i.e. the houses started are completed a year later, and we can use the statistics to provide a 'leading indicator' of what completions will be. In most European countries permits are used instead of starts, but with few exceptions the correlation between permits and completions is very high (usually over 0.97, except for

Italy). Construction statistics are the source for information on construction in the UK, as well as the *Annual Abstract of Statistics*. Sometimes it may be necessary to telephone a government department in order to obtain the latest statistics, not yet available off the shelf. In these cases patient searching will eventually lead you to the right extension, sometimes after as many as eight wrong leads. Note the name, number and extension of the source, because you are sure to need it again later.

Service Industry Statistics

Besides the sources mentioned above, these often have their own measurements. In the tourist industry, for example, numbers of visitors to the country and number of bed-nights in hotels are of obvious relevance.

Industry Statistics

Devised for the use of an industry, these statistics often contain exactly what the analyst needs. There are two very frustrating exceptions— high growth new industries, and industries dominated by one large supplier. Both these types of industries are of great interest to the rest of the commercial world, but there is nothing to be done about getting their statistics off the shelf. Fieldwork will be needed. The source for statistics on industrial output in the UK is the Business Monitor series, available through the Department of Trade and Industry.

Deflated Statistics

Deflated statistics of value are needed where there is no measurement of volume available, and here the analyst must choose a deflator. Normally the deflator used is the index of wholesale prices. Its use is shown in Table 4.4.

Table 4.4. Value of Unteland Production of Decorative Brassware, 1990 to 1995—Million Unteland Dollars

	1990	1991	1992	1993	1994	1995
Value in $U of year (A)	3.1	3.8	4.2	4.5	4.9	5.2
Wholesale price index (B)	100	104	110	120	127	135
Value at constant 1990 prices $(\text{A} \times 100)$ over B	3.1	3.6	3.8	3.8	3.9	3.8

In Table 4.4 the analyst may have gone back to the original series and found it indexed with 1988 as year 1, equalling 100. In order to make clear the way that the deflator works, he has divided the series from 1990 by the 1990 index, to get 1990 as the start year.

Personal disposable income, which is how much money the nation has in its pocket and the bank, always requires to be deflated to be understood. Let us take an example here to show how any series can always be re-indexed back to a starting date of our choice. See Table 4.5.

Table 4.5. Personal Disposable Income in Unteland, 1990 to 1995— Billion Unteland Dollars

	1990	*1991*	*1992*	*1993*	*1994*	*1995*
Value in $U of year	1909	1989	2287	2700	3104	3507
Retail price index (1988 = 100)	120	131	145	158	170	179
Retail price index (1990 = 100)	100	109	121	132	142	149
Value at constant 1990 $U	1909	1825	1890	2045	2186	2354

In adjusting the RPI to make 1990 equal 100, we have simply divided the series by the first observation,

$$\frac{131 \times 100}{120} = 109.2$$

which is the index for 1991.

Consumption Statistics

Consumption statistics are usually disappointing from a published, government-sourced direction. The annual **Blue Book** (*National Income and Expenditure*) provides data on consumption of various consumer goods, but generally the detail is not very fine. Nevertheless, this source can provide some background on long-term trends: for example, the growth in coffee-drinking. Much privately sourced information exists, obtainable at a cost, from such sources as Attwood, Gallup, and many others. Information on these sources should be sought from the Market Research Society.

Retail Statistics

More properly, retailing statistics, these are the speciality of A. C. Nielsen, for grocery outlets. They are very useful for short-term snapshots of the market, and can aid in estimating the size of the national market.

Net Acquisition of Financial Assets

This statistic derives from the Central Statistical Office and is published in *Financial Statistics*. (See C. W. Pettigrew, 'Financial Balances of Industrial and Commercial Companies', *Economic Trends*, December 1978.) It is of interest to the office equipment industry (including telecommunications systems, data processing, typewriters, and so on) because it provides a clear indicator of how much spare cash there is in the commercial sector. Sales of office equipment clearly are dependent to some extent on the profitability of the business sector, and this is exactly what this indicator signals: how much spare cash the business world has to buy stocks, bonds and shares. The indicator leads by up to a year and can be used like GDP to show the sensitivity of sales to companies' ability to buy financial assets. But it is more useful than GDP in some ways, because it leads (like housing starts lead completions) by about a year.

Take the cumulative balance of companies' liquid assets for four quarters (which equals a moving annual total) and plot it. Do the same for the orders and for sales of the office product being investigated (e.g. PABXs or typewriters). Peaks and troughs in the first series will lead those in the second series for mature products.

Moving Annual Growth Rates

These are useful in showing the dependence of a market on the larger market in which it belongs. Fig. 4.2 illustrates the way in which deliveries of metal window frames move in cycle with completions, though they are more volatile. The fact that permits (or starts in the UK) lead completions by about a year means that the next year's trend is always known.

This section has described the collection and analysis of background statistics. Their projection forward is not at issue yet: all the analyst has sought to do so far is to understand what the history of the industry has been up to now. In every case the analyst has looked at at least five years' data and in some cases he will look at more, in order to get a view that is not too influenced by the ups and downs of the business cycle.

What to do if there are no statistics? As will be seen, the analyst does the best he can. But to neglect to look for what statistics are available would be a real mistake.

Fig. 4.2. Moving annual percentage changes in value of domestic deliveries of metal window frames and non-residential building completions in Unteland (cu.m).

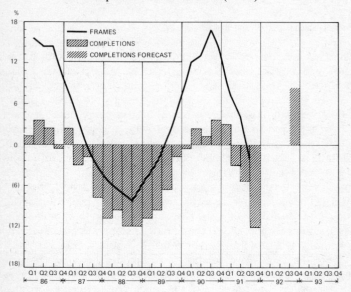

Literature Search

This means the reading of articles, press cuttings, magazines and books on the topic in question. A good business library will have an index, and the analyst can start to look at what is available. Reading trade magazines is very useful, because you pick up the names of the industry leaders, some of the issues that trouble it, and find out the companies who advertise or do a lot of public relations work, reflected in the number of news items about their products.

Computerised data banks can be employed for a literature search, but do not use one without the help of a professional and not before you have a very clear idea of the information you want to get. To give an example, 'Could you please get me some information about the cigarette industry?' would be an invitation to be inundated with a tonne of computer information on cigarettes and health, cigarettes in the USA, in Turkey, in Europe, in Asia, in Australia, in 1980, in 1985 or in 1990 as appropriate; all this will come flowing from the data bank. What do you want to know? The best plan is to wait until you have completed some of your fieldwork before you employ a data bank, because by then you will have some key questions still outstanding. This advice is given because the analyst does not know what are the important questions until he has most of the answers in his hand. The data bank cannot be scanned and skipped in the same way as trade magazines can be read and understood—all that it provides is a list of articles which may or may not be of interest. For statistics, occasionally, a data bank may be a direct source and a handy one for rapid work, but beware! They can never be as up to date as the original source and that can sometimes matter.

Besides reading books and magazines, the analyst often needs examples of sales brochures from suppliers of consumer durables and industrial products. These are obtained by shop visits or by writing to the company in question and requesting details of a particular product. For some industry products such brochures do not exist because the products are sold personally, but generally there is quite a lot of printed information on products available to the public and the market investigator.

Do not neglect to approach major market research agencies and consultants, particularly companies that publish research, like Frost and Sullivan, in order to find out if there are any reports in existence that can be bought from your department budget. Weeks of work can sometimes be avoided by buying inexpensive relevant material. The British Overseas Trade Board publishes a very useful *International Directory of Published Market Research*, which should be consulted.

Fieldwork

Fieldwork comprises visits to persons gaining their living from selling the product under investigation or from representing the industry that produces it, or to those who gain some of their living by analysing it, regulating it or in some other activity that makes them aware and knowledgeable about the product or service at issue. In this chapter, we are looking at how to organise the business of visiting them. In Chapter 6 the persons who should be included in the sample are discussed. The stages of fieldwork will be the following:

(*a*) drawing up the list of contacts,
(*b*) approaches to contacts,
(*c*) clinching the interview,
(*d*) arranging the timetable,
(*e*) visits

Listing the Potential Contacts

As he reads through the literature, the analyst will have been listing potential contacts in order of importance. The list should be bigger than the number of interviews desired, by a factor which differs according to the information required and the circumstances of the company. Some examples may illustrate this.

Contacts with Buyers at National Retail Chains

These buyers are the experts on the products they buy and their time is worth a lot of money to you but also to them. Getting an interview is like obtaining an invitation to a Royal Garden Party.

Contacts with Industrial Buyers Whom Your Company Supplies

There will be problems of holidays, travel and sickness among the contacts sought, but you should count on reaching 90 per cent of the list you draw up with the aid of your sales manager.

Contacts with Professionals

The doctor, the architect and the lawyer are busy men. Their time equals their income. Approaches have to be made with great care, your seriousness has to be evident, and nine out of ten may conclude that the pay-offs for giving information are too small to justify the time.

Contacts with Small Businessmen

Deeply suspicious, under pressures most of the time from staff and clients, the small businessman is like the professional when approached.

Information from Competitors

While it is relatively easy to obtain interviews with competitors, the chance of getting useful information is very small. Normally, all that the analyst can hope for is information on the size of their marketing headcount (the number of people employed in the marketing department) and perhaps some chance facts of marginal relevance to the market. This is because the competitor's interest is in having as large a share of the market as possible and his meeting with someone else with the same goal is like an encounter with a competitor in an interview for the same job: an occasion for courtesy laced with every kind of deception. The competitor will inform you that the market is, despite all evidence to the contrary, already in decline or expected to decline very soon, and will prove his point by reference to US or Japanese experience (stressing his company's multi-national coverage). Do not believe a word. A visit to a competitor is useful to obtain some idea of the size of their marketing headcount, but that is about all.

Approaches to Field Contacts

A letter or telex setting out the purpose of research, the reason why the research is being carried out, and the hoped-for date of the prospective meeting is still the best way of obtaining a meeting, using a promise to telephone later rather than a request for a written reply. Here is an example of a letter addressed to a buyer of packaging at a brewery. The name of the buyer has been found by a previous telephone call and the buyer is addressed in his own language—never send a letter in English to a foreign buyer.

TRANSLATION

From: Mrs Sharon Shore   To: Mr Ugo Untel
    Market Analyst   Brasseries Barfords
    Canstack Incorporated   2222 Unteland
    London W.1.

Dear Mr Untel,

Recent press reports of which you will be aware have described the advantages of the unique Canstack system for merchandising canned goods. I am writing to request an interview in order to discuss the potential for this new product in the brewing industry, as seen by an expanding brewer currently regarded as in the vanguard of merchandising techniques.

    I shall be visiting Unteland between July 12th and 19th and hope to make contact with you for an interview which should take up no more than 30 minutes of your time. I shall telephone during the week of June 20th in order to confirm a suitable time and date and I hope to be seeing you in July.

Yours truly,

Sharon Shore

The features to note about this letter are:

1. *It is short and to the point.* It gives the minimum of information needed to establish a joint interest.
2. *It says little about the purpose of research*, but does explain that selling a product is the final goal.
3. *It flatters the buyer* (recipient of the letter). He expects to be flattered.
4. *It engages the buyer's curiosity.*

5. *It makes no promises.*
6. *It gives no exact details of when the meeting is to take place.* There is no point in trying to be precise at this time. In fact, it helps to be imprecise even about the time you (or your secretary) will telephone.

In this hypothetical case a woman writes the letter. In many cases it will be written by a man. In all cases (in 20 years' experience) a woman has a better chance of clinching an interview by telephone than does a man, provided that the buyer is a man. That is why a female secretary is so often used to finalise the interview date. The reason for this is not sinister. Most men prefer to grant favours to a charming young woman rather than a charming or even distinguished man. They receive no impression of the personality of the person seeking an interview through this secretarial contact, and this can also be of help in breaking through the inertial barrier to reach the target interviewee.

Clinching the Interview

Telephone follow-up has to take place within the broad time limits set in the letter, and as the analyst or preferably his secretary makes the calls, he or she needs a map and a drawing in front of them to arrange the travel and timetable. She needs to explain: 'Mr Thruster will be in Gloucester on Tuesday morning and wonders if he could see you on Tuesday afternoon at Stroud?' Interviewees appreciate the logistics of travel. It is useful to note where interviewees say 'You can visit me at any time during the day', because the day can then be organised around contacts who have very tight time-schedules, leaving the flexible calls to be filled in as best as is possible on the day in question.

Use the interview clincher to obtain as precise directions as possible on how to reach the company being visited. Even if you are coming by taxi, there may be special tricks to learn.

Arranging the Timetable

Generally the analyst needs to allow at least 90 minutes per interview. Some will be very much shorter, some may be longer, but 90 minutes should be regarded as a minimum. Yes, it is possible to get all the information you might need in 30 minutes from a coherent, cooperative, hard-pressed executive; but what normally happens is that the buyers (or other interviewees) give you more time than they had planned to do in the first place.

How many industrial interviews can you undertake per day? In a capital city it should always be possible to get three and with luck you may manage five. A lot depends on the type of information you are after. In one case a company was seeking information about roller-towels installed in factories and offices, and it was found possible to do eight to ten interviews every day because the information was not closely guarded by respondents. The analyst in this case simply 'knocked at the door' of the factory, i.e. asked the receptionist who was responsible for handling the roller-towel contracts and if it was possible to talk to him. He had one refusal in eight approaches and was able to get responses from a big sample in very rapid research. But this example was concrete, everyday, cost little, offered the chance of saving money in the future and required no expert to understand the product. Imagine trying to arrange a series of interviews with managing directors of small companies about their attitudes to use of shire horses as a publicity medium! Not quite an opportunity for speedy in-out research.

One other hint about the timetable: make sure that there is adequate time for travel. Always err on the side of generosity because it is easy to get lost.

Finally, always take the trouble to confirm the arrangements for the final visit in writing, usually telexes, as this can save you a great deal of embarrassment. It is useful to write the names and addresses of all the companies you intend to visit on small filing-cards, which you can take with you as you travel—suitably annotated with the name of the contact, date of visit, notes on the location and so on. These can even be useful for when you have a typewritten list of contacts prepared in your final report, as they can be arranged into any order you like (e.g. by segment or alphabetically).

Visits

Chapter 6 will be concerned with how you address questions at an interview; here it is sufficient to mention the practicalities of field visits. First, always ensure that your secretary or a colleague knows where you are and can contact you while you are interviewing, as this can save you a lot of time if another interview has had to be cancelled through sickness or other unforeseen events. Secondly, ensure that you have your copies of telexes or letters of confirmation about the interview, as these can open doors that might otherwise be closed, owing to the unforeseen absence of the contact with whom arrangements have been finalised. Try to stick to the rule that you never look at your watch during an interview. If you find you have overrun your schedule because your respondent has given you an enormous bonus of all sorts of useful information, request permission at the *end* of the interview to phone on to the next contact to explain you are just leaving.

Occasionally, you may be obliged to accept the hospitality of your contact or to offer to take him to luncheon. The more this can be avoided, the more efficient will the field research be: information obtained over a drink tends to evaporate rapidly. The view that meals between businessmen are required to cement cooperation is widely shared, but if you compare the output of analysts who subscribe to this view to those who do not, the difference will generally favour the abstemious.

Reports on visits must always be written up on the day of the visit, if the value of the visit is to be maximised. One of the most accomplished analysts I know always writes his reports (up to two typewritten pages long) in his car before going on to the next interview. These interview reports may not be used directly in the final report, but it is useful to have an answer to the question: 'What did the X Corporation tell you, anyway?' The final report, of course, is the distillation of information from many field visits.

Calculating Person-Hours Work

The number of interviews should be divided by the number of interviews per day in order to obtain an estimate of person-days of fieldwork. For background desk research, literature reading and statistics, it is best to allow at least 15 days for beginners and reduce the time afterwards, depending on their skill. Report writing and editing should normally take at least ten days for research including over 30 interviews and then two days per week of fieldwork. This can be reduced with experience. If someone else is responsible for editing (a very normal and useful arrangement), keep a note of the date and time at which they receive your manuscript, in order to avoid responsibility for lateness being laid on you rather than the editor.

Quick-and-Cheap Research

The most enjoyable research, for some temperaments, is for something complicated but with very tight time limits for results. In such circumstances it is possible to obtain a great deal of information, but it is not possible to sort out the relative weight of different items of information with any ease. Such research, often associated with acquisitions that require rapid ratification, should always be clearly labelled 'Quick-and-Cheap' to all recipients, to ensure that they are aware of its limitations. Quick-and-cheap research is usually broadly correct in its perceptions of a market; after all, if you are constrained by time to finding out the basics of a market, you will be pretty clear whether respondents report it to be flat, fast growing, or in decline. But there will be errors in the research that a full-scale report would not make. Quick-and-Cheap research is worth mentioning because it reminds us that even marketing analysis can be both time- and resource-constrained. In an ideal world there will be no quick-and-cheap research. In a badly run company there will be no marketing research at all.

Key Concepts

Desk Research. Research carried out in the office and libraries, comprising reading and analysis of trade statistics, published articles, trade journals, sales brochures and other information available without personal consultation.

In-House Research. Reading of statistics, visit reports and other information available inside your company and interviews and correspondence with company employees knowledgeable in the market being investigated.

Deflated Statistics. Reduction of money measurements of sales to value expressed in terms of the prices for one specific year, usually by means of the retail or wholesale price index for retailed or industrial products. This provides a rough indication of the volume of sales where volume data are unavailable.

Fieldwork. Visits to buyers, sellers and users of a product or service in order to obtain first-hand information about its current and future market.

Quick-and-Cheap. Information obtained and presented rapidly to meet a deadline, signalled to be such by use of this expression.

GDP. Gross Domestic Product, the most common measure of the value of the national output.

Exercises

1. The series below shows the Unteland GDP in Untel dollars, personal disposable income per head, national consumption of canned and frozen peas in tonnes, the retail price index and the GDP deflator from 1990 to 1999. Devise a way of showing cyclical effects on pea consumption graphically as clearly as possible, and explain the relationships. *Note:* The figures for Unteland GDP and PDI are in $ of the year: they are not deflated.

	1990	1991	1992	1993	1994	1995	1996	1997	1998	1999
National sales of peas, canned (tonnes)	89	87	91	99	106	97	88	94	108	98
National sales of peas, frozen (tonnes)	93	106	117	112	160	109	88	94	108	98
GDP in billion $U of year	741	834	947	1011	1118	1258	1443	1484	1548	1788
PDI per head, $U of year	2041	2289	2548	2744	3039	3374	3869	3979	4142	4670
RPI (1990 = 100)	100	114	127	135	148	160	180	192	204	224
GDP deflator (1990 = 100)	100	110	120	128	141	152	170	174	180	198

2. An international company with a turnover of £2000 millions per annum is investigating a number of prospects for diversification. In which cases below would you judge that quick-and-dirty research would be adequate and when would you advocate at least 5 man-days' research?

(i) An anti-pollution product to be sold in Europe, currently manu-factured in the USA. Legislation in Europe is stated to match American standards, and the growth in demand is expected to be even higher.

(ii) Solar panels have been offered on contract for sale in the UK, at £3,000 each. Sales of £60 millions per year are promised.

(iii) A new anti-jackknifing device for towed caravans claims to have potential for 100 per cent use on caravans. The product will cost £30 and penetration in France has reached 80 per cent in new caravans in three years. Estimate the British potential.

(iv) As for (iii) but estimate the European potential outside Germany and France.

5

The Size and Representativeness
of the Sample

In this chapter we shall look at the question of how many buyers (or specifiers) ought to be questioned in order to obtain adequate or, as it may be called, **actionable information** on the market. How much information is required before a businessman makes a decision depends on his temperament, experience and desires with regard to the market.

How Certain Do You Need To Be of the Answer?

At the worst, some businessmen require no information from the market-place at all, because they are already certain of the answer, although they lack any real knowledge of the market-place. This type of entrepreneur generally makes a mistake in the end, although it is much better for profits if he makes his mistake at the start. At the other extreme, there are businessmen characterised by an extreme reluctance to make any changes to the products they sell in the market-place, even in the face of considerable pressure from competition and customers, and these temperaments require more and more research of a more and more detailed character before they will do anything. This situation is characterised as 'paralysis by analysis'. Gigantic expensive surveys taking over nine months to complete are loved by managers of this type, and their response to the results is always disappointment and a need for more research.

The analyst should try to recognise managers of this type and press them with regard to the question: 'What do you plan to do if the segment of the market you are interested in turns out to be larger or smaller than a certain size, or if the buyers turn out to be more willing to experiment than other buyers?' The person requesting research is, of course, nervous and imaginative and will always be trying to get extra assurance by asking the buyer more questions: for example, 'Would you prefer a year's guarantee plus one free maintenance visit in year 2, to a two-year guarantee with no free maintenance? How about an 18-month guarantee with free maintenance in the next six months?' This is an exaggeration, of course, and questions cannot be posed exactly like that. But someone like this (assuming you both work for the same company) must be controlled and it must be explained that you cannot ask all those questions and get reasonable answers because respondents become tired, resentful and confused. The cost per interview must be spelled out in detail, and you need to get into an argument about the use of the results. If you work for an agency, on the other hand, such a manager may offer a lot of work for two years, or more.

Experience is the second factor that controls your need to be certain of the answer. If you are a brand manager concerned with **fast-moving consumer goods** (**FMCG** or **FMCP** for products), you will have experience of using a great deal of market research in modifying the products you sell. Small samples may be quite adequate for your purposes: you know how to evaluate the results.

The desires of the manager are also of relevance. If he plans to launch a new product based on the needs of a key customer, he may only require a small sample of other professional buyers just to check out whether his instinct is correct. If eight sampled potential buyers say 'No, I don't like it', he will revise his plans. He is quite happy with half the sample saying they like it, and half rejecting, because he plans to launch even if some buyers dislike the product. He is sure of himself because of past experience of **buyers' inertia** (reluctance to change), and so he will accept minimal enthusiasm from a small sample. But the sample will be adequate to give him certainty that he is making a mistake if seven or eight of the sample of eight say 'No, I don't like it' and give good reasons.

So the answer to the question 'How certain do you need to be of the answer?' varies according to who is asking the question and what they want to do with the answer. Certainty costs a lot of money and time, and as a general rule most businesses are able to tolerate a great deal of uncertainty in market research results, because they understand the environment in which they work and have a platform of certainty based on their sales to existing customers which they can use to evaluate results of field surveys.

How Large a Sample Do You Need?

The next question to pose is: 'Given how certain you want to be of the result, how large a sample do you need to obtain that certainty?' The answer depends to a large extent on how significant the factor or product you are researching is in the population to be investigated.

Consider an example: an aerosol spray is developed to provide an impermeable seal against dampness, and the product manager, so far concerned only with selling spray products for shoes, has no idea of how large the market might be. The size of the market and the number of sales need to be estimated because there will be a small investment in mixing equipment and tanks to hold materials and marketing costs will be high. The product is intended mainly for householders.

What is the population that needs to be investigated? As a first attempt, you might decide that it will be all householders, and you could decide to use a national random sample to ask 1,000 householders: 'Do you suffer from damp on any of the walls in your house or flat?' This brings back results in this case that 2 per cent of the population of householders in Unteland have such a problem.

Estimating Proportion of Population with an Exclusive Characteristic

The analyst can be very sure of the validity of the answer from a national random sample of 1,000 persons. Statistical theory shows that, when a population is dominated by one or two mutually exclusive characteristics, e.g. red balls and white balls in a bag, or householders suffering damp or not suffering damp in this case, we can set tight limits on the proportions in the total population with the same characteristic. Unteland is unique in having agencies offering truly **random samples**, of course, as samples of this type (which can and will include remote farmsteads) are extremely expensive. Table 5.1 is part of a table reproduced in full in Appendix 4.

Table 5.1. Range of Error of Estimates of Percentages of Population with One Characteristic at 95 per cent Confidence Levels (Plus or Minus)—for Random Samples

Percentage	Sample size							
	25	50	75	100	150	200	500	1,000
98 or 2	5.6	4.0	3.2	2.8	2.3	2.0	1.3	0.9
97 or 3	6.8	4.9	3.9	3.4	2.8	2.4	1.5	1.1
95 or 5	8.7	6.2	5.0	4.4	3.6	3.1	2.0	1.4
90 or 10	12.0	8.5	6.9	6.0	4.9	4.3	2.7	1.9
80 or 20	16.0	11.4	9.2	8.0	6.6	5.7	3.6	2.5
75 or 25	17.3	12.3	10.0	8.7	7.1	6.1	3.9	2.8
70 or 30	18.3	13.0	10.5	9.2	7.5	6.5	4.1	2.9
60 or 40	19.6	13.9	11.3	9.8	8.0	7.0	4.4	3.1
55 or 45	19.8	14.1	11.4	9.9	8.1	7.0	4.5	3.2
50	20.0	14.2	11.5	10.0	8.2	7.1	4.5	3.2

From Table 5.1 we see that, because we have a sample of 1,000 and a figure of 2 per cent, we can be reasonably sure that the total population of households in Unteland contains no more than 2.9 (i.e. 2.0 + 0.9) per cent of households suffering from damp and the number will be no less than 1.1 (i.e. 2.0 — 0.9) per cent. The expression 'reasonably certain' refers to samples of two mutually exclusive variables in a population with only those two variables, and means that 19 times out of 20 (or 95 times out of 100) a sample would indicate correctly that the total population had characteristics between the limits indicated. The table tells us that if we had found that 50 per cent of our sample (bottom right hand of the table) suffered from damp, the population in total might contain between 46.8 per cent and 53.2 per cent suffering from damp. If the result were so large, the sales development manager would probably not ask for any more information—it's a large market. A popular story in the marketing world concerns two salesmen who arrive on a small undeveloped island to sell shoes, one telegraphing back 'Returning on next boat, no one wears shoes' while the other reports 'Send large consignment urgently, no one wears shoes', which illustrates the difference between a salesman and anyone else. In either case there was no need to sample. No one encountered wore shoes and it was a small island. For populations of large countries, however, a random sample of everyone in the nation is needed to reach a hypothesis about the nation as a whole. You might go into a car park in Hamburg and record the number of Mercedes and the number of cars that were not Mercedes in order to make a hypothesis about the number of Mercedes in the population of cars in W. Germany—but this would be an error. Because Hamburg is different in characteristics from other places in Germany, the analyst might be happy to use the car park sample as a means of making a hypothesis about the percentage of cars that are Mercedes in a 20-mile radius of the car park, but that is all.

Inadequacy of Sample Data for the Management Decision

Let us go back to the example of the damp. So far we know that between 1.1 per cent and 2.9 per cent of households in Unteland suffer from damp. The entrepreneurial development manager says: 'Let's assume that 5 per cent of these householders can be persuaded to buy our product in the first year. From your figures it could mean 400,000 customers or 150,000! But we break even if we sell 320,000. You must be more precise.'

In fact the marketing analyst might feel very nervous about the results so far. The fact that a house suffers damp is far from indicating that householders are willing to start spraying its walls with a new product. Would it not be more sensible to start with existing sales of products against damp and assume that the new spray might win a share of the market?

The entrepreneur agrees that this is a valid approach, and the analyst visits a number of do-it-yourself stores and finds that products against wall damp in Unteland are limited to bituminous wallpaper and electrolytic systems. He discusses the problems of using these products with the store proprietors and finds that the first is messy and the second is expensive. The new product is shown to five national do-it-yourself experts, who are very enthusiastic—there is no doubt, they agree, that the new spray will take half the market of bituminous wallpaper within three years at the suggested price.

Sampling Another Population–Retailers

The problem now is to find out how big that market for bituminous wallpaper is in square metres per year. The population to sample now becomes retailers of bituminous wallpaper (it has been decided that sales to builders' merchants will not be taken into account in deciding whether to enter this market, as the entrepreneur is reluctant to base his case on anything other than the retail trade). Now the problem is to find out how much bituminous wallpaper is sold nationally on the basis of a sample.

There are 4,380 do-it-yourself retailers in Unteland. Like retailers in other countries, the Unteland shopkeepers do not mind giving a little information so long as they are not giving an indication of the total value of their business, so research is possible. Further calculation with the entrepreneur establishes that as long as the average do-it-yourself (DIY) shop sells more than 15 rolls a year, the total market will be adequate, i.e. more than 320,000 units a year. A questionnaire is developed as follows:

TELEPHONE QUESTIONNAIRE TO RANDOM SAMPLE OF UNTELAND DIY RETAILERS
Good morning. I am telephoning on behalf of Shoesprazee, the company that makes spray-on shoe shiners. We are thinking of launching a new spray against damp walls, and I am telephoning a number of DIY stores in order to estimate how large the market might be. We think our product will compete against bituminous wallpaper. Is that a product you can sell?

YES/NO (If no, close interview)

What do you think of the idea of our product? Here's how it would work (read sales brochure). Note retailer's comments ....
....
....

To get some idea of the size of the market, we are asking retailers like yourselves how many rolls you sell in a year. How many is it? ....
Is the market growing or are sales fairly static for this product?

Growing _____   Static _____

Do you think our product will compete?

YES/NO   Why? ....

Thanks for your help. In order to calculate the size of the national market from the sample, I need to know how big your business is, simply in terms of numbers of employees. Are you a one-man shop? YES/NO. How many employees? ....

Thanks again for your help.

Note some features of the questionnaire. The tone is informative, the questioner is frank about the reasons for his interest. But there is no leading question. The analyst cannot ask 'Do you sell more than 15 rolls of bituminous wallpaper a year?' because the retailer will say 'Of course!' He will sense that selling over 15 rolls makes him more important and successful. There is no point in asking how many rolls the retailer will sell next year because, if you ask this question, the replies will show a great upsurge in the market based on each retailer's wish to grow. The question is framed as it is to stop this sort of boasting but allow the retailer to explain that this is a growing market, if indeed it is one.

There is a reference to the size of establishment, framed in a way that does not upset the retailer's desire to keep details of the size of his business private. Unteland has no dominant retail outlets that would kink the results if they were missed out, it is believed (but see below). The questionnaire is used on a random sample of retailers—the names are chosen from a complete list of the 4,380 retailers, numbered from 1 to 4,380, and tables of random numbers are used to choose the companies to approach. The retailers of Unteland have an unusual characteristic in that they never refuse to help. If there were refusals, it would make the strict application of statistical methods of assessing the size of the total population's use of the product impossible. (Non-response invalidates probability sampling, although methods of compensation exist. Jackson, 'Case History Evidence of Errors Associated with Non-Response in Industrial Market Research', [*Commentary*, July 1966] refers to the literature and illustrates the problem in a commercial context with three case histories.) The results of the interviews are shown in Table 5.2.

Table 5.2. Numbers of Bituminous Wallpaper Rolls Sold by Unteland DIY Retailers in Latest Year

Rolls sold	1–4	5–9	10–14	15–19	20+	Average
Observations	5	5	7	5	3	11.76
(no. of outlets selling)						

Only eight out of the 25 sold 15 or more rolls. Can we be sure yet that the average sales nationally are less than 15 rolls? As we will see, the answer is—not yet.

Of course, if all the retailers had volunteered, 'Sales are growing very fast for this item, and every time I reorder I double the amount required', it would not be necessary to establish that 15 rolls is or is not the national average now, because the market next year would be much larger. Hence the question on growth.

The size of the sample needed, therefore, depends a lot on how significant the factor investigated turns out to be within the sample. If, by luck, the average sales of the DIY retailer needed to be only two rolls per year, then the sample of 25 retailers would easily have established that the average sales of retailers were over two rolls per year.

Establishing Average Sales from Sample

The analyst goes back to his sample statistics and sees what can be derived from them. The detailed results are shown in Table 5.3, and the calculations the analyst carries out are also given.

From Table 5.3 the analyst calculates the **standard deviation** of the sample, which is written as 'S' in statistical notation. S is calculated by means of a programmable calculator and is found to equal 6.935.

The analyst now needs to use the **sample mean** (found to be 11.76) to work out the possible limits of the **mean of the population** as a whole or, put another way, to find out what sort of average sales per outlet nationally is compatible with the findings about this sample. The predicted range of the population mean is found by the formula,

$$\bar{x} \pm \frac{Sx}{\sqrt{n}} t$$

where $\bar{x}$ is the sample mean
   Sx is the standard deviation of the sample
   n is the number of items in the sample (25 in this case)
   and t is the value you find in a t table for both upper and lower limits in Appendix 5.2.

Table 5.3. Number of Rolls of Bituminous Wallpaper Sold by 25 Unteland Retailers in Latest Year

Number Sold	Number of observations	Total	Number sold	Number of observations	Total	Number sold	Number of observations	Total
0	0	0	5	0	0	10	3	30
1	0	0	6	1	6	11	0	0
2	1	2	7	1	7	12	2	24
3	2	6	8	1	8	13	2	26
4	2	8	9	2	18	14	0	0
Subtotal	5	16		5	39	—	7	80
15	1	15	20	0	0	25	1	25
16	1	16	21	0	0	26	0	0
17	2	34	22	0	0	27	0	0
18	1	18	23	1	23	28	1	28
19	0	0	24	0	0	29	0	0
Subtotal	5	83	—	1	23	—	2	53
Grand Total							25	294

Sample mean $\bar{x} = 11.76 = \dfrac{x_1 + x_2 + x_n}{n}$

Sample standard deviation $6.936 = S_x = \sqrt{\dfrac{\Sigma(x - \bar{x})^2}{n-1}}$

The analyst decides that the entrepreneur will only be happy with 98 per cent certainty, so he decides to use the column referring to 98 per cent certainty (0.02 in the table).

The **t value** is read off the Appendix 5.2 table as referring to 24 degrees of freedom. For tests of this type, $t = n - 1$, that is, the number of degrees of freedom is one less than the number of items in the sample.

He then calculates the range of the sample mean, using the following data:

$$\bar{x} = 11.76$$
$$Sx = 6.935$$
$$n = 25$$
$$\sqrt{n} = 5 \ (\sqrt{\ } \text{ means the square root})$$
$$t = 2.492$$

The analyst now substitutes in the formula and the result is

$$11.76 + \frac{6.935}{5} \times 2.492 \qquad \text{for upper limit}$$

$$11.76 - \frac{6.935}{5} \times 2.492 \qquad \text{for lower limit}$$

That is $11.76 + 3.4564 = 15.2$ for upper limit
and $11.76 - 3.4564 = 8.3$ for lower limit

The result shows that the total population of retailers is predicted to have an average sale of between 8.3 and 15.2 rolls per year at 98 per cent confidence levels, thus making it possible that sales are as high as 15 rolls.

Increasing the Sample

The entrepreneur is now asked if he wants to extend the sample? With further sampling it will be possible to be more certain. Mind you, if the entrepreneur would be satisfied with 95 per cent certainty, it would already be clear that 15 rolls is ruled out as the population average. (This can be verified by recalculating, using the 95 per cent, i.e. 0.05, score.)

The entrepreneur wants to be very sure, so the analyst carries on. Another five retailers are duly sampled, using random numbers once more, with the remote possibility that a retailer already sampled could turn up in the sample again. This possibility is important, because many statistical laws depend on 'random sampling with replacement', a concept which it is unnecessary to explain fully here. The results are

8, 9, 10, 12 and 14. The mean is now calculated as 11.57 and S (the sample standard deviation) is 6.28. The analyst uses the formula

$$\bar{x} \pm \frac{Sx}{\sqrt{n}} t$$

substituting 11.57 for $\bar{x}$, the sample mean; 6.38 for Sx the sample standard deviation; and 30 for n, the number sampled. The limits of the mean for the total population (all retailers) is therefore

$$11.76 \pm \frac{6.38}{5.477} t$$

From the table, he sees that t is 2.462 for 29 degrees of freedom $(n-1)$ so the limits are

$$11.57 \pm 2.87 = 8.7 \text{ to } 14.44$$

The analyst can therefore inform the entrepreneur that the statistical odds for the average sales being over 14.44 are about 50 to 1 against.

Confidence Limits for Random Samples of More than 30

Where random samples of over 30 are employed, it is possible to use the normal distribution tables, as set out in Appendix 6. Take, for example, a continuation of research on retail sales of wallpaper (excluding large outlets), which gives the following figures:

Total sample size (n) = 40
Average sales $(\bar{x})$ = 11.98
Calculated standard deviation (Sx) = 6.82
σ = 6.82

The sample standard deviation is assumed to be equal to the population standard deviation, σ, in cases like this where you have more than 30 samples, hence σ is the same as Sx.

We can now calculate the range for the population mean (the average sales of the item at all retailers) by using the formula. Range for mean of population is

$$x \pm \frac{\sigma}{\sqrt{n}} z$$

at the degree of certainty you select.

A 95 per cent level of certainty (95 per cent confidence level) is chosen, so substituting in the equation we have

$$11.98 \pm \frac{6.82}{\sqrt{40}} z$$

We look up the table and see that z is 1.96.

So we calculate that national average sales of this item will be

$$11.98 \; \genfrac{}{}{0pt}{}{+}{-} \; \frac{6.82}{6.324} \times 1.96$$

$$11.98 \pm 2.11$$

We can be 95 per cent confident that the national average is thus between 9.87 and 14.09.

Sampling Businesses in Practice

Unteland would be unique in the pattern of its business if the size of businesses was normally distributed. In the practical world, as a generalisation with many exceptions, there is a tendency for 80 per cent of the sales to be made by 20 per cent of the outlets. This is called the **80/20 rule** and it means that while statistical methods of calculating the population mean can be applied, a more precise result can be obtained by sampling the **strata** (different size groups) independently and randomly.

Let us continue with this example. The entrepreneur informs the analyst that if he look at the sample carefully, he will see that it is in fact kinked due to some exceptionally large outlets being included in the sample. Unteland has recently opened some DIY gigantimarkets, all with over 200,000 square metres selling space. Since these have come into existence, the 80/20 rule is beginning to operate. A friend of the entrepreneur who works for a DIY journal says that the breakdown is in fact as shown in Table 5.4.

Table 5.4. Estimated Volume of Retail DIY Trade in Unteland by Surface Area of Store—1990

Surface area	Number	Per cent	Volume of sales ($mn)	Per cent	Sales per outlet (av. Value)
Less than 200,000 sq.m	4174	95.3	1,670.1	42.4	0.40
Over 200,000 sq.m	206	4.7	1,228.3	57.6	5.96
Total	4380	100	2,898.4	100	0.66

The analyst sees that you could certainly make a grave error if the gigantimarkets were not included in the sample. Looking back at the records of the telephone interviews, he finds that there were two outlets with over 20 employees included which stated that their sales were 25 and 28 rolls a year, double the sample average. On investigation they turn out to be gigantimarkets. This is one of those flukes, because the choice of outlets was made in an entirely random way.

Perhaps a sample of the gigantimarkets should be made and the results put together with the standard retailers. The gigantimarkets selling 25 and 28 rolls should be removed from the first sample.

Getting information about the gigantimarkets proves very difficult, for they are centrally controlled and only someone with access to the computer knows anything about the volume of sales. Finally, however, data on five gigantimarkets are obtained through another five helpful buyers. See Table 5.5.

Table 5.5. Number of Rolls of Bituminous Wallpapers Sold by 5 Unteland DIY Gigantimarkets in Latest Year

Outlets	Rolls
Husky Hobby	25
Brico King	75
Park and Buy	88
Tool Chest	90
Giant	110
Total	388
Average	77.6

The analyst has to inform the entrepreneur that this is not a random sample, but is in fact a **partial census**. There is a definite bias in that only friendly companies will help. The annual sales of these five gigantimarkets are known, and represent 6.1 per cent of total gigantimarket sales in the latest year. An estimate can be made by grossing up from the 388 rolls sold by companies accounting for 6.1 per cent of national sales to give a rough estimate of national gigantimarket use of 6,361 rolls. This is not a statistically backed estimate, since there is no way of knowing whether the national average is higher or lower or what it might be. The analyst discusses this projection with the entrepreneur, who decides that straight-forward grossing up is all right. 'The five you talked to seemed fairly typical', he says.

The analyst now puts together the estimates. See Table 5.6.

Table 5.6. Estimated Annual Average Sales of Bituminous Wallpaper per DIY Outlet of All Types—Unteland—Rolls

Type of outlet	Av. no. rolls sold pa			Total outlets of this type	Projection to national market ('000)		
	Low	Central	High		Low	Central	High
Under 200,000 sq.m	8.1	10.5	12.9	4174	33.8	43.8	53.8
Over 200,000 sq.m	na	30.9	na	206	—	6.3	—
TOTAL	—	—	—	4380	—	50.1	—
AVERAGE PER OUTLET					—	11.4	—

The results are just at the limit of being attractive; as a result of sampling the two sectors, the analyst gets an estimate of just below 12 rolls per outlet. Of course, there is a chance that the national average is higher, but the entrepreneur has been provided with all the information possible and a good measure of the risk. Normally double-checks by other research methods would resolve the decision problem.

Some Practicalities of Consumer Sampling

In this chapter so far some ways of establishing upper and lower limits which depend upon statistical methods have been briefly outlined. These are extremely important in consumer market research because in consumer markets one has a very large population, which can be sampled randomly and which approximates to a normal distribution.

In consumer sampling two or three levels of research can be carried out:

(*a*) *sequential sampling*, using a Bross chart (usually with own staff),
(*b*) *samples of 30 up to 100*, using own staff,
(*c*) *samples of over 100*, using market research agencies.

A Bross chart is shown in Appendix 7, and it is used to research preferences between two products or services at speed in order to find out which of two choices is preferred. (See 'Sequential Analysis: a reappraisal for Market Research', by E. J. Anderton, R. Tudor and K. Gorton, *Journal of the Market Research Society,* October 1976, and 'What Price the Humber Bridge Toll?' by the same authors, *IMRA Journal,* Winter 1979, Vol. XI, No. 1.) The researcher requires a random sample to make the use of the method valid, and approaches to persons in the High Street which approximate to this should only be recorded as preferences applying in that place. The method can be extended to national telephone samples, and here it can be extrapolated to apply to national preferences among phone subscribers. Preferences are recorded as a movement towards one side or other of the chart, and when the line reaches the outside limit, the hypothesis is established at 95 per cent confidence limits (in the case of the chart in Appendix 7) that there is a significant preference for one product or service over another. This means that over 50 per cent of the population, faced with this choice, state that they prefer one product to the other. The method is inexpensive, rapid, and good for price research, as, for example, 'Would you prefer to buy a normal washing machine or one with an all-electronic system at an extra cost of $20?' The question of what is an acceptable price to the public can be settled rapidly.

Samples of 30 up to 100 persons for consumer goods by your own staff are often practical. Interviewing the public is sometimes seen as undesirable by office workers—a silly prejudice—so in practice limits of this type impose themselves. Interviewing the public is hard work. A High Street position is usually necessary because of cost, and the results should not be extrapolated nationally.

Samples of 100 or more are usually carried out by professional agencies. Where a questionnaire is not very detailed—for example, 'Have you visited a department store within the last week?'—the researcher may opt to buy a question from an omnibus survey. This type of survey is run regularly, with questions purchasable by any company that wants to obtain information, up to a limit imposed by consumer fatigue. The results are very reliable even when not strictly random, because the user gets the benefit of the agency's expertise in sampling and posing questions to the public.

Practicalities of Sampling for Consumer Goods Markets

One of the surprising facts of commercial life is that although the science of statistics is well understood, the application of it to samples of the population who are potential or existing customers for consumer goods is comparatively rare. The reason is that the truly random sample is so expensive. Names drawn from a list, for example, on a basis of starting with a random number and then counting every x units to cover a certain percentage of the total population are not regarded as truly random samples. This type of sampling, called **list sampling** or quasi-random sampling, is convenient, but there is no easy way to calculate upper and lower limits from the data because sampling error is not known.

Cluster sampling is another type of sampling with some random elements, to which the calculation of sampling error cannot be applied. This type of research generally uses different geographical areas that resemble the total population as far as possible, with a random choice being made among the areas (or groups). Each person in the selected area is then interviewed. This is a popular method of research, as it reduces the cost of travel.

There are other methods of sampling based on probability but unable to make direct use of the science of statistics to calculate error, use confidence limits and so on, including multi-stage samples that divide and subdivide the areas to be investigated. The example of the investigation of DIY stores above was one where **stratified random sampling** might have been applicable. We saw that one stratum of the market, the DIY stores, could be investigated on a random basis, and if it had been possible to investigate gigantimarkets the same way, we could have had two statistically based estimates of the characteristics of two separate populations.

For all the methods cited above, except for true random sampling, agencies will generally not talk about confidence limits and usually will eschew claims for the statistical representativeness of their work. Agencies can be pressed to set limits on their estimates by clients who do not understand the limitations of the science of statistics, but normally an agency will not make unsupportable claims to please an entrepreneur desperate to reduce his uncertainty.

In practice, however, *methods of sampling which are not based on probability* are well understood by the entrepreneur. 'Industrial Survey Sampling' by Dwight L. Gentry and William A. Hailey (*Industrial Marketing Management*, July 1981) warns against the temptation to present data as deriving from a probability sample when non-response has been encountered.

Quota sampling is often employed as an inexpensive way of getting samples, but, once again, the methods of statistics used for calculations of the range of error of estimates of the population cannot be employed. For quota sampling the researcher seeks out respondents to match the known characteristics of the total population: for example, if the population of users of denture cleaners is made up of 40 per cent over 60, 30 per cent aged 50 to 59, 20 per cent aged 40 to 49 and 10 per cent all other, the researcher will seek a sample that matches this breakdown and cease sampling in a particular segment when sufficient interviews have been obtained.

Practicalities of Industrial Sampling

In industrial markets the most practical way of carrying out research is to ask the person who commissions it to state what sort of a sample he thinks is needed to be certain about market characteristics, in order to make the resulting decisions required for business expansion. The sample selected may be a partial census of the total population, designed to be as representative as possible, given a limited amount of information held on the total market. The entrepreneur will usually have five to ten key customers and potential customers in mind but, in many cases, there will be a need to sample some large group whose needs are not well known—for example, the customers of the company's customers who buy an end-product for which the original customer supplies the raw material. The type of aluminium supplied for lithographic plates can be specified by the few buyers of the product, but the prospects for aluminium sales for lithography depend on the future of this printing method. How many printers should be seen? For a statistically valid sample, numbers of at least 25 chosen at random all around the country will be needed. In practice, this is often too expensive if personal visits are required, and because of the 80/20 rule there will be a need to see several large companies that account for 50 per cent of demand. A good rule of thumb is always to go for 25 interviews as a goal, and never accept less than 15 in any downstream investigation. The reason is that experience shows that with a smaller sample the quality and quantity of information is just not adequate. This does not mean that, if a market is segmented, visits are needed to 25 outlets in each segment, but that 25 as a total is a minimum goal in a national market.

This figure of 25 is no more than a rule of thumb. It represents what many companies can afford and feel happy with, but it is not always enough. It represents enough for an analyst to be able to extract useful information about the market. Below 25, there is a chance that the picture of the market will be inadequate. Consider research into a construction product handled by roofing companies. The company specifying was interested to find out why its product was preferred to others by roofers, as there was no single obvious reason. At least 25 interviews were realised to be necessary in each country in which the company operated, and in the end a sample of 200 in each country was employed because the company in question felt happier with those numbers. In this case, the company was wealthy enough to foot the bill, but money and time constraints are often crucial.

Sampling Segments

If detail is required about some segment of the market, it becomes necessary, once again, to have a reasonably sized sample. In the lithographic plate market, for example, it might be found that the fastest growing sector was in-house stationery printing at large companies. If it were important to find out whether this sector had special needs or was liable to saturate rapidly, a detailed survey of 25 outlets might be needed, even though this sector represented only a tiny proportion of the total market.

Problems of Grossing up to National Market Size

Because the structure of industry and the service sector is often unclear or in a state of flux (with a movement towards amalgamations), it may be difficult to appreciate how kinked the market is by the 80/20 rule (see above p. 73). A national survey run on a regular basis for over ten years in one European country was known, by cross-checking with industry deliveries, to underestimate the true size of a particular market by a factor that varied between 55 and 65 per cent. The size of this error did not stop the major customer from employing the national survey, because the company valued the information on changes in the market, which were signalled by the sample. However, there is a lesson to be learnt from the problems of sampling exemplified by this survey: take care when extrapolating to the size of the national market. Always double-check with other available statistics, such as total production minus exports plus imports, or listen to the views of market experts. The size of the error possible with a sample is enormous. If, for example, the true percentage of the population with the characteristic investigated is not 0.2 per cent but 0.4 per cent, the market may be described as being twice as big as it really is. Errors of over 100 per cent are quite common and, although it may upset the recipient of the information, it is sensible to advise him or her that experience of grossing up to the size of the national market from a sample shows that large errors are possible. Work out the probable lower and upper limits of the forecast and state them boldly, even if the limits seem extremely wide.

Lack of Statistical Confidence Levels for Industrial and Distributor Samples

It is possible to calculate how many interviews are needed to achieve 99 per cent confidence levels in a kinked population in which 80 per cent of the purchases are made by 20 per cent of the purchasers but the process is complicated and outside the scope of this book. (See 'Sampling and Weighting of Industrial Products', *IMRA Journal*, Vol 5, No. 2, May 1969.) The analyst must follow this simpler logic in solving the problem:

1. *Investigate the Structure of the Market from the Point of View of Purchasing Power*
   In looking at retailed stationery products, or pharmaceuticals, the analyst will find that one outlet dominates the UK market, or that in groceries some twelve companies account for over 60 per cent of UK sales. Clearly, it will be essential to see all these dominating outlets in order to estimate demand for a potential product for the appropriate UK market if it is intended for the retail market. In such a case the analyst needs to explain the structure of the market to the entrepreneur and agree that all these dominant outlets should be approached. It will also be found that there are hundreds to thousands of small outlets that each account for a very small number of purchases.

2. *Agree on How Many Dominant Outlets/Customers are to be Interviewed*
   Likewise for other markets where there are outlets accounting for over 4 per cent of the total market, explain the situation to the entrepreneur and try to agree that it is worthwhile attempting to interview every outlet accounting for more than 4 per cent of the total market. It may not be possible to see them all because of refusals, cost or policy, but at least the entrepreneur will be party to the decision.

3. *Sample the Numerous Smaller Outlets/Customers*
   Where there are more than 100 other important outlets or customers, the most economic way of obtaining information will be to sample these outlets by telephone. Use may then be made of the calculations outlined above, if a probability (random) sample is obtainable, in order to estimate the confidence limits for calculating the average purchase, with samples of 30 wherever possible. Note that in some cases three strata, i.e. three size levels of enterprises engaged in purchasing, can all be sampled. The office products market, for example, where every business is a potential purchaser, has few dominant purchasers outside the Civil Service, and it is useful to divide it up into three or even four levels of purchasing power defined by size—say offices with less than 50 employees, from 51 to 100, from 101 to 500, and those with over 500 employees at one site.

Methods of Deciding on Sample Size Used in Commerce

The main constraint in business is the cost of sampling, and businessmen engaged in regular market research tend to settle on the number of interviews that 'feels right'. Twenty-five interviews per country are often accepted, provided that all the most important potential customers are interviewed. For markets where there is no dominance by a top handful of outlets, samples of 30 are common, with 100 or more as delightful exceptions. In all analysis there is a **learning curve** (an expression denoting the way that production increases per resource input in manufacturing, and applied to other processes where efficiency goes up after time) which applies to the analyst and his client, the entrepreneur. The analyst learns how to manage with limited time and money, and the entrepreneur learns how the fact of market segmentation may cause large samples to be necessary at the start but may ultimately allow him to concentrate on one segment of main interest, where smaller samples are required.

This chapter has shown that sampling is used in business as a means of reducing uncertainty, and the size of sample required in investigating any particular market depends on how certain the entrepreneur needs to be of the answer. The methods of sampling based on probability will give answers between defined limits that are correct 90, 95, 98 or 99 times out of a 100 (depending on what the entrepreneur is happy with), but these are usually expensive to employ and non-probability-based samples will often be used instead.

Sampling enters the business world when the entrepreneur is uncertain. Always insist that everyone who claims knowledge of some factor 'based on personal contact' is using some sort of sample, and a very small sample can be worse than none at all. The most common failure of new products is based on the enthusiastic reception of a new product concept by a handful of potential customers. Every time the analyst doubles the size of those sampled, whether consumers or industrial buyers, the risk of a mistake decreases. How big should the samples be? It needs to be large enough for the entrepreneur to be certain. The analyst must make it his task to ensure that the entrepreneur's certainty is adequately based.

Key Concepts

Actionable Information. Information on market characteristics that can be used by a management because it is relevant to decisions they are making, comprehensible, and trustworthy.

Buyer's Inertia. The tendency of any buyer to continue to buy what he has bought in the past.

Leading Question. A question inviting only one response because it is framed in such a way that the respondent is strongly motivated to reply with that response.

Certainty. The subjective assurance of management that knowledge of the market derived from specified samples, market analysis or from such other sources as personal experience is or will be adequate to allow them to act in the market.

Confidence Level. A statistical measurement of the degree of reliability of a sample by reference to the number of times out of 100—95 or 90 per cent are often employed—that such a sample would give estimates of the total population correctly between defined limits.

Standard Deviation. A measurement of the extent of variability (or dispersion) in a data set. It is based on the difference between each value in the data set and the mean of the group.

Random. A statistical term denoting that every unit in a population has a known chance of being selected and that no unit has no chance of being selected, thus permitting the application of the laws of probability. Random does not mean haphazard.

Non-random. Any sample selected by methods that do not give equal chances to each unit of being selected and to which the laws of probability therefore cannot be applied.

Sequential Sampling. A method of random sampling that continues until an adequate sample has been made to validate or invalidate a hypothesis at determined confidence levels.

The 80/20 Rule. That there is a tendency in many populations, particularly those involving human enterprise, for 20 per cent of the population by number to produce 80 per cent of the value. The 80/20 rule refers to the tendency for distributions to be kinked, and is not an absolute rule that the bias will be exactly 80/20.

Exercises

1. Using a Bross chart, interview a group of fellow students or members of the public in some central place like the High Street, asking each one: 'Do you intend to vote for or against the present Government at the next election?' Record each result as a movement to one or other side of the chart, ignoring 'don't knows', and note how long it takes to establish what the result will be. How useful would this result be for forecasting the preference of the whole population if there were an election (*a*) tomorrow, (*b*) in three months' time, (*c*) two years ahead? To what population could you apply these results? If you fail to reach an answer with the sample, how would you suggest that preferences should be investigated?

2. The sales manager for the North-West region of France gets his representatives to report on the retail prices of their main competitor's washing machine, Model X95, asking them to note what price is charged at the next five shops they visit or pass, thus including retailers to whom they do not sell. The results (in French francs) are FF999 at ten outlets, FF1,099 at three outlets, and the following prices: FF909, FF919, FF939, FF949, FF959, FF969 and FF979. Estimate the average price charged in the North-West region for this model, giving the range in which the average is 90 per cent certain to fall. Why are the prices below a round number?

3. The market for a revolutionary new scanner in hospitals in Unteland is related to the potential purchasing power of the different health boards in

each of the cantons, plus the Central Health Ministry purchases and the private sector. The budget pattern is shown below.

Health Budgets by Administrative Area and the Private Sector in Unteland—1997—Percentage Breakdown

Cantons		
Faxe	14	
Stellan	13	
Columbia	7	
Spielan	6	
Subtotal	40	
Central Health Ministry	29	
All Private Hospitals	31	
of which:		
Bassin		2
All others less than 2% each	—	29
TOTAL	100%	

Management asks the analyst to visit the central purchasing officer in each canton and the Central Health Ministry to find out their purchasing prospects for the new scanner. The analyst's plan to also visit 35 of the private hospitals also is vetoed by management as too expensive. Does this invalidate estimates of total market size? Management asks if results from the public sector have any statistical degree of confidence attaching to them. How should the analyst reply? How could the analyst obtain information on the private hospitals more cheaply than by personal visits?

6
Industrial Marketing Research

When carrying out a market survey, you will find that desk research can often yield a large amount of the information required, particularly with regard to statistics on market sizes, consumption, import/exports and additional background data concerning a product market. However (for both industrial and consumer research), completely up-to-date information is needed, including present and future opinions, trends, changes in technology, demand, competitor images, distribution methods and so forth; it is therefore essential to talk to people in the industry in order to build up a comprehensive picture of the market.

This chapter will cover:

(a) sample structure and drawing up lists of contacts,
(b) methods of approach and arranging interviews,
(c) planning the schedule,
(d) use of aides-memoire and questionnaires,
(e) conducting the interview,
(f) writing up the interview report,
(g) telephone interviewing,
(h) postal questionnaires,

As an introductory work this book does not treat of standards of conduct in marketing research, and readers should contact the professional association in their country (the Industrial Market Research Association in the UK) on these issues.

Groups Likely To Be Interviewed

When conducting an industrial market research survey, the drawing up of the sample and ensuring that the sample consists of the right companies in the right sector of the market form an important part of field research and require a certain amount of time that is often overlooked when estimating the timing of a survey. The sample will depend upon the type of product or market to be researched. Tables 6.1 and 6.2 show examples of industries in which a market survey may be carried out and the groups of people/companies that should be interviewed in each industry.

Table 6.1. Type of Company Likely To Be Included in an Industrial Sample

AUTOMOTIVE	Manufacturers, distributors
SECURITY/FIRE	Manufacturers, factories, warehouses, offices, banks, supermarkets, retailers
CONSTRUCTION	Manufacturers, builders, builders' merchants, plumbers, architects, surveyors
TELECOMMUNICATIONS/ BUSINESS SYSTEMS	Large commercial companies, offices, banks
DISTRIBUTION	Manufacturers, wholesalers
NEW PRODUCT OPINION RESEARCH	Wholesalers, retailers, end-users/buyers

Table 6.2. Type of Interviewee Likely To Be Included in an Industrial Sample

AUTOMOTIVE	Managing director, marketing director
SECURITY/FIRE	Security manager
CONSTRUCTION	Managing director, marketing director, chief architect
TELECOMMUNICATIONS/ BUSINESS SYSTEMS	Communications manager, data processing manager, office manager
DISTRIBUTION	Sales manager
NEW PRODUCT OPINION RESEARCH	Sales manager, chief buyer, buyers, consumers

As can be seen, the mix of potential interviewees can be very varied, but if several types of company are all engaged in the same industry, then it is essential to visit a sample of each, in order to obtain a total picture of the industry and to build up a report based on the views of each type of company, which may vary widely and may affect the ultimate requirements of the product or market differently in each sector. Often, in industry, a minority of large companies account for the majority of the market. As mentioned on p. 73, the 80/20 rule, by which 20 per cent of the total number of companies tend to account for 80 per cent of sales, applies in many industries. In these cases the target will be as many of the large establishments as possible (normally 20 to 30 large company interviews will be adequate). In actual fact large companies although dominating the markets all over Europe, are very few compared with the total number of companies of all sizes, as Table 6.3 shows.

Table 6.3. Total Number of Businesses in UK, France and Germany ('000)

No. of employees	Number of businesses ('000)	% of total businesses
1 to 9	4660	83.2
10 to 49	743	13.3
50 to 199	143	2.5
200 to 499	39	0.7
500 +	15	0.3
Total	5600	100.0

(Source: Arthur D. Little)

Industry Structure—Drawing up the Sample To Represent the Whole Industry

The structure of an industry can often be obtained from government product statistics or from the association of the trade in question. Where the industry is dominated by a few large companies, it is evident that as many as possible of these should be interviewed and that, if all the top companies in an industry are visited, the task of assessing the market accurately becomes relatively easy. Based on the information obtained, it will be possible to make a good estimate of the total market size and future demand. Where it is evident that the market-place consists of a large number of smaller companies, or where a survey is being carried out, for example, in the security industry, as shown in table 6.1, then it is not possible to visit all the potential customers in the market and a carefully structured sample must be drawn up, to represent the national market as best as possible. Again, the National Statistical Office or trade association can usually provide statistics on the numbers of manufacturers, wholesalers and outlets for each industry/product sector, together with value of production accounted for by each.

Microcosm

From this information the importance of each sector can be estimated in terms of percentage of the total, and this can then be applied to the sample mix. For example, if manufacturers, wholesalers and retailers are to be interviewed in, say, six different product categories, the proportion in which they are interviewed should as near as possible equal the proportions that make up the total industry. This follows in turn for each product type within the sector, i.e. if food manufacturers account for three times as much of production value as wine and spirits manufacturers, then the sample should be weighted accordingly. In other words, the final sample should form a microcosm of the total market under survey.

List of Contacts

Having established the framework of the sample, you must draw up a list of potential interviewees. In many industries, where the researcher already has some experience, the names of the largest, most important firms will be known to him, and it will just be a question of finding out the address and telephone number. For lesser known industries, names of companies can be obtained from the various company directories that are published, or from the trade association, which will normally be prepared to send a list of members, and which will include all those of importance. Directories of associations are available, listing hundreds of associations from all kinds of industries—manufacturing, wholesaling or retailing—and should be a must for a market researcher. The company directories usually give name, address, telephone and telex number, and frequently additional information on the number of employees, sales and breakdown of activities, which can be of assistance in preparing the sample.

Allowance for Refusals

Based on the established sample structure, the list of contacts is then drawn up and, in each contact type, about 25 per cent additional contacts should be added to allow for refusals. In certain sectors, including large retail chains in the UK, the allowance may need to be much greater.

Grouping by Geographical Location

It is helpful to group the contacts according to geographical location to simplify the setting out of the schedule when actually making the appointments. At this time any remote locations can be singled out and assessed as to their value to the survey, before making special trips, which cost additional time and money.

Personalised Approach

If possible, the name of the person to be visited should be obtained, in order to avoid addressing the request for an interview to a title only, such as chief buyer, managing director, communications manager, etc. This may require more work, such as further searches in directories or a short phone call to the company, but will pay off in terms of a better chance of success in obtaining an interview.

Method of Approach and Arranging Interview

Having drawn up the list of contacts and names of people to be interviewed, your next step is making an approach and obtaining an interview. For industrial interviews, requiring possibly a minimum of one hour of the respondent's time, it is preferable to make initial contact by letter. This is courteous, enables the request to find its way to the right person if it was not so directed at first, and gives the respondent time to consider the request. Sending a letter also makes final confirmation of the interview easier and quicker. The potential interviewee is told in the letter the preferred dates and advised that a telephone call will follow after a few days to confirm whether an interview will be convenient. Thus considerable telephone time is saved in finding the right person, explaining the research that is being done, and possibly having to call back, perhaps more than once, because the person you wanted is out.

However, the letter approach can add a week or ten days to the survey timing and, with deadlines to meet, this is not always practical. The alternative then, is to spend two to three days making intensive telephone calls, often requiring much patience and perseverance, before definite appointments are finalised.

Initial Telephone Approach

The actual telephone approach made to establish a firm appointment is one of the most difficult and nerve-racking parts of market research. Once the appointments are achieved and the schedule neatly planned out, the rest of the survey appears relatively straightforward. For the uninitiated, picking up the phone to begin this task is certainly an experience to be faced with some trepidation. For those who have been through the ordeal several times, it becomes no easier with each subsequent occasion, and it has to be said that it is always with some dread that the researcher eventually compels himself to pick up the phone and dial the number. It is, without doubt, one of those jobs where it is tempting to find something else to do first, in order to postpone the evil moment.

Psychological Effects

One may ask what it is that causes such fear and trepidation? After all, the most harm anyone at the other end of a telephone can inflict is a few words of abuse and an abrupt replacement of the phone in your ear; the worst outcome that can befall is that one ends up with no interviews at all out of the trial sample of fifty and you are faced with convincing your superior of the unfortunate truth that people in this market are just not willing to talk. Perhaps it is the fact that one is just over-conscientious and anxious to obtain all the important key interviews and therefore fears failure, or simply that it is a case of hurt pride or severe discouragement when one meets an abnormal number of refusals. It is true that after two or three refusals in succession, picking up the phone to try yet again can be almost unbearable. But the truth of the matter is that, generally speaking, about two out of three attempts in industrial markets do meet with eventual success and often the companies one expects to be the most troublesome turn out to be the easy catches. The main point to remember is to keep cheerful and optimistic and to dig up that reliable stand-by, the sense of humour, whenever the going gets tough.

Bypassing Human Barriers

Probably the most difficult part of the telephone approach is bypassing all the intermediate human obstacles met with on the way to reaching the real custodian of all the knowledge and information you require. The optimistic, if slightly apprehensive, researcher always nurtures a certain hope that, having given a brief explanation of his purpose to whoever answers the telephone, he will be plugged straight through to a charming character who is just ready and willing to receive him any time and give answers to all his questions with enthusiasm and competence. This is rarely the case. First, there is the switchboard, whose operators, in spite of being very efficient at their main function, have an infuriating habit of never being able to understand the purpose of market researchers, no matter how painstakingly and how many times it is explained; then comes the person to whom the switchboard connects you, who may be, and at this stage usually is, entirely the wrong person; the next transfer takes you to a third person, who again may or may not be quite qualified to deal with your problem but does think he knows who is and will pass you 'straight through'; and last, but certainly not least, is the secretary of the *Right Person*. Of course, if the name of the contact has previously been established, life is made a lot simpler, although you normally still have to find your way past the foreboding secretary, who will want to know every detail of your objective before ascertaining whether to allow you to interrupt her extremely high-powered and otherwise occupied boss.

However, the contact's name has frequently remained unobtainable by any other means, and it is therefore necessary to explain the purpose of the call to several people of the type mentioned above, who can vary widely from vicious and protective guard dogs to sweet, helpful things, but whose interests unfortunately are as remote from yours as an ice-cream maker's from a telephone engineer's. All one can do in these trying circumstances is exercise patience and perseverance. Having reached the secretary of your sought-after respondent, you will find she will probably do her utmost to ward you off, since this is one of the things she has been trained to do and she prides herself on it being one of the things she does best. She may try the 'letter' approach, i.e. tell you that, for this kind of request, it is always necessary to write a letter explaining your intentions before making any other contact with the company. If you are smart enough, you will ask her the full name of her boss (in order to address him correctly in the letter) and then call back a little later, asking for him by name with the confidence of an old friend or long-lost uncle and be put straight through without question. If she does not use this tack but merely wishes to know sufficient to be able to inform her boss of the nature of the caller and thus give him the opportunity to rush off to an important meeting, you may find that you are about to be connected to the person you have just spent long and expensive minutes trying to locate.

Talking to Potential Respondent and Clinching Interview

Once you are 'face-to-face', telephonically, with your prey, you will begin your approach story, which by now you can reel off with confidence and fluency and thus concentrate on sounding pleasant, well-versed in your field and convincing in your purpose. One bright aspect of this otherwise depressing activity is that you will generally find that the right person will listen with interest (since you are interested in *his* field), is quite sympathetic to your cause and understands, if he is a good businessman, the need for market research and the mutual exchange of information, discussion of problems and needs for the future. Provided that he has no arrangements to leave on an extended trip, has no good reason to feel that the information he is asked to part with is too sensitive, and does not possess an inherent, deep-seated hatred of market researchers, he will probably *ask you* when you would like to visit. Concealing your surprise and gratitude, you then suggest that, since you will be passing through Untetown next Tuesday (if only to visit him and because this would fit in with the rest of your schedule), you could drop in at 10.00 am. If this is convenient to him, then you mark up one success and start the whole procedure over again. If he cannot make that time, suggest another time on Tuesday or, if Tuesday is completely out, you may have to let him suggest the day and possibly the time and fit it in your other appointments accordingly. Some shuffling may be necessary and occasionally, if appointments pile up, you may have to call an interviewee back and see if he can possibly change the established time to another, in order to accommodate someone else.

Respondent's Payment

It must be remembered that setting up an industrial market research schedule is not easy. You are asking people for their time and, more often than not, offering nothing in return except perhaps the hazy promise of future benefit with regard to fulfilling product demand or offering a better service to the market in general or, for some respondents, an ego trip by flattering them with your desire to pick their brains. Occasionally a respondent may ask for a copy of your results in return for his time, and there is usually no problem for the researcher in complying with this request, once he has obtained the agreement of his superior and always assuring that anything confidential to the sponsor company is removed from the copy. Remember to make a careful note of this request so that it is not forgotten by the time the report is issued, thus avoiding any bad advertisement for market researchers. Sometimes a respondent with a flair for business will agree to give his time only if he is paid cash for it. This happens rarely but when it does it tends to be expensive—so make sure it is spent on an interview you cannot do without.

Coping with a Refusal on the Telephone

The 'letter' approach has already been mentioned. If the potential interviewee insists on a formal written request himself, this is in the majority of cases a 'put-off' reaction and a positive response is rarely obtained. On other occasions the researcher will be told on the spot, politely or otherwise, that an interview is not possible, and that is that. When met with a refusal, retain your dignity and a polite tone of voice. Refusals are by nature fairly brusque and the long-suffering market researcher may easily become disheartened. However, you do not have any right to an interview and therefore no reason to become ruffled when refused. Nevertheless, thank your unachieved target and terminate the call pleasantly. You will do the reputation of market research no good by behaving otherwise. One point of etiquette: always replace the telephone receiver after your respondent has put his down.

The Schedule

When planning the schedule, it is important to set up the interviews logically, allowing enough time to carry each out in a calm, unrushed manner but equally to be as economical as possible on timing and travel. Despite all the difficulties of obtaining the actual interview, it will usually be possible to arrange the successful meetings more or less to your convenience. This means laying out a plan with the locations of each interview in some geographical order.

Timing Logistics

Before confirming the set times of the interviews, it is necessary to check that the planes, trains, etc. can in fact get you there for the approximate time of day you have scheduled. When this has been established, you can draw up the precise time of each interview. On average, industrial interviews last about 60–90 minutes. Some will be only 30 minutes and some have been known to last for two to three hours. Working on the basis of the average, then, allow sufficient time for travel between each. If you are taking a train to another town, this may cost you another hour or two. If the following interview is located in or near the same town, perhaps 10–15 minutes by taxi will be sufficient. If you are driving around in your own or a hired car, then you have much more flexibility, since time is not wasted travelling to stations and waiting on platforms. However, if you do not know the areas you are visiting, you must be armed with good maps and allow time for losing the way (especially around industrial estates), having to stop and ask for directions and finding a place to park the car, although this is usually no problem in industrial interviewing, as most large companies have ample parking space for visitors.

Coping with Problems and Remaining Calm

The important thing is not to become flustered while travelling but to ensure you arrive calm and composed. It inevitably happens that things do go wrong on journeys: trains are late, cars break down, the road on the map does not resemble the road in reality and occasionally your interviewee will turn up late, owing to meetings or some other delay, thus threatening to throw the whole day's schedule into turmoil. For an inexperienced researcher the combined effect of all these little inconveniences can cause exasperation and discouragement. However, with experience, one becomes used to these daily aggravations, and learns that the only way to take things is just as they come. The worst that can happen is that an interview may be lost if a schedule is running very late, but just as you have to be flexible yourself, so, you will find, are the majority of others, and it is rare that an interviewee who has said he is prepared to see you cannot reorganise his own schedule if required.

Practicalities to Remember for Marketing Research Travel

Here is a list of the things you will need:

CHECKLIST

Airline tickets	Road maps
Train tickets	Driving licence
Timetables (useful in the event of changes of plan)	Business cards
	Pocket calculator
Money, credit cards, chequebook	Questionnaires/aides-memoire
	Plenty of paper for writing up
Typed list of interviewees' names, addresses, telephone numbers	_____
Note of hotel bookings	For international research:
	Passport
	Dictionaries

Timing and Costs

These will normally be set by your superior. As an example, for industrial research comprising 20 interviews (per country), the following timing might be required:

Activity	*No. of days*
Questionnaire design and testing	3
Arranging interviews	3
Conducting interviews	6 (at 3 to 4 per day)
Report writing	5
Total	17

Costs vary with the amount of travel necessary, whether domestic or international, and on company policy with regard to the category of hotel and method of travel. Within one's own budget/company policy, one must use commonsense about costs. As already stated, geographical remoteness must be weighed against the importance and potential value of the interview, and when plans go wrong, sound judgement must be used to decide on the best action to take. For example, if one is fog-bound at an airport, the plane is cancelled and the next one to leave is full in economy class, you may use company money more wisely by paying the extra for a first-class seat on that flight than spending it on another night in a hotel and on lost working hours just biding time until the next available flight. Again, if an interview has to be changed for some reason, requiring an additional day's expenses that was not budgeted for, judge the extra cost against the value of the interview in question. If in doubt, there is the following useful alternative: after carrying out several interviews on the same piece of research, you often begin to get a feel for the way they run; with this experience, it may be possible to switch the interview to the telephone, rather than going in person and upsetting the schedule or the budget.

Extending Deadline Non-Agency Research

It may be necessary to ask for a deadline extension if insurmountable difficulties are met with obtaining interviews, or if the research is being carried out just before a holiday period and the relevant interviewees are prepared to see you but not until such and such a date a few weeks hence. This is usually not a problem with management. If the information is required badly enough, then it is worth waiting another three or four weeks to get the best information possible, rather than be presented with a rushed job that has only covered half the necessary ground. Delays can also be caused by the sudden cropping up of a more urgent assignment for which everything else has to be relegated to second place.

However, within these limitations, the timing set out in the terms of reference should be adhered to as closely as possible, both to maintain a good and reliable market research service to general management and to keep costs to a minimum. Time is money.

Questionnaire or Aide-Memoire

An industrial market research questionnaire requires careful design, thought and testing if it is to be effective. Even when the final questionnaire is produced, the market researcher will find that changes may need to be made during the course of interviewing. The main points of an industrial market survey are listed on the checklist in Appendix 9.

An aide-memoire is generally used when the questions to be asked are broad and fairly general. However, if the research is more complex, perhaps because the product is one that has many facets, such as size, applications, varying types and models, resulting in different distribution methods, profit margins, and so on, then a detailed questionnaire may need to be formulated so that questions can be asked and answered in a methodical manner to ensure that nothing is missed. Part of an industrial questionnaire is shown in Fig. 6.1. This questionnaire is for use in a survey on builders' merchants to discover their position in the construction industry, the amount of trade passing through them, their discount structures, profit margins, etc. In order to do this, it is necessary to visit not only builders' merchants but also their suppliers and customers. The questions in the figure are directed at the manufacturer of construction materials.

Even if the questionnaire is fully structured, always leave time and space for free discussion and general questioning at the end, as often the most interesting and important facts are picked up in this way and they may also form the basis for further questioning/cross-checking at subsequent interviews. The interviewer who leaves with nothing but a neatly filled-in questionnaire, with all the appropriate ticks and data in all the right boxes but no comments or talk around the subject, will find himself writing a very sterile report, with little or no qualitative data. Any particularly sensitive questions relating to turnover, profits, company policy etc. should be left until last. It is by no means certain that they will be answered, and it is best not to cause hostility and jeopardise the rest of the interview by asking such questions at the beginning.

Unstructured Interviewing and Conducting the Interview

Using a formal questionnaire means that each question is asked in order. The answer is noted down, with any additional comments, and notes are taken about general information given in open chat at the end.

Using an aide-memoire means unstructured interviewing, which requires more attention to the way the respondent is talking and careful steering of the questions and answers to make sure the interview keeps on the right track and that all the required information is obtained. This requires practice and experience. Some respondents tend to go off at a tangent and talk about subjects that

Fig. 6.1. Questionnaire

MANUFACTURER

Name _____
Location _____
Interviewee _____ Position _____
Financial affiliations _____
Turnover _____
Products _____

1. Can you give an indication of breakdown of turnover:

   (*a*) Builders   _____ %
   (*b*) Councils   _____ %
   (*c*) Government   _____ %
   (*d*) Builders' merchants   _____ %
   (*e*) Other   _____ %

2. What percentage of work or trade is for original work _____ %
                                      for repairs _____ %

3. What movements have taken place over the past few years in (1) and (2)? (increase/decrease)

4. Which sectors are growing most rapidly?

5. Can you give an indication of sizes of discounts?

   (*a*) by products
   (*b*) by quantities

6. Are these discounts increasing, static, decreasing?

7. What payment terms do you stipulate?

8. Is it your policy to encourage builders' merchants, or to sell direct to builder, etc? Why?

9. What is the reaction of a builders' merchant if you begin to sell direct to a builder? (Cut out your products/other lines, etc.)

10. Do you feel builders' merchants offer sufficient services to the end customer?

11. Are there additional services you would like to see offered. What/why?

12. Do you give exclusivity in an area?

13. What is your opinion on the increase in cash and carry warehouses?

14. General comments (future trends, etc.)

may be interesting but nevertheless are not relevant to the task in hand and therefore eat into valuable schedule time. Patience and tact are required to return the respondent to the question posed and to keep him there.

Assessing Value of Interview

Some interviews will naturally be much more valuable than others. Interviewees who ramble tend to be those who cannot give good, full answers to the questions anyway, and, having covered the important points, you should terminate the visit fairly quickly and gain time for other interviews, which may turn out to be more profitable. A respondent who knows his job, understands the question and is willing to reply, will do so competently and fully in an economical amount of time, and you will leave feeling that it was an hour well spent, with a few pages of very useful and relevant information under your arm.

Using Information Obtained to the Benefit of Subsequent Interviews

You will probably use points from some interviews to reformulate or modify the questionnaire slightly or as prompts in further interviews. For example, one respondent may make a point that a certain supplier has changed his method of distribution or changed his discount policy and that this has adversely affected the respondent's business. This point, which may not be mentioned at the next interview, could be raised by you. The respondent may then reply 'Oh yes, indeed' and continue to talk expansively about the importance of this change to his business, or he may dismiss it as unimportant. This way, you establish whether certain aspects of the industry mentioned by one respondent as important are of general relevance or are merely of note only to the odd one company you have visited.

Controlling the Pace

Without looking at your watch, you must control the pace of the interview to ensure that all points are adequately covered in the time available. The important questions should be asked first. If something very important and interesting arises, a little extra time may be allowed to discuss it, or a note can be made to return to that point at the end of the interview, if there is time. Again, judgement must be used during the interview to decide just how important each issue is.

There will usually be one or two questions on which the respondent cannot be very helpful, so time will be gained here. Controlling the pace means sensing the atmosphere. If the respondent is pressed and not over-cooperative and you feel he is likely to throw you out in ten minutes, endeavour to cover the first, important questions as quickly as possible (this may mean getting the bare answers and very little extra information around the subject), as without these answers the interview will be next to worthless. Steering an interview according to the climate, without becoming harassed, rushed or even impolite, thus causing even more irritation to the respondent, is an art that comes with experience.

Understanding and Clarification of Responses

Having covered the important questions, pause for a moment's thought to be really sure that they have been adequately answered, that all comments and remarks tally and are logical, and that you understand everything that has been said. Marketing researchers often have to work in a field in which they have had a crash briefing and are not equipped with in-depth knowledge of the product/industry. Do not be afraid to admit this, and if a question arises from anything the respondent has said, then ask it and settle the matter there and then, rather than be left puzzling over it when trying to write the report; if you do not, you may end up either omitting a point that may be important or having to follow up with expensive phone-calls, at which time it is far more embarrassing to be asking silly questions than it would have been on the spot. Occasionally the researcher may not have had the opportunity to see the product under survey 'in the flesh' before the research, apart from pictures in brochures. If, during an interview, the researcher can be shown the product in question, what it looks like and how it works (particularly if it is something complicated), this will help his understanding and appreciation of the market under survey and will enable him to carry out subsequent research with greater ease and confidence.

General Chat

Once confident that the important information is obtained, proceed with the rest of the questions, which will tend to be more straightforward and therefore progress more rapidly. This is another reason for placing the longer, more difficult questions first, since both researcher and respondent will be more enthusiastic at the beginning of an interview and, as time draws on, will want to see the questions flowing and the end in sight. Then you will come to the general chat, when you prompt the interviewee to talk about anything else of relevance that you have not covered, or you may return to a topic which was mentioned earlier as being important and which you wish to discuss further.

Sensitive Questions

Finally, you arrive at any sensitive questions which will have been placed at the end of the questionnaire, such as sales, profits, future company policy on certain issues, and so on. Some respondents will surprise you by handing out the answers readily and without hesitation. Try to act as though you had never expected otherwise, write them down and thank him. If a respondent is not willing to answer these questions, a little persuasion in the way of reassurance of confidentiality can be given, but too much insistence or pressure should never be applied, as it will produce no results other than to upset the rapport, make the respondent distrustful of the whole interview and create an awkward atmosphere on departure.

Keeping the Door Open

Always ask if the respondent would mind if, at a later date, you gave him a call to check on or clarify any point that might come up during report writing. After a well conducted, amicable interview, most respondents will be quite prepared to accept this request and will be very pleasant in the event that you actually need to call them.

Need to Write Up Rapidly

It is essential to write up visit reports quickly. A fully completed questionnaire may contain much useful information, but if it is written up several days later or not until it is incorporated in the actual report, it will be completely cold, and difficult to recall and to write up in a lively or flowing style. While it is still 'warm' from the interview, it is ten times easier to write up, and it is surprising how many small but relevant points that were mentioned around the questions and answers but not actually recorded at the interview will come to mind, and these will add to the depth and readability of the report. Another good, practical reason to write up each interview as the schedule progresses (each evening, for instance) is to avoid amassing a backlog of questionnaires and interview notes that have to be dealt with at the last minute. An exceptionally good interview can take as long or even longer to write up than the interview itself. So, given three or four hour-long interviews a day, a bad dose of writer's cramp is in store for those who fail to keep ahead of the task.

Analysis/Tabulation Sheets

If the industrial interview has brought forth a large amount of statistical information or questions on product sizes, models, brands and other generally numeric data, the best way to write it up is by means of an analysis sheet, with columns for each response, headings indicating the questions and, in the left-hand column, the name of each company visited. If there is a question concerning a choice of, say, three answers, e.g. a product size of less than 50 kg, 50 to 500 kg and more than 500 kg, it is clearer to make a column for each size and fill in the answers with a tick. Calculating the total in each category can then be done at a glance, a much simpler and faster procedure than sorting out totals from a single column. See Figure 6.2.

Figure 6.2. Analysis sheet

UNCLEAR AND MORE DIFFICULT TO COUNT		CLEAR AT A GLANCE HOW MANY COMPANIES ACCOUNT FOR EACH SIZE			
Company	*Product Size (kg)*	*Company*	*Product Size (kg)*		
			L 50	*50–500*	*M 500*
A	L 50	A	X		
B	M 500	B			X
C	L 50	C	X		
D	50–500	D		X	
E	M 500	E			X
F	50–500	F		X	
G	L 50	G	X		

Tabulating all the data in this way enables the summary for the final report to be written up and analysed fairly easily. If the interview produces mainly qualitative data, then it is generally better to write up each report separately, keeping the format logical, i.e. each topic covered chronologically in separate paragraphs, so that the final report can be written in similar format, incorporating, as a whole, the data from each interview.

Telephone Research

With regard to interviewing, this chapter has dealt so far with personal interviewing, since the nature of much industrial research demands face-to-face contact. The questions are complex, requiring in-depth responses, with further probing to obtain explanations, followed often by an open-ended discussion developing as a result of the respondent's answer to a particular question. Giving an adequate reply often means opening a drawer or filing cabinet to find papers on a given subject and perhaps calling in a colleague who is more qualified to give information on certain points. All this requires careful and patient handling and diplomatic reactions to any impatience or annoyance that develops on the part of the respondent. Over the telephone, which creates a barrier between the parties, this kind of interview becomes virtually impossible and the quality of information that can be obtained will be much reduced. You should use telephone interviews for industrial research, therefore, only when you are obliged to do so because of timing and cost restraints, except in the following two instances.

Telephone Interviews for a Fragmented Sector of Market

When the personal interviewing of an industrial sample has been carried out among the large, most important companies and a sample of the smaller companies making up the market structure is required to be surveyed, the telephone can sometimes be employed. In this case a *short* questionnaire may be compiled, using simple questions requiring brief, straightforward answers in order to interview perhaps 30 of the smaller firms. The type of question to be asked would obviously be defined by the experience obtained from the personal interviews. For example, you may have discovered at these interviews that a certain new system is becoming important and replacing an older model. You may then telephone this small sample to ask them if they have already installed this system are planning to and when, and why or why they are not in favour of installing it.

This example shows the way in which information may be obtained in addition to that already gathered at the personal interviews, to supplement the conclusions already drawn and to add credibility to the reliability of the numbers that are going to be put forward in the final report. When making such a telephone call, and finally reaching the person who is going to be able to answer your questions, you must make sure that you explain yourself correctly at the outset, in order to gain cooperation. Announce your name and company clearly and pleasantly, and give a simple but well defined background to your mission. Then ask politely, 'Would it be convenient to talk for a few minutes now or could you suggest a time to call later?' During the telephone interview, the researcher will gain a feel for the willingness of the respondent to talk, and if he appears cooperative, then further discussion may take place. Again, as with the industrial interview, it is a matter of assessing the atmosphere and encouraging the maximum out of your respondent without causing annoyance. Once the scales are tipped too far, it is impossible to reverse the situation.

Telephone Interviewing as Follow-Up to Personal Interview

The second instance when use may be made of the telephone in industrial interviewing is for follow-up after a personal interview. This is a comparatively pleasant task, since the researcher and respondent have already met and have probably established an agreeable rapport over a cup of tea or coffee; therefore further contact by telephone will not require all the initial introduction, explanations and anxious waiting for a positive/negative reaction. After the niceties of 'How are you?', 'How did the rest of your trip go?' and the weather, the contact will be quite willing to give you a bit of additional information or clarify some query that has arisen as a result of subsequent interviews or during report writing.

There will always be these queries during marketing research, either as a result of misunderstanding or conflicting information given by different respondents. When you have these kinds of discrepancies in your information, it is dangerous to try to draw conclusions without verifying the facts first, and, even if it means several of these follow-up calls, it is essential that they be carried out. Taking notes during an industrial interview, with the mind half-concentrated on the steering and diplomatic handling that has been discussed, puts pressure on the interviewee and such 'bugs' in the data are not always immediately apparent. This is normal and it is only when you are tabulating the results or trying to write logical qualitative statements that you will notice the 'bugs' glaring at you, necessitating your tracking them to their source in order to eliminate them. So, for each industrial survey, probably two or three of these 'clarification' calls can be expected.

Postal Questionnaires

Like telephone interviewing, postal questionnaires in industrial marketing research, although having one or two advantages, put serious limitations on the type and amount of information that can be obtained, and should only be used where other methods are precluded by budget or time constraints. The following are the advantages and disadvantages of Postal Questionnaires:

Advantages	Disadvantages
Cheapness	Non-response
Covers larger universe in less time	Ambiguity
	Impossible to probe
Anonymity—respondent can remain unknown	Bias
	Simplicity required

Cheapness

The postal questionnaire is, in comparison to personal and telephone interviews, an economical way of carrying out an interview. The cost amounts basically to the cost of a postage stamp plus the time of a secretary to mail out the questionnaires.

Coverage

With a large industrial sample of several hundred, the postal questionnaire allows a greater number of interviews to be carried out, with faster results, than trying to cover such a large area in person or by telephone.

Anonymity

The respondent can remain completely anonymous, which may give him more incentive to respond.

Non-response

The main disadvantage of the postal questionnaire is that recipients do not reply. Statistics show that companies receive a vast number of such forms to fill in and that, as a result, they are often thrown straight into the waste paper basket. A normal rate of response without any kind of follow-up is less than 10 per cent.

Tips from agencies handling numbers of postal questionnaires include advice to try to get the letters delivered on a Monday morning, to stick stamps on the envelopes for returns rather than frank the envelope, and to use an 'urgent' sticker. The most important tip is to keep the questionnaire on one sheet of paper, for if it is long and bulky, it will be thrown aside.

Simplicity

The questionnaire must be both short and simple, generally with yes/no answers or with a set of alternatives by which the respondent places a tick. Complex, searching questions cannot be included, thus limiting the depth of information that can be obtained.

Ambiguity

Even though the questionnaire may have been well tested, there is always a chance of misinterpretation by individuals, and with no interviewer present to clarify or explain questions, there is nothing that can be done to avoid this problem.

Probing

Whereas in industrial interviews answers can be enlarged·upon by probing from the interviewer on various interesting points, this is impossible with postal questionnaires.

Bias

The recipient of the postal questionnaire can of course read through all the questions before completing the questionnaire, and this can bias his answers.

When to Use Postal Questionnaires

(*a*) When the sample needed is large (e.g. 500 +).
(*b*) When the universe is fragmented, i.e. the 80/20 rule does not apply.
(*c*) When the information required is short and basically straightforward.
(*d*) When the budget or time available is highly restricted.
(*e*) For double-checking on data already established.

Covering Letter

It is important to attract the attention of the recipient of the postal questionnaire sufficiently to stop him from throwing it straight into the waste paper basket. A friendly, personal tone should be used, in a manner which captures his interest and convinces him that this knowledge is of importance and use in the survey. The company conducting the research should be open about who they are and why they seek the information requested, in order to allay any suspicion. If the research is done by a body such as a government department or large national company that is looking for information to improve services offered to the community at large, then the response rate may be higher than for an industrial company that is merely trying to obtain information for its own ends, often from competitors. Another important point to emphasise in the covering letter is that of confidentiality. The recipient must be assured that his replies will be treated in strictest confidence. It is essential to provide a *stamped addressed envelope* for the return of the questionnaire and this should be pointed out in the letter.

Maximisation of Rate of Returns

As has been mentioned, the response to a questionnaire is generally very low. To maximise the returns, it is frequent practice to offer a 'sweetener'—some form of encouragement to the recipient either to interest him in replaying or to make him feel obliged to fill in the questionnaire. One common practice is to undertake to send, for each returned and completed questionnaire, a sum of money to a named charity; this has been shown to increase the rate of return to between 10 and 20 per cent. Another way to encourage cooperation is to offer each respondent a copy of the summarised findings. This of course removes the possibility of anonymity, but that is not necessarily of the utmost importance to respondents when weighed against other advantages.

Follow-Up

Another way to increase the final response rate is to send a follow-up letter. This of course must be carefully prepared and phrased in order not to cause any offence. When mailing out a follow-up, you should include another copy of the questionnaire in case the first has already been destroyed or the recipient cannot be bothered to search for it through his papers.

In summary, the postal questionnaire is not recommended for complex industrial surveys. It is used where information sought can be obtained through short, simple questionnaire design and where the sample to be covered is large and fragmented. It may also be used as a complement to personal interviews. Some researchers refuse to use postal questionnaires because they claim that the results are unrepresentative. But postal questionnaires will remain in the armoury of marketing research because, in certain difficult markets, they will offer more information than no research at all.

Key Concepts

Conducting Unstructured Interviews. Patience and diplomacy are needed to guide the respondent through the questions and obtain the maximum amount of information in a reasonable time. Information from interviews may improve the questionnaire and be of benefit in subsequent interviews. Controlling the pace and dwelling on important issues are important, as is cutting time short on questions where the respondent cannot be helpful. Any points that are not clearly understood should be clarified, and the door should be kept open for future contact. Important questions come first, then general discussion and finally sensitive questions.

Telephone Research. Use for interviewing the fragmented sectors of the market and for follow-up to personal interviews.

Postal Questionnaire. Not generally recommended for industrial surveys; use where information sought is straightforward and the sample is large, or as a complement to personal interviews.

Exercises

1. A product offering economies in the behaviour of gas-fired furnaces for central heating systems is to be launched by your company. In order to make significant savings, the user's total fuel bill must be in excess of £160,000 per year. What is the most efficient way of finding out how large the potential market is for your product?

2. Design a postal questionnaire to find out, from a sample of commercial companies, what their present usage and future purchase/installation plans are for photocopiers with reduction, collation and stapling facilities.

7

Consumer Research—Continuous Research and Questionnaire Design

At some point in the life of almost every business, no matter how industrial, there will be an interface (meeting) with the person who buys the product and whose custom is highly valued by the manufacturer. Even the manufacturer of a raw material—for example, the producer of glass for bottles—may need to go to his customer's customer to find out if the needs of that individual could be better met by a modification to his product that he wants to suggest to the bottle manufacturers and the dairies who fill milk bottles for distribution (e.g. would the customer tolerate green bottles for milk?). In the shopkeeping sector retailers wanting to explore the possibilities of new sites have to observe the way people use the shops in the area, and if they want to measure the potential for their stores, they will have to ask questions of the public.

But it is for consumer goods, particularly mass-marketed, fast-moving consumer goods, that consumer market research is an essential part of growth in the market. The analyst will be asking the following questions:

1. How are the company's existing products perceived by the public?
2. What is the public's awareness of their brands?
3. What profile does their product have with the public?
4. What sort of profile should new products have to achieve market success?

In this chapter the topics that will be covered will be:

(a) continuous research for existing products,
(b) continuity and significance in continuous research,
(c) research on new consumer products,
(d) research using outside agencies,
(e) designing a consumer questionnaire,
(f) research on a retail outlet.

Continuous Research for Existing Products

Continuous research is research carried out at any regular interval. The interval is most frequently one month or one year but it can extend even to every two years. Because it is continuous, it is necessary to conduct it in the same way every time, and for this reason market research agencies are usually employed. Each question posed will be exactly the same, every time, in order to ensure that the results from year to year or month to month are comparable. The sort of questions that are asked will include variations of those below:

1. 'What brands of (product) do you know?'
2. 'What brands of (product) on this list do you know?' (prompted brand awareness)
3. 'What slogan do you associate with Brand X?'
4. 'How do you rate Brand X and Brand Y in terms of value for money?' (other factors depending on the product concerned)
5. 'How do you rate Brand X in terms of (certain characteristics)?'

The last question posed above will use scales, which are generally arranged to give five or seven different ratings. For example, a cleaning product will be judged on its ability to clean and the scale employed might be schematic, as in the sketch below, with respondents invited to place an X at the appropriate point.

Very effective   Average strength   Weak

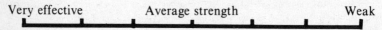

   In some questionnaires 'Very effective' might be associated with 7, 'Average strength' with 4, and 'Weak' with 1. Scales associated with numbers have to be used with telephone interviewing. For toothpaste, degrees of 'freshness' might be of relevance; for food products, their wholesomeness or nutritional value, use of natural ingredients, similarity to home-cooked products; and so on. Continuous research will be concerned with the very basic facts of consumer acceptance of a product that are the foundation of day to day success, so its questions will all be basic and will change very little if at all. If a detergent used in washing up suddenly offers a new plus over existing products in counteracting skin problems, a new question about this factor will probably have to be added to future continuous research, but such occurrences will be rare. Continuous research is used as a means of double-checking the marketing policy of the company, and so becomes one essential element of the total marketing picture.

   Consider the elements of the marketing mix for a consumer product for which no continuous market research is undertaken. The marketing director selling Turn-On sunglasses knows his market share, his expenditure on advertising, his distribution system and the price profile of the competitive products. In so far as his sales and market share are buoyant, he has a lot of information about the market and he believes that he is leading consumer trends. What more could continuous consumer research give? Quite a lot. The answers to the question, 'What brands of sunglasses to you know?' will provide a useful input on how effective is his advertising campaign. Consider the data in Table 7.1.

Table 7.1. Advertising Expenditure, Unaided and Aided Brand Awareness and Market Share, 1991

Brand	Unaided brand awareness (%)	Aided brand awareness (%)	Share of total annual advertising expenditure (%)	Market share (%)
Turn-On	25	65	17	21
Regard	23	62	24	19
Forensic	41	78	30	23
13 Others	na	na	29	37
Total	—	—	100	100

From this data it is clear that Turn-On is running a much more effective advertising campaign than is Regard. The high market share and high awareness of Forensic sunglasses has been achieved by a relatively high expenditure on advertising, and the Turn-On product line manager will expect some reduction in market share as Forensic's rapid growth begins to slow as it reaches the limit of ultimate potential (there is only a limited amount of room for large brands in any market). The Turn-On policy is to set its advertising agency a target for brand awareness and this policy is working well.

Market share is partly determined by the efficacy of the advertising done both in the current and the previous year(s) for many products, and it requires monitoring at least to a level where brand awareness is known, as the example shows. There are many studies of effects of changes in advertising expenditure on sales, market share and profits (see Peter T. Fitzroy, *Analytical Methods for Marketing Management* McGraw-Hill, for a good summary of literature and some examples). But for most market analysis purposes advertising expenditure, market share data and brand awareness will be all the information required by management. The reason why more detailed modelling is not required is that other marketing activity, such as promotions, price reductions and changes in patterns of distribution, all affect market share. Collecting the 'cleaned' data is expensive and time-consuming: the share of total advertising of one brand is not controllable, and management does not want a complicated picture.

The Problem of Significance

The findings of research based on samples will generally show a movement upwards or downwards in brand awareness, or usage of the product in the latest week, estimated market share, and rating of the product as excellent and above average by a certain percentage of the sample. Does the increase or decrease represent a significant change or not?

Table 7.2 provides an example and Fig. 7.1 shows how the data should be presented. The confidence limits are taken from the table provided in Appendix 3. This specific example is given by way of illustration and references to statistical sources will be needed for other percentage breakdowns. A graphical presentation is most useful because the eye can immediately perceive whether there is any real movement upwards or downwards.

Table 7.2. Unprompted Awareness of Ponty by Year—Samples of 100 at 95 per cent confidence levels

	1990	1991	1992	1993	1994
Per cent aware	4	5	4	6	12
Lower Limit	0.1	0.6	0.1	1.2	5.5
Upper Limit	7.9	9.9	7.9	10.8	18.5

Fig. 7.1. Confidence limits of 95 per cent for national percentage unprompted awareness of Ponty by sample of 100.

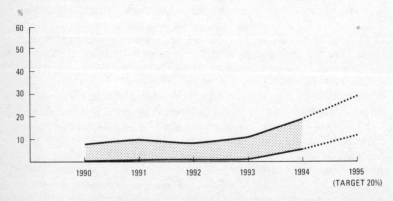

The same data is presented in Figure 7.1. From the graph we can see that brand awareness has not really shifted that much: it is possible that the brand awareness has remained steady at 7 per cent over the whole period, not a very satisfactory situation. If the advertising agency plus an adequate advertising budget can push awareness up to 20 per cent, using the same sample size, it would be clear that a real advance in awareness has taken place. Alternatively, if a sample of 1,000 were used, the confidence bands would become much closer together and management would have a much better idea of real progress.

Own Research on New Products

Using agencies is of course expensive and companies often use their own resources for 'quick-and-dirty' research. There is no harm in this, provided that experience of evaluating the results of own research is carefully cultivated so that results can be interpreted, and provided that the 'real world', in the form of adequate samples of the total population of the country, is consulted from time to time. To take an example, a panel of factory workers may be used to evaluate all new frozen food products and can provide an excellent coarse-screening for products in general. With carefully designed research in-house, blind testing of two products can produce usable results as to whether product ingredient changes are detectable with samples of as few as 30 employees. The Bross chart approach mentioned in Chapter 5 has been employed in the laboratory of consumer goods companies like Reckitt & Colman to check on preferences for new products with a sample of company employees, and has performed well.

Such initial research provides a pre-screening of the factors that are going to be important in any final national consumer research. The analyst will be required to compose a questionnaire for internal research, and will discover most of the problems of question-posing in a relatively inexpensive way. The problems of composing a questionnaire are outlined later in this chapter. Of course, any research carried out inside a company is not a valid picture of the rest of the world. Experience in interpretation is needed, and claims that the product is 'bound to go' because 25 employees like it, should be avoided. Finally, it is sometimes possible to do better research within the company than without, by extending it to at more than one site and the sample to different grades of employee, or by increasing the number of tests per year with the same basic panel in order to discount the effect of their gratitude for attention, which tends to make them kinder than they should be.

Outside Research on Own Products

A good market research agency will be able to steer its client away from most of the errors of questionnaire construction that can arise, will advise on sample size and will offer hints on interpreting the results. The work of clarifying what exactly the analyst is trying to find out can be assisted by the agency, but that question will always remain the basic concern of the analyst. One of the tools for creating the questionnaire will be discussions.

Discussions

A *discussion* uses a group of up to eight users or specifiers of a product or service, permitting them to talk about how they perceive it and any connected issues which require examination. An excellent method of learning how people talk about the product and the needs it serves, the discussion provides what is called *qualitative* rather than *quantitative* research.

A discussion on breakfast cereals could reveal that one of the preoccupations of the housewife might be how much fibre the cereals contained, and these and other topics arising in the discussion could engender a whole qualitative hypothesis that the territory of competition was moving away from sugar-based, vitamin boosted products with on-pack and in-pack premiums targetted to children, towards a more sober, family-oriented but fast-food fibre-rich cereal, which tastes good with skimmed milk.

Two or three discussions will clearly aid the advertising, the packaging, the premium policy and new product developments, but all of this will require *quantitative* back up: for example, 'How many cereal buyers look at the contents list for fibre?'

At least two or three discussions on any given topic are needed in order to avoid being over-directed towards some hypothesis which later proves to have been a quirk of the discussion group. Almost all types of marketing will use discussions at some time, because of their usefulness and inexpensiveness in directing research more closely towards the right track.

Security officers, doctors, small businessmen, garage workers, plumbers—all of these might find themselves invited to join a discussion at some time. There is no reason why anyone doing market analysis should not use a discussion group. These simple rules are suggested:

1. Never run one discussion group only, have at *least* one other.
2. Try to avoid dominating personalities who will kink the results.

3. Don't let the person who wants to use the research be present if at all avoidable—they will tend to hear what they want to hear.
4. Try to keep the numbers about eight.
5. Serve some refreshments.
6. Videotape or tape the proceedings. Edited material can be used as part of a good presentation later on.
7. Try to let the discussion run itself rather than directing it: if it does require steering, the touch of the hand on the tiller must be very gentle.

Discussions help to destroy stereotypes: let the new emerge.

Designing a Consumer Questionnaire

The only way to learn about questionnaires is to devise one, test it and find out how it is understood. The example given here is based on a consumer questionnaire for a different product to the one named, so it is only partly 'pre-tested' and not yet perfect, and provides an example of some of the obvious pitfalls. The main rules for consumer questionnaires are:

1. Be as brief as possible.
2. Ask short, easy-to-understand questions.
3. Don't ask leading questions.
4. Do not provide motives for respondents to lie.
5. If you can get the information confirmed by examination of other evidence, do so.

Our example of a questionnaire makes many errors. The product to be researched is called a 'plastic sack-bin' inside the company developing it. It resembles a large, smartly coloured kitchen bin with a swing-lid, but is in fact completely disposable, can be tied up like a sack and is made of a semi-flexible plastic and foil laminate. It is to retail at the cost of five plastic sacks, and because of its strength it will take about 10 per cent more rubbish than can be crammed into any existing garbage sack. The entrepreneur asks the analyst to forecast demand for the product.

The analyst runs a discussion with eight housewives working in the company in order to find out what might be important with regard to the future of the product, and finds out that the factors mentioned are the price, the volume of the product when collapsed, the rigidity of the product when assembled, its ability to withstand foraging dogs and cats, and the way the product looks. Product pluses are the avoidance of the need to remove or insert plastic sacks into another container, the sturdiness of the product and the lack of need to wash the bin. The panel does not like the name of the product. The analyst decides that some pictures of the product will be needed to show the sample to the public, since misconceptions as to its size collapsed and erected are only too likely. He decides to call the product a disposable kitchen bin, guided by the discussion group's views. Potential will be determined by how many people now use sacks for kitchen bins and how many say they will buy the product at the quoted price. This potential should be cross-checked by finding out what housewives are paying for refuse containers now. The first draft questionnaire runs like this.

DRAFT 1—DISPOSABLE KITCHEN BIN QUESTIONNAIRE
I am carrying out some research on a new kitchen product among housewives. Can you help me?

[RESPONDENT IS NOT A HOUSEWIFE—close interview]
How old are you?............... Do you work?............... What is your husband's job? ....
How many plastic sacks do you usually use per week? ....
Do you buy these or are they given free by the local Council? BUY ☐ FREE ☐
How much do they each cost? ....
How do you use your plastic sacks in the kitchen? (Tick one)

1. In a kitchen bin   ☐
2. In a dustbin   ☐
3. In a special sack supporter   ☐
4. Hanging from the wall   ☐
5. On the ground   ☐
6. In an open bucket   ☐
7. In a bucket with a lid   ☐
8. Some other way   What? ....

Why do you do this? ....
Which brands do you use, or do you change brands frequently? ....
....
What do you most dislike about plastic sacks?

(*a*) tendency to burst   ☐
(*b*) need to remove from bins   ☐
(*c*) smelliness   ☐
(*d*) cost   ☐
(*e*) need to clean bins in which they
      are supported   ☐
(*f*) ugliness of bins or sack-holders   ☐
(g) something else: what? ....

Now I want to tell you about a new product and find out what you think of it. It is a disposable kitchen bin. Here is a picture of it assembled.

[SHOW PICTURE 1: PRODUCT NEXT TO 20 LITRE KITCHEN BIN]

As you see, it looks very much like a kitchen bin. You see how it has a flap and it can stand up even empty. Here it is full and put out for the dustman.

[SHOW PICTURE 2]

Here is a picture of the product as you would buy it at the supermarket.

[SHOW PICTURE 3: PRODUCT NEXT TO ROLLS OF PLASTIC SACKS]

Do you think this product will be useful? [NOTE COMMENTS] ....
....
The new disposable kitchen bins will cost $U4 for a packet of five, enough to handle the average rubbish produced in a week by a family with two children. Could you tell me whether you will buy the new product when it is launched or will you continue with your current sacks?   YES............ NO.............

Thank you for your help.

Faults of the Questionnaire

This particular questionnaire contains a good few of the mistakes that can be made. The first thing that needs to be done is to consider the person who is answering the questionnaire. Say it is a woman. Her reaction to being approached by a researcher may be one of curiosity, or of fear of being buttonholed for a long time. She will want to give a good impression of herself and may even regard the questionnaire as a test of her efficiency or prestige (in fact respondents sometimes ask: 'Did I get it right?', indicating that the questionnaire is regarded more as an intelligence test than a request for information). The analyst therefore needs to go through the questionnaire and remove, as far as possible, all motives for the person questioned to run away or give untrue answers to the questions.

The first thing to tackle is the length. A questionnaire that is clearly very short has much more chance of being answered than a long one. How many questions do we really need here? The analyst has a question about what users dislike about sacks, which might serve the purpose of finding out what are the pluses of the disposable kitchen bin. But an open question 'Do you think this product will be useful?' could be analysed afterwards to pick up reasons why the new product is liked and its advantages over existing systems. In fact, the analyst has put in this question to ensure that the respondents register a positive attitude to the new product—this is a real leading question. So this question could be deleted as providing little useful information and should be deleted from the point of view of accuracy. Someone asked this question will be persuaded by their answer to think positively about the disposable kitchen bin. But the analyst is not trying to sell the new product—he is interested in negative as well as positive attitudes to it.

Let us now consider the introduction to the questionnaire. It is reasonable, and the only thing that might be added during the interview is 'It will only take three minutes to answer'. This can sometimes make all the difference between losing or retaining a potential respondent. The draft questionnaire asks if the respondent is a housewife but the goal of the research is to find out the opinion of the person currently buying garbage sacks, and this could be a man in some cases. The question should therefore be rephrased to take in both men and women. For example, 'We want to have the opinion of persons who normally buy the groceries for themselves or the family. Are you the right person to ask?'

The next question, 'How old are you?' is quite crazy! The age of the respondent may be of interest to the entrepreneur for disposable kitchen bins, but it will probably not be important. It is a well known fact that younger people are more interested in new products than older ones, and that there is a high-earning segment in their thirties who will lead in use of new products. So the entrepreneur may decide that he does not really need that information anyway.

But to ask, badly, 'How old are you?' at the start of an interview is to break even the rules of politeness. If data is wanted on respondents' ages and social groups, questions about this should be posed at the end of the questionnaire, as we shall see. An estimate of the age of the respondent is all that is required normally, because data on the age of respondents is usually not that important. Information on the job of the respondent and that of the spouse can also be posed at the end of the questionnaire.

Next on the draft questionnaire comes the question 'How many plastic sacks do you usually use per week?' This is a leading question and invites respondents to lie about their use of the product. This question is really dangerous, because if all the respondents feel that they need to state they use them, there will be an overestimate of the market available for penetration. There are many people who never use plastic sacks. This question cannot be posed here. Instead, the logical next question is, 'What sort of thing do you use for your kitchen rubbish?' and respondents should be presented with attractive cartoon pictures of the different ways of handling kitchen rubbish, coded R, M, T, J, P etc. Why is this preferable? The reason is that respondents will be liable to lie about how they handle rubbish, because they regard it as socially unacceptable to let rubbish lie in a lidless bucket rather than in a kitchen bin with a plastic sack. Every effort must be made to show the alternative ways of handling kitchen waste as attractively as possible, and the coding by letters will be arranged so that there is no perceived 'best answer'. The interviewer will refer to answers by the code rather than saying: 'Oh, I see, you put your rubbish in old plastic shopping bags'. The interviewer will not discourage multiple answers: 'Sometimes, this, usually this'. The cartoon picture, too, will have to make clear that each container is in exactly the same attractive kitchen, in order to remove the danger of confusion with dustbins as well as to show that there is no association of open buckets with ill-equipped kitchens.

There are certain consumption habits and practices on which respondents give notoriously unreliable answers, and this is one area. In one case cited by Professor William Rathis of the University of Arizona, consumption of beer was investigated and 85 per cent of respondents stated that they drank no beer in an average week. When a census was made of the garbage, it was found that only 25 per cent of households drank no beer in one particular week (*Herald Tribune*, 7 January 1982). There are many other examples of falsehoods about alcohol consumption.

As regards falsehoods, a visit to the respondent's kitchen will give much more reliable answers than any questioning outside it. If that is possible within the budget and time-frame, because there will be many refusals, it will provide a better solution. (This book, as an introduction only, cannot cover standards of conduct in marketing research, and readers are advised to contact the professional association in their country [the Market Research Society in the UK] on these issues.)

Frequency of use is the next question, with a particular interest in plastic bin-liners, of course. Against each picture, respondents will tick a five-point scale of usage comprising 'Always, Usually, Sometimes, Very Seldom, Never'. Users of plastic bin-liners will be asked, 'When did you last buy any bin-liners?' and the interviewer will persist in his questioning until he finds the exact day. The next question will be 'How many did you buy?' Such energetic persistence is required because research by William A. Belson (*The Design and Understanding of Survey Questions*, Gower Publishing Co.) has shown that a large percentage of respondents do not understand or answer correctly questions of the type, 'How many have you purchased in the last 7 days, not counting today?', and questions about 'typical weeks' are just too vague to be reliable.

Question about Usage of New Product

The draft question is confused: the fact that respondents will buy the new product does not necessarily mean they will give up sacks completely. It is at this point that the difficult question about respondents' intentions to use the new product have to be posed. Experience of question-posing about new products shows three points to be of importance:

(*a*) information on the price of the new product must be provided,
(*b*) reminders about the price of competing products are useful,

(*c*) if respondents can rate how probable their purchases will be on a five-point scale, accuracy will be increased. (See Gordon Heald, 'The Relationship of Intentions to Buy Consumer Durables with Levels of Purchase', *British Journal of Marketing*, Summer 1970.)

In fact, the nearer any offer of a product gets to a real market situation, the better can consumer behaviour be examined—hence a test-market is preferable to field research if it is economic. Bearing in mind the need to ask clear questions, and the question of how frequently people will buy, posing the question looks a very difficult task. The analyst decides it is unsafe to assume usage of the new product as a *complete* substitution for existing products in the short run, and this complicates the questionnaire. Finally, after a lot of work, this imperfect solution is tested.

This new disposable kitchen bin will cost $U4 for a packet of 5, enough to handle the rubbish of one family of two children for a week. Five disposable kitchen bins will carry as much garbage as 6 sacks costing 80 cents. Please look at this list and tell me which statement best describes how you will probably buy the new product.

1. I will certainly buy the disposable kitchen bin　　　　　☐
2. I will very probably buy the disposable kitchen bin　　　☐
3. I may buy the disposable kitchen bin　　　　　　　　☐
4. I probably will not buy the disposable kitchen bin　　　☐
5. I will certainly not buy the disposable kitchen bin　　　☐

Now I would like you to tell me which of these statements describe how often you will buy.

1. As often as I buy sacks now　　　☐
2. Occasionally　　　　　　　　　☐
3. Very rarely　　　　　　　　　　☐

Respondents preferring either of the last two descriptions would be asked how often that would be. This is perhaps not the best solution to the problem; if the question on frequency of use could be separated, it might remove the temptation to make up for a disappointing probability of use by talking about buying a lot.

Finally, the respondents might be asked a few questions about occupations if that is necessary: often the data does no more than reassure the recipient that the sample was not hopelessly skewed by the presence of too many low- or high-income respondents. Typical wording might be, 'In order to classify your answers statistically, could you help me with a few questions about yourself and your family?' As Mr A. N. Oppenheim suggests (see *Questionnaire Design and Attitude Measurement*, Heinemann), there is usually no need to do anything other than estimate the age of respondents. His suggestions for job classification should be followed, a combination of 'What is the name of your job?' and 'Please describe as carefully as possible the work that you do', reducing unclassified jobs to 10 per cent of the sample. The same question can be posed about the work of the respondent's spouse. Questions about the numbers in the household, their ages and whether they work will also be posed, and there are elaborate rules for assigning respondents to certain social classes, which are outside the scope of this book but well within the competence of consumer market research agencies. For international comparisons and a company's own 'quick-and-cheap' research, the whole business of social classes and occupational prestige has, thankfully, to be dropped in any case, and ownership of consumer durables, educational levels, patterns of expenditure on holidays and so on becomes more relevant as a means of classifying the sample. With changes in working habits, potential changes in the status of women, the growth of a whole series of jobs based on computer technology, and the disappearance of many old occupations, the social scaling is in danger of directing attention to the wrong factors in any case.

Social class data is employed for advertising purposes, of course, because some products (e.g. telephones) are purchased by top class persons who have comparatively low incomes (e.g. they are starting their careers). But this sort of fact is usually well known or commonsense, so that the loss of class data in 'quick-and-cheap' own research is not that important. The size of the household's total income and the number in employment in the household are very relevant to the prospects of more expensive convenience products, but direct questions about the income earned cannot be posed with the certainty of getting reliable answers.

Second Draft Questionnaire

The next questionnaire, reproduced below, is still not perfect, but some of the worst errors have been eliminated. After field testing with further respondents, it should be possible to devise the final questionnaire.

DRAFT 2—DISPOSABLE KITCHEN BIN QUESTIONNAIRE
I am carrying out some research on a new kitchen product. The questionnaire will take 4 minutes. Can you help me?

We want to have the views of the person in a household who usually buys the groceries. Are you the right person to ask? YES☐   NO☐→ Close interview.

I have some pictures here of ways people hold their rubbish in the kitchen before they take it out to the dustbin. Please have a look at this picture and tell me which methods you use for rubbish in the kitchen.

[PRESENTS CARD]

R	□	T	□
M	□	P	□
J	□	L	□

How often do you use these methods?

(For one ticked)		(For second ticked)		(For third ticked)	
Always	□	Always	□	Always	□
Usually	□	Usually	□	Usually	□
Sometimes	□	Sometimes	□	Sometimes	□
Very Seldom	□	Very Seldom	□	Very Seldom	□
Never	□	Never	□	Never	□

[WHERE APPROPRIATE]

You buy plastic sacks to put in your kitchen bin. When did you last buy one?

[PROBE] Date............ = ... days ago.
How many did you buy?...... How many are left now?......
Now I want to tell you about the new product. It is a disposable kitchen bin.
Here is a picture [OR SAMPLE] of it assembled.

[SHOW PICTURE 1]

As you see, it looks very much like a kitchen bin. It has a flap which opens
and closes easily and it stands up even empty. Here it is tied up with its built
in metal tie and put out for the dustman.

[PICTURE 2]

Here is a picture of the product as you would see it at the supermarket.

[PICTURE 3]

This new disposable kitchen bin needs no plastic bin-liners. It costs $U4 for
a packet of 5, enough to handle the rubbish of a family with 2 children for a
week.

The questionnaire would continue as on p. 117 with the question on
buying intentions, but with a large space left for the comments and
criticisms of respondents. The questions about the household and the
notes of the sex of the respondent and so on would come at the end of
this questionnaire.

Going from Intentions to Buy to Forecasting Sales

Gordon Heald of Gallup has argued that for products that have a
comparatively low household penetration—for example, below 65 per
cent—consumers' statements that they will buy require scaling down,
while for products with higher penetration rates, their purchasing

intentions need to be scaled upwards. This argument makes good sense. Where TV sets or vacuum cleaners have a high penetration, the users become dependent on them and will replace them rapidly if they break down (at an unforeseen future time); householders who have not enjoyed the benefits of any particular product can put off their purchase much longer without discomfort.

The need to scale down buying intentions for completely new products is the most pressing problem for the market analyst, however, as most companies already selling consumer durables will have worked out scaling factors for the difference between intentions and purchases, based on years of experience. How much does one need to scale down from the 90 per cent of consumers who say they will buy the new product?

The first rule to obey is to ensure that respondents rate their probability of buying in terms of 'Certainly', 'Very Probably', 'Maybe', 'Probably Not' and 'Will Not'. Concentrate attention on those who definitely will buy the product. The Germany agency Contest-Census stresses the same need to scale intentions, and uses a seven-point scale (rather than the five-point scale mentioned here), with only the top box employed as a predictor. Jan Standaert, the French international market research consultant, working with fast-moving consumer goods, adds the three top boxes (certainly, probably, maybe), and if they come to 70 per cent, judges that a product has a pretty good chance of succeeding in the market. M. Standaert always includes price data and double-checks with prices 10 per cent below and 10 per cent above the projected price.

Nigel Spackman of Research Surveys of Great Britain suggests a second way of making results more valid. If the sample is directed to persons who have equipment which is nearer to the end of its life (3 to 5 years for much office equipment, 8 to 12 years for consumer goods), then their statements about acceptance of the new product will be more reliable. According to one agency, the time scale of many 'intentions to purchase' in industrial markets is five years, i.e. if the respondent says 'I will definitely buy', the analyst should mark it down as something that may happen any time in the next five years. RSGB stresses very thorough consumer briefing on the product and then might apply a 100 per cent weighting to those who definitely would buy, 50 per cent to 'probably' and possibly 20 per cent to 'maybe'. A conference in Toronto, at which almost 200 products were considered, came up with no magical formula to cover all products, however, and no agency claims to have a universal magic formula. Judgement needs to be applied and some further experience of researchers is mentioned here in order to aid that judgement.

Dr Kurt Hammerich of Dr Raymon Muller Institute, Hamburg, has suggested a rule of thumb for food products that development is worthwhile if 30 per cent of the population will certainly buy. Of course, this was related to steady experience of testing the market and to the economies of scale that were specific to the particular food producers. Another agency, IFF of the UK, suggests that first-time buyers' intentions give only an indication of the size of the pool from which purchases may be drawn, although it stresses that, for replacement purchases of consumer durables, econometric models will provide better forecasts. A colleague who worked for a producer of the archetypal replacement product, the electric bulb, also found that even for this 'necessity' there were cycles of sales which moved with the economy and personal disposable income. However, it will be the completely new product that will pose the problems.

The purpose of these references to the experience of researchers is to arm the analyst with warnings that purchase intentions do not equate directly with sales, in case the entrepreneur misconstrues a semi-enthusiastic reception as a potential market landslide. Like Donald Osborne of the DOR agency (UK), the analyst may take the 'very likely' buyers as the 'total potential' market, and then make guesses as to how long it will take to realise that potential, e.g. 'We should be able to realise one half of the potential in three years'. The realisation of the need to scale down intentions to buy should not be the fruit of bitter experience, and enough hints have been given here to show that underestimating potential from intentions to buy is less of a problem than overestimation. The analyst joining an innovative company will find many guidelines for scaling down that are private to the company concerned.

Surveying New Sites for Retail Outlets

This topic can only be treated briefly here, but it should be stressed that quite a volume of information can be obtained on potential at retail sites with a Saturday audit of shoppers. A team of more than two is generally required to get an adequate coverage and research can have three aims:

(a) to find out the area served by the shop or site,
(b) to investigate traffic patterns in the High Street or shopping centre,
(c) to find out reasons why particular stores are favoured.

The catchment area covered by stores can be discovered by asking users about where they live, and purchasing power can be measured by questions on ownership of household consumer durables, numbers of earners in the household, jobs, cars and so on. A simple check by 'rateable value' of the shoppers' home addresses (a valuation for local tax in the UK) may be applied. All this data is used on a *comparative* basis, of course, either to measure one site versus another *or* to look at the catchment area of one store versus a competitor. Questions on how long the journey takes from the home to the store door need to be posed, in order to discover any advantages enjoyed from siting and parking facilities. Questions can also be devised to find out why particular shops are favoured or disliked on the basis of variety of offer, service, prices, catering facilities and so on. The traffic census requires researchers to count the number of persons passing particular places on foot and going in one direction. The data is then used to show flows of shoppers and ensure that the relative desirability of particular sites as places where shoppers pass can be measured. A practice run is recommended, as, even with the use of a hand-held counting machine, the job can be exhausting or defeated by the sheer volume of shoppers, and it may be necessary to count with breaks or over a shorter period of time. A peak shopping hour is required and the area to be covered depends again on whether comparisons are being made between different sites and whether changes in parking sites may affect the flow of shoppers.

Even the independent shopkeeper may find the need to make such comparisons when seeking a new outlet. He will of course only carry out an investigation when he is unsure whether the new site is better than the existing site. It needs to be stressed that undertaking such a survey is not a large task. A list of the cars by type and manufacturer entering a car park over four hours at a shopping centre can also provide an inexpensive way of checking relative prosperity. One thing about doing any of this research is that it removes the subjectivity that everyone suffers from: the tendency to look at places and see what we want to see, so that a Birmingham suburb may be regarded as 'scruffy' by one person and 'charming' by another. As social changes take place invisibly and one suburb goes up and another down, only a careful check may allow the developer to spot changes that may mean a lot in terms of relative purchasing power.

Summary

1. Continuous research is mainly used as an aid to assessing marketing success and setting targets. Recipients of the information need to be reminded of its significance.
2. Internal research with panels of employees can be an inexpensive way of carrying out research, but it requires experience in order to evaluate results.
3. Consumer questionnaires require very thorough testing and retesting. They must be neutral, informative about any new products researched

without being sales pitches, brief, comprehensible and free of leading questions.

4. Intentions to buy completely new products always require some scaling down and the degree to which this applies depends on the product's household penetration, whether it is perceived as an alternative to an existing product, the loyalty of users to products of this particular type, and other factors that make a general rule for scaling down impossible. Intentions to replace existing products often require scaling upwards.

5. Intentions to buy should be graded by respondents at least as 'Certain', 'Probable', 'Maybe', 'Probably Not', 'Definitely Not', and main attention should be devoted to 'Certain' buying intentions in looking at potential sales.

6. Retail outlets can be surveyed rapidly by teamwork on Saturdays and can provide comparative information on sites, shops and shopping centres.

Key Concepts

FMCG. Fast-moving consumer goods. Any repeat-purchase consumer product found in the shopping trolley from razor blades to baked beans, usually low in price and branded.

Brand Awareness. The percentage of persons remembering the name of a brand of product, either by connecting it with a product spontaneously (unprompted brand awareness) or after being reminded by looking at a list (prompted brand awareness).

Product Manager. The marketing executive with responsibility for a particular product. Often called a product line manager because a range of products is handled.

Advertising Expenditure. The amount of money spent on advertising a product on television, in newspapers and journals, on radio and by poster (billboards), as quantified in published audits of expenditure produced by companies such as Media Expenditure Analysis Ltd.

Own Company Panels. Groups of employees used to test new or existing company products on a regular basis.

Leading Questions. Questions which invite the respondent to give one particular answer.

Group Discussion. An informal gathering of about eight existing or potential users of a product or service to be investigated at which information on their attitudes to it and the language they use to describe and evaluate it are collected.

Questionnaire Testing. The process of using draft questionnaires with small samples to check if the order and wording of questions is satisfactory. It also refers to the double-checking of the same sample of persons to find out what they understood by the questions they answered in a completed questionnaire.

Prompt Card. A list of alternatives shown to a respondent to allow him to see the alternative choices available.

Catchment Area. The area from which a shop draws its customers.

Shopping Traffic Census. A count of persons passing particular points between certain times in shopping areas.

Exercises

1. Design questionnaires for three of the following new products or services:

(*a*) A do-it-yourself (DIY) anti-intrusion kit for the home to sell at £20.

(*b*) An infra-red scanner for heat loss in the home, to be rented from a DIY retailer, the rental cost to be decided by research.

(*c*) A cheap family medical self-diagnosis kit, which will include items judged to have best sales prospects up to a price for the total kit that will be attractive to at least 5 per cent of respondents. Items to be researched should include a thermometer, scales with tables of optimum weights, a blood-pressure measurement system, a pregnancy test kit, a handbook, analgesics, bandages, and stomach-pain remedies with a shelf-life of over five years if they exist.

(*d*) How advertisements for solicitors should look, if they were permitted to advertise, in a small town, and for a London practice.

(*e*) Gas explosion incidents, although very, very infrequent, can sometimes be bunched through the erosion of old pipes and their collapse in drought conditions when laid down in clay. A campaign of reassurance to the public is to be prepared against this eventuality. Find out what information the public needs.

(*f*) A canned soup wants to claim to be an example of 'La Nouvelle Cuisine'. Is it a credible claim to the soup buyer?

(*g*) A national canned beer wants to claim to be a real ale. Is it a credible claim to the beer drinker?

(*h*) A petrol-burning, flame-thrower snow-melter is used in areas where there is heavy snow in Germany. What prospects does the product have in the UK?

(*i*) A smaller-length bathtub with a seat and sloping back offers economies in water use, comfort, a better use of space and a good base for a shower. Previous attempts to sell such a design foundered because new house buyers did not like the product. Design a new product and devise a questionnaire to test the public's reaction.

(*j*) A supermarket is considering putting its butcher full-time on a counter in one corner of the premises. Find out if customers will use his services.

2. Write a prospectus to local retailers and the Chamber of Commerce in two local areas competing for some of the same shoppers, outlining the advantages of retail site audits for the expansion of shopping facilities, the re-siting of stores or planning car-park sites, suggesting a price for your services. Carry out any research requested as a team.

3. *Use of an Omnibus Survey Background*. The Van Hypolinus company in Flapp sells a range of pre-sliced smoked salmon from the best sources of supply in the world. These products are of the highest quality and retail at a high price. Van Hypolinus has one major competitor in the Unteland market, Ernst Kuhl, which has a similar range of products, marketed at somewhat

lower prices. Distribution is made through normal channels for a food product, but Van Hypolinus is present in a limited number of retail shops only.

The Marketing Problem. In the spring of 1993 Van Hypolinus was aware that sales in units were stagnating. Very large price increases had been made during 1992 and it was suspected that the price relation between Van Hypolinus and its principal competitor had reached a point where more and more consumers were buying the cheaper alternative. However, it was not known what consumers thought of the two brands, or how loyal they were to either. Knowledge was also lacking on the *extent* to which Van Hypolinus and its products and their competitive equivalents were known, and on the kind of people who knew and bought these products. Finally, it was thought desirable to learn more about the occasions on which people ate gourmet products, and on the types of outlets in which they bought them.

The Marketing Research Solution. It will be obvious that the subjects for investigation range from ones which require large, fully representative samples, e.g. levels of brand and product awareness and use, to ones which are normally approached with smaller samples and detailed questioning, e.g. brand images. However, large samples are expensive for one set of reasons, and detailed questioning of particular groups is expensive for another set of reasons. Furthermore, Van Hypolinus had no information on consumers that would have enabled it to short-cut the sampling process and select the right kind of respondents easily. In any case it was desired to find out all this information relatively cheaply.

The solution adopted was to participate in an omnibus survey, aiming to obtain some information on all the subjects defined earlier, but not in too much depth. Because in an omnibus survey the client pays pro rata according to the number of questions, and because it is not possible to have very complex interview techniques, the questions have to be as few and as simple as possible.

THE QUESTIONS

(*a*) Basing yourself only on the information given under 'The Marketing Problem', draw up a questionnaire of 14 closed-ended questions. The form 'Which of the following brands (or products) do you know (or use)?' counts as one question.

(*b*) Bearing in mind that omnibus survey results are normally analysed only on the basis of age, sex, social class, income and region, suggest additional useful analysis breaks (these are not normally very expensive).

8
Export Marketing Research

Research in export markets poses three important questions:

1. Do you need to do anything beyond desk research?
2. If visits are required, should they be carried out by outside agencies, by the analyst, or by someone from the sales force?
3. Can an export test market be mounted with minimal field research?

Export research is expensive but attractive to persons who enjoy travel. The surest way to turn off the tap for funds for export research is to waste money on badly planned research abroad. This chapter gives the answers to the questions posed, with a side reference to problems of obtaining market information by use of the sales representatives.

Scope of Desk Research

One of the first questions about any export market is, 'Is it big enough to justify trying to enter the market?' In many cases the answer is easy—almost any country in the EEC, for instance, may already be large enough to constitute a market. But there may be a question about the oil states, where the answer is not so readily available. Most construction products, almost any mass-consumer product and any low-value, high-volume product require that the market be of a certain size to be attractive to the supplier; and a rapid check that the market is of that size can be made by looking at statistics of population, gross domestic product per head and any other available data.

For construction products, for example, statistics are often available from the Export Library of the Department of Trade and Industry at 1 Victoria Street, London SW1, which it is best to visit in person if data on more than one country is sought. By using the data available for whichever countries collect it, and by estimating the relation between gross domestic product per head and expenditure on construction or numbers of dwellings completed, or whatever data is available, you can construct estimates for other countries in the same area. The very rough estimates derived can give a clear idea of just how big the market is, and they can save huge expenditure on wasteful field research, if, as is sometimes the case, it is found that some seemingly promising export market is as tiny as a suburb of a provincial town. In the case of one construction product, multi-client field research costing over \$20,000 and covering Africa and the Middle East was found to match the estimates already made by desk research so closely that expenditure on such surveys was seen to be a bad investment. An example of the sort of data used to make an estimate of the size of any particular market is given in Table 8.1. Though dating back to the 1970s in this example, the method remains equally valid in the 1990s. This particular table comes from the business news bulletin *Business Europe*, which publishes tables of 'Market Indicators' every year. Only a few of the relevant indicators are included here because of space, but other indicators include trucks and buses, telephones, radios, energy consumption per head, and gross domestic product as well as imports and exports.

Table 8.1. Selected Indicators of Comparative Market Size–Middle East

Country	Popula-tion 1983 (mn)	GNP/ capita 1982 (*)	TV sets 1983 ('000)	Steel consump-tion ('000 tonnes)	Energy consump-tion per capita 1982*	Market size (%)
Bahrain	0.3	N.A.	125	100	11,316	1.2
Egypt	45.1	690	3,500	1,950	618	14.2
Iran	41.8	1,621	3,000	5,360	1,025	23.4
Iraq	14.5	2,150	800	440	680	7.5
Israel	4.2	5,612	1,000	630	2,458	8.9
Jordan	3.6	1,875	350	450	891	1.9
Kuwait	1.6	25,850	750	570	3,421	5.4
Oman	1.0	6,828	60	330	681	1.4
S. Arabia	10.1	15,838	1,750	7,875	3,026	26.3
Syria	10.1	1,957	500	210	991	4.6
U.A.E.	0.8	30,000	250	N.A.	19.046	4.0
N. Yemen	6.2	750	25	N.A.	122	1.2
Total	139.3	2,588	12,110	17,915	1,155	100.0

*Coal equivalent in kg
*Source: *Business Europe, February 1985*

Population is a basic determinant of market size, and 12 of the countries listed in Table 8.1 are smaller than the London conurbation. Gross National Product per capita should be compared with the figure for the UK to arrive at some feeling for the comparative spending potential on consumer goods. From the same source, a figure of $6,967 per head is derived for the UK and we see that five countries—Bahrain, Kuwait, Qatar, Saudi Arabia and the United Emirates—are all higher than the UK but only add up to the population of the London conurbation. However, the comparative wealth per head of these countries signals a good market for such high price-ticket consumer durables as Rolls-Royces and antiques, which can support high marketing costs per unit. *TV sets* give a feel for the mass consumer good market and we can compare the total number installed to annual sales of 2 million sets in the UK. *Steel consumption* gives an important indication of the size of the construction market, and *energy consumption* is another statistic that supports estimates of wealth per head. Finally, the *market size* gives an indication of the size of each country's market.

Other indicators, not shown here, often give a measure of how far a country is behind the European average and therefore how much potential there is for expansion (the barefoot versus the shod). Telephones per head in many countries shows such a vast difference when compared with European standards that a huge potential is indicated in telecommunications investment. Some figures, like those for cars, trucks and radios, are of interest in their own right to the manufacturers of these consumer durables. Housing starts and housing completions will be available for some countries to give an indication of the value of the house-building market. In every case the analyst can use the indicators to obtain some estimates, by analogy with the home market, of the demand for a particular product, be it a bathroom cabinet, costume jewellery, a diesel generator or electrical cable.

The analyst should beware of using this method of grossing up by extrapolation from known figures about his home country except where some very general indication of the size of a market is required. Extrapolations from the size of the US market to the size of the European market (of 16 or 17 countries) are liable to err up to as much as 100 per cent, depending on product, and calculations of the European market based on only one country are also dangerous. Time and time again, in investigating markets as various as margarine packaging, telecommunications cable, language schools or security systems, real differences between the size, shape and competitive parameters are revealed within the many countries of Europe. For example, diesel generators may be important as security against electricity supply breakdowns in one country, while they are bought for use as a method of saving costs at peak-usage periods in another country in Europe. The relative size of the market in two countries may be kinked by this fact.

It always goes back to the question posed in Chapter 5—'How sure do you need to be?' The analyst should ask to what use the information he is providing will be put. If a market of £5 million is of interest, and extrapolation shows that the market is £50 million, enough research has already been done, because the possibility of error is improbable. Horses for courses—if someone were preparing a very elaborate prospectus for a company marketing wood-burning stoves and showed a proportionally large use of wood as a fuel in the UK based on extrapolation from Sweden, there would be little credence in the figures. Every case is different and what the analyst has to do depends on what needs the information serves as well as the nature of the product investigated.

Use of Import and Export Data

Analysts should be wary of the use of import and export data for developing countries. Generally, apart from the OECD countries, export and import data is difficult to obtain, out-of-date, unreliable, and incomplete. One way round the problem of the lack of statistics is to take export data from the 15 major exporting countries to each developing country under investigation and add it together to give an estimate of the imports. This crude method is sometimes the only means available of arriving at any reasonable estimate of imports of a particular commodity. If time allows and the statistics exist, extend the data to as many countries as possible, as Eastern European, Indian, Pakistani or Far Eastern suppliers may be important.

Other Information

World Bank summaries, reports from the local consulates, reports commissioned for the US Congress on trade in certain countries, and special bulletins on particular markets can all be sources of information. Within the UK, a visit to the Export Library is essential. In Europe the libraries of the Chambers of Commerce, listed in Appendix 2, can usually be consulted. Trade associations are an important source of information in Europe.

Visits to Export Markets

The analyst, having completed the desk research, may find that no further information is required. However, in some cases the entrepreneur may really need further information before the business of export can begin. Who should carry it out?

Table 8.2 summarises the advantages and disadvantages of using three different information sources—the agency, the analyst and the sales manager himself.

Table 8.2. Criteria for Selection of Field Researchers in Export Markets Requirement

| | Relative Strengths | | |
Requirement	Local agency	Analyst	Sales manager
Knowledge of lanaguage	***		
Knowledge of local market	***		
Knowledge of product		*	***
Lack of bias	*	**	

Knowledge of the language is not an essential requirement for getting market information but it can reduce the cost of research by eliminating the need for translators and speeding up the whole business of getting information together. English is a major commercial language and it is possible to do an adequate job without any knowledge whatsoever of the language of the country researched. However, a rule applies by which English alone always fails to catch the part of the market in the middle, i.e. where the many industrial buyers in middle-sized enterprises are situated, or the enterprises so tied into their language and culture that they are unaware of the possibility of importing. An ability in the language of the country investigated is a great plus, even where the product is visible on the shelves of supermarkets, because there will be a need to talk to those who buy it. Exporting within the EEC, as well as outside, is part of *l'esprit de conquête* of the best European (that includes British) manufacturers, and exploiting that 'will to export' does mean that the exporter must eventually employ staff who speak the language of the country to which his company is exporting.

The management and workers of many outstanding exporting companies believe that export selling is necessary for their own personal good, for that of the company and even for their country. Their selling policy abroad will normally display an evolution from local agents and exclusive dealers to a single national exporter and finally the setting up of a national office. At this point they will appoint someone who speaks, to a faultless standard, the two (or three) languages required, and they will pay him very highly. Where mechanical products are exported, it will be necessary to wait three or four years for profits, as a back-up for maintenance and repairs is developed, but this will be weathered by the export-oriented company.

Languages are important in exporting, and so they are important in export market research. If the aspiring marketing executive wishes for a career in exporting, learning a language as part of a business course is a good way to start. A student who tackles an important world language like Spanish, Chinese or Russian will have a real plus when he enters the job market, but should make sure he is in a company that wants to export. In 1965 40 per cent of Britain's exports went to English-speaking countries, but this had declined to 26 per cent by 1977 and the increase of other languages is steadily continuing (see 'Languages and our Trading Future', *Trade and Industry*, 26 May 1978).

Knowledge of the local market is exactly what the agency has got, and it can be worth paying for it. A good market research agency can do wonders but, even more than in the home market, the analyst will need to double-check all client references that the agency supplies.

Knowledge of the product belongs principally to the sales manager but occasionally an agency that is expert in the product area may be found. There are great advantages in the sales manager doing the research himself, particularly if he is experienced in export markets: the go/no go decision will be taken faster, he will meet the persons he has to deal with and assess their reliability personally, and he will decide himself what represents a reasonable target. What then can the analyst offer? His best contribution may be a certain objectivity, which the sales manager may lack, and he may be called in only because of previous failures by the sales force to target export sales correctly in different countries. Lack of bias will particularly be manifested in detailed consideration of competitive products, the drawing up of a short-list of at least three possible agents (rather than one), and the listing of several leading potential customers to be approached by the sales manager. But really the main thing the analyst will have to offer is his time. It needs to be used very efficiently in the expensive task of export research.

Salespersons as Market Analysts in General

Both the analyst and the salesperson represent their company, and the salesperson knows the product and the foibles of purchasers very well. Why is it worthwhile having an analyst at all?

The answer, well known to anyone in the marketing research world, is that the salesperson has a different task to do and a different motivation. In most cases the salesperson's earnings are related to what he or she sells; the analyst's salary does not have so direct a dependence. The salesperson lives on goodwill; the analyst relies on goodwill to get inside the door but is not afraid to raise questions which admit the possibility that the prospective purchaser may have a higher regard for a competitor than for his own company. The salesperson is used to communicating orders and selected information about customers; the analyst is trained to provide comparatively detailed information about attitudes, normally double-checks information wherever possible, and can concentrate on the task of compiling such information because that represents the whole of his or her task.

In practice, where a sales force is used to collect information about existing customers, the information is often patchy and unreliable. Where respondents tell lies, the salesperson is motivated to believe them, and such falsehoods (generally boasts about the size and prospective growth of the company) are very common. The salespersons do not have the motivation to communicate that the analyst has; they will often hang on to very useful bits of information until the moment that they can pass them on directly to the managing director in a way that enhances their importance. Salespersons can be excellent at their jobs, and they can occasionally aid in giving information; but they should not be asked to undertake large-scale information-collecting exercises, except on a one-off basis. (See David Grace and Tom Pointon, 'Marketing Research Through the Salesforce', *Industrial Marketing Management*, Vol. 9, pp. 53–8, 1980.)

The Sales Manager in Export Markets

Given all the caveats above about saleswomen and salesmen in their home markets, it still remains true that the sales manager (and perforce the export sales manager) is well able to prospect an export market. He will be used to looking at a prospective customer and saying 'Not worth the effort!', and skilled in sorting out the true from the false because of his experience in coping with the sales force's forecasts and targets. The role of the analyst in export markets therefore can become one of aiding the sales manager to use his time to the best advantage in the highly expensive task of prospecting the export market.

Task for Field Research—the Advance Party

The whole task of the market analyst in the export market is to reach a go/no go decision regarding export potential and, if the signal is go, to ensure that the sales manager goes directly to the identified potential customers or agents when he makes his visit. Therefore, the analyst will often accompany the sales manager on a second country visit, after a first visit during which the analyst will have located the important contacts and learnt how to find his way round. Competitive information will be the main thrust of research. Do not give too much weight to respondents who tell you that the market is over-saturated, cut-throat and generally without a place for a new entrant. These statements of doom are always made and in some cases the imminent collapse of demand is predicted with great assurance. Ignore the warnings but look carefully at what is on offer at what price, because if your company has something of better value to offer, it will find a market. Table 8.3 gives a checklist of information needed in the export market.

Table 8.3. Checklist for Export Research

Size of existing market—Volume —Value	*Competitive suppliers* Names, market shares
Characteristics	Position in the market
Openness, volatility, other	Characteristics, strengths,
Major customers	weaknesses
Names, size, addresses	Export activity
Volume purchased pa	Major importers
Suppliers—how rated	Trends in supply
Prices paid	*Distribution system*
Special requirements	Mark-ups
Attitudes to imported goods	Merchandising
Likely potential	Characteristics
Products sold	*Direct sale or agents*
Description	Short-list of agents
Prices	*Tariffs, cascade taxes, quotas*
Trends in demand	*Standards and Approvals Required* Government constraints Tendering procedures

Problem of Timescales

There is no possibility of arranging lightning visits to many developing countries, and the analyst needs to prepare management for this fact. In Thailand, in many Middle Eastern countries and even in oil-rich countries of South America and Africa, it may be necessary to besiege potential contacts for weeks in order to obtain an interview. Paradoxically, this problem of delay is greater for projects under the aegis of the central administration than it is for the directly commercial sector.

Telephone around to others selling similar but not competing products in the countries to be investigated before setting targets for a visit. In the case of some very large public works contracts it may be that a company is not considered as a serious contender unless it is willing to wait ten weeks for an interview. The timescale of the export market may be very different from that experienced in the OECD countries, and it is as well to be ready for the painful adjustment required.

Continuous Export Market Research

In some companies with world markets the analyst will take on the world as the field for his daily work. The task will be very different from the occasional investigation of an export market and will almost certainly permit regular travel to seminars and conferences as well as visits to particular countries. Table 8.4 shows some of the sources of information used by export marketing professionals.

Conferences, seminars and exhibitions can provide a very useful background and a direct feel for a foreign market. With persistence and discretion, it is possible to talk to many potential buyers at trade fairs in order to obtain a clear idea of their requirements, size, the prices they pay and future prospects. But it does require careful behaviour, or the analyst will find himself thrown out of the exhibition hall. Consumer research at exhibitions open to the general public does require permission from the organisers of the exhibition. But the analyst should be able to chat to a few people around the exhibition without attracting too much attention—that's what trade fairs are for. Exhibitions do not give a good idea of how much spending power is in the market—people go to boat shows to feed their dreams, after all. Having said all this, exhibitions abroad remain a source of information on export markets.

Visits abroad, if the potential market size justifies them, are essential in putting confidence brackets on your forecasts. The analyst gets a better feel for the strength of competition and a better handle on what the market needs. Areas for new market and product development can be better identified and some idea of the timescale of development can be acquired. Without such visits the first step towards selling has yet to be taken.

Finally, it goes without saying that all the standard tools of marketing research can be applied in an export market with only changes in the language of labels and questionnaires. A local agency will need to be employed. Modifications in the product may be required for the export market, and the marketing research will be used to come back to potential buyers with a market-adapted product.

Table 8.4. Some Examples of Intelligence Sources

Source	Advantages	Disadvantages	Effectiveness for forecasting purposes
Press material Commercial (Newspapers)	General awareness of market scene	Often ill informed. Verification required	Doubtful
Technical	Provides detail of products in well informed way. Useful competitor information	Reports post-factum	Good as library back-up
Development plans Surveys, 'white papers'	Authoritative, frequently detailed. Enables evaluation of product suitability in market place	Require careful scrutiny to separate facts from politics	Good
Agents/associated companies	Close proximity to customer provides authenticated data	Quality/integrity of personnel determines volume/quality of feedback	Variable from excellent to fair
Direct customer contact	Opportunity to probe forward thinking in general terms and follow up specific leads in forward planning	Time constraints	Very good
International conferences/ seminars/planning groups Open participative	Provides opportunity to meet many key people in one place at one time and discuss topics of common interest		Excellent
Non-participative		Reliance on secondhand and sometimes biased information, which may need verification	Fair but use with caution
Exhibitions	Give first-hand experience of competitive products and prices	Give exaggerated impression of market dynamism	Doubtful

Exercises

1. Choose a product that is mainly supplied by domestic producers in your national home market. Prepare a letter to potential exporters from another country, attaching a one-page summary of the main facts about the home market but limited strictly to one page. Offer your services to fill in the details on the home market, at an appropriate price plus expenses for the number of days' work required, and suggest how many days will be needed. Despatch the letter to five potential clients, preferably in their native language.

2. Using *import* data, check on the share of British, French, Italian and Japanese goods of the following type in imports into Germany in 1960, 1970, 1980, 1990 and/or the latest year.

Cars	Electrical cable	Polyethylene (all types)
Decorative laminate	Television sets	Chocolates
Mild steel plate over 9mm thick	Washing machines	Glassware

Present the information in tables and comment on trends.

3. Using *export* data from OECD countries plus East Germany, India, Pakistan, Thailand and Taiwan, show imports from those sources in the following countries—Nigeria, Venezuela and Saudi Arabia—of any the products listed above.

9

Forecasting for an Existing Product—Quantitative Techniques

This and the next two chapters examine some statistical techniques that can be used as an aid to forecasting. The focus is on the application of these techniques in real situations where the manager has to cope with seasonality, sudden changes in demand levels, competitive manoeuvres such as price cutting, and upturns and downturns of the economy. Examples are taken from the colour television (CTV) market and the market for new cars.

Three methods of quantitative analysis will be discussed:

(a) extrapolation with steady growth,
(b) extrapolation with decreasing growth rates over time,
(c) moving averages to show the underlying trend in a market subject to major fluctuations from outside influences

The use of seasonal adjustment will then be illustrated.

All the techniques put forward in this chapter have one thing in common: they assume that you have a good series of statistics for past performance available for a number of years (generally at least four). If you do not have such a series, you may find it useful to look at Chapter 2. You will also notice that forecasting for the total market in which your company operates is suggested before you go on to examining your own company's sales.

Quantitative Demand Analysis

Quantitative demand analysis requires several years of historical data for sales, preferably month by month. The objective is to identify major influences on the sales of the product concerned, as set out in Table 9.1.

The headings in Table 9.1 are self-explanatory. Efforts by the

Table 9.1. Factors Influencing the Demand For a Product and Quantitative Demand Analysis

	Market Influences	*Quantitative Demand Analysis*	
Direct Marketing Forces	*Industry marketing efforts* ● price ● physical distribution, personal selling ● advertising/ promotional mix ● product quality	Multivariate regression Correlation analysis	Econometric modelling
Environmental forces	*Seasonal variations* ● consumer habits ● seasonal influence	XII, (X eleven), other seasonal adjustment methods	Projection and classical time series analysis. Box-Jenkins
	Cyclical swings of the economy ● economic prosperity/recession	Smoothing techniques	
	Long-term development in ● population ● income ● technology	Long-term extrapolation	
	Non-recurrent events ● strikes, wars, droughts, freezes etc.		

industry to boost demand, called *direct marketing forces*, include all the advertising and promotional activity, the price, the quality of the product and physical distribution which make up what we usually call the marketing mix. These direct marketing forces can, in some cases, even have a counter-cyclical effect. One interesting example is when the cost of having a telephone installed was reduced in Germany in 1975 by the introduction of a payment spread over 12 months, with great benefit to consumer demand at the time when the economy was in recession.

The second category of market influences are called **environmental forces**. They include those systematic forces—the trend, the cycle and the season—which are influenced by the economic environment and the calendar and are largely repetitive over a long period of time.

Before undertaking quantitative demand analysis, you should be able to identify which factors are of relevance to the progress of sales. Usually in most mature markets that are not much affected by the level of marketing expenditures but rather vary with the economic environment, **projective techniques** and **time series analysis** are quite adequate for analysing and forecasting the sales movement.

As the names of these methods suggest, they concentrate on projecting what happened in the past and assume that future time will resemble past time. In **buoyant markets** characteristic of products in their fast development stage, fluctuations in sales are mainly due to the underlying demand factors, and the techniques involved in quantitative demand analysis, namely **regression** and **correlation** should be used to try to discover the factors most likely to account for a significant amount of the variations in sales. Trying to establish the relations between sales (usually called the dependent variable) and other demand factors (called explanatory variables), and estimating and testing these relationships by means of a regression analysis, is called **econometric modelling** in statistical jargon. But let us start with a very simple case of forecasting, using **extrapolative techniques**.

Extrapolation from Past Data

When can we appropriately use this method? The answer is quite simple: when products show a very regular pattern in their sales, as illustrated in Fig. 9.1. The reasons why there should be such regularity should be examined in case a long established pattern is in fact likely to change. Products for which there is a large demand but a limited supply may show a pattern of regular development so long as supply and demand are out of balance and the supply constraints remain regular. In the case of public monopolies, such as the telephone system in some countries, supply of equipment goes on at a regular pace in most years and demand has not yet been completely saturated, leading to very stable sales. In such cases there is no need to make any detailed search for methods of forecasting, nor to consider the influence of the environment, as the passage of time itself offers the most important basis for prediction.

The example below shows how extrapolation works. In this example, as in the others that follow, the mathematics are worked out to provide you with an easy point of reference for your own calculations, but it is important to note that you will be able to work out the best-fitting line for your data and most of the other calculations at great speed if you use a calculator with statistical functions and a good user's manual.

EXAMPLE 1. FORECASTING TELEPHONE DEMAND BY EXTRAPOLATION (Using a Trend Line)

Fig. 9.1 shows the chart that describes the park of residential telephone stations installed in Unteland for the 15-year period from 1984 to 1998. We can observe that all the dots representing Y (park of stations) at each time period X scatter along a straight line, showing a **linear**

Fig. 9.1. Number of telephone stations installed in Unteland ('000 units).

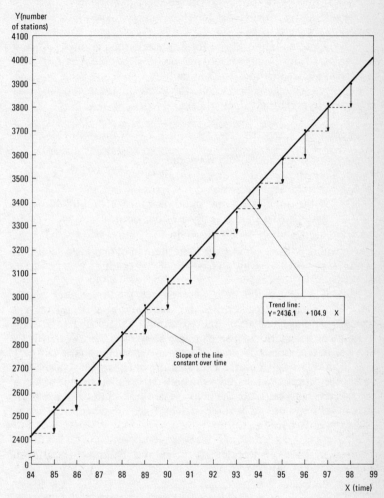

Trend line:
Y = 2436.1 + 104.9 X

Slope of the line
constant over time

relationship between the variables X and Y.

The formula expressing the linear relationship between Y and X is given as

$$Y = a + bX \qquad (1)$$

Here the park of stations installed (Y) is shown as a linear function of time (X). The parameter (*b*), called the **slope** of the function, measures the constant year-on-year increase in the park of stations, independent of the level of the park installed previously. This can be explained in terms of economics by the limited capacity of the telephone authority, which can only satisfy a certain amount of demand in a year. The parameter (*a*) represents the park of stations existing at the start (X=0), taken here to be 1984.

The method commonly used for estimating the parameters (*a*) and (*b*) so that the resulting equation (1) best fits the actual data is called the **least-squares method**, and it is employed in many calculations of trend. The formulae generated by the least-squares method are used here to determine the values of (*a*) and (*b*),

$$b = \frac{\Sigma XY - n.\overline{Y}.\overline{X}}{\Sigma X^2 - n.\overline{X}^2} \qquad a = \overline{Y} - b\overline{X}$$

where *n* is the number of observations,
$\overline{Y}$ and $\overline{X}$ are the means (average) of all values of Y and X over *n* periods of observations,
ΣXY is the sum of all the multiplications of Y and X over *n* periods (the sign Σ designates the sum),
ΣX^2 is the sum of all the squared X values over *n* periods.

The meaning of these symbols and the method of making calculations of this type will be easily understood if the example given below is worked out by the reader.

Table 9.2 shows the data of Figure 9.1 and includes all the calculations needed to determine the equation for the trend line. As is typical in trend calculation, the years have been coded to simplify subsequent calculations. The example shows the 'park'—that is the number of telephones or stock of telephones, similar to the 'car park' as a term referring to all the cars that are in existence. As each year passes the number of telephones installed increases, and the object of the exercise is to calculate the increase per year so that the size of the park in future years can be forecast. This fixed increment is calculated as *b*, and is 104.9.

Table 9.2. Park of Residential Telephone Stations Installed in Unteland ('000 units)

Year	Coded year (X)	No. of stations (Y)	X.Y	X²
1984	$X_0 = 0$	$Y_0 = 2,425$		0
1985	$X_1 = 1$	$Y_1 = 2,539$	2,539	1
1986	$X_2 = 2$	$Y_2 = 2,653$	5,306	4
1987	$X_3 = 3$	$Y_3 = 2,758$	8,274	9
1988	$X_4 = 4$	$Y_4 = 2,885$	11,420	16
1989	$X_5 = 5$	$Y_5 = 2,968$	14,840	25

Year	Coded year (X)	No. of stations (Y)	X.Y	X^2
1990	$X_6 = 6$	$Y_6 = 3,079$	18,474	36
1991	$X_7 = 7$	$Y_7 = 3,182$	22,274	49
1992	$X_8 = 8$	$Y_8 = 3,269$	26,152	64
1993	$X_9 = 9$	$Y_9 = 3,356$	30,204	81
1994	$X_{10} = 10$	$Y_{10} = 3,459$	34,590	100
1995	$X_{11} = 11$	$Y_{11} = 3,585$	39,435	121
1996	$X_{12} = 12$	$Y_{12} = 3,705$	44,460	144
1997	$X_{13} = 13$	$Y_{13} = 3,817$	49,621	169
1998	$X_{14} = 14$	$Y_{14} = 3,906$	54,684	196
Total	$\Sigma X = 105$	$\Sigma Y = 47,556$	$\Sigma XY = 362,273$	$\Sigma X_2 = 1,015$

$$n = 15$$
$$\Sigma X = X_0 + X_1 + \ldots + X_{14} = 105$$
$$\Sigma Y = Y_0 + Y_1 + \ldots \ldots + Y_{14} = 47,556$$
$$\Sigma XY = X_0.Y_0 + X_1.Y_1 + \ldots \ldots + X_{14}.Y_{14} = 362,273$$
$$\Sigma X^2 = X_0.X_0 + X_1.X_1 + \ldots \ldots + X_{14}.X_{14} = 1,015$$

$$X = \frac{\Sigma X}{n} = \frac{105}{15} = 7 \qquad Y = \frac{\Sigma Y}{n} = \frac{47,556}{15} = 3170.4$$

We determine the equation of the trend line as follows:

$$b = \frac{\Sigma XY - n.\overline{Y}.\overline{X}}{\Sigma X^2 - n\overline{X}^2} = \frac{362,273 - 15(3170.4)(7)}{1,015 - 15(7)^2} = \frac{29,381}{280} = 104.9$$

$$a = \overline{Y} - b\overline{X} = 3170.4 - 104.9 (7) = 2436.1$$

Therefore substituting the values of *a* and *b* in equation (1), we obtain:
$$Y = 2436.1 + 104.9$$
This equation is shown by the straight line superimposed in Figure 9.1.

An immediate prediction for 1999 ($X_{15} = 15$) can be derived from the above equation by substituting X by $X_{15} = 15$:

$$Y = 2,436.1 + 104.9 (15) = 4009.6 \text{ (rounded to 4010)}$$

So, assuming a constant environment, we can predict that the park installed in 1999 will reach 4010 stations, an increase of 104 stations versus the actual park of 3906 stations in 1998.

Extrapolation with Steady Changes in Growth Rates

The previous example has shown the park of telephone stations growing at a constant rate. How does one deal with trend extrapolation if the rate of growth is not constant, but increases or decreases over time? Let us look at Example 2.

EXAMPLE 2. FORECASTING THE PERSONAL INCOME FORMATION IN UNTELAND BY EXTRAPOLATION (Using an Exponential Trend Curve)

Fig. 9.2 shows the plot of personal income formation in Unteland during the 16-year period from 1990 to 2005. We see that all the dots scatter along a curve that we suspect is growing exponentially, i.e. its slope is steadily increasing (or decreasing in other examples) as time progresses.

Fig. 9.2. Personal income (non-agricultural) in Unteland ($U billions).

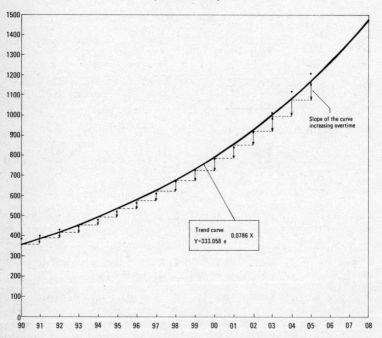

So the formula we choose to fit the relationship between Y (personal income) and time period X, can be of the form

$$Y = a.e^{bX} \qquad (2)$$

which shows (Y) as an exponential function of (X). Since this formula in its initial form does not express the linear relationship between (X) and (Y), the least squares method cannot be applied immediately. An initial transformation of the equation (2) is needed so that the transformed data can express a linear relationship between variables. Taking the logarithm of both sides of equation (2), we obtain

$$\log Y = \log a + bX$$

Substituting log Y by (y) and log a by (α), we have

$$y = \alpha + bX \qquad (3)$$

which shows that logarithms of Y vary linearly with time X (Figure 9.3).

Applying the least squares method to expression (3), we can estimate α and b:

$$b = \frac{\Sigma Xy - n.\bar{y}.\bar{X}}{\Sigma X^2 - n.\bar{X}^2} \qquad \alpha = y - bX$$

Fig. 9.3 shows log y moving linearly with time X. This has been achieved with **semi-logarithmic graph paper**, which shows that growth is at a steady average rate in this case (a straight line) by reducing the plotted increases period on period according to the logarithmic scale, so demonstrating the underlying logic of growth in the way that is easiest to project—a straight line.

Fig. 9.3. Personal income (non-agricultural) in Unteland using log scale ($U billions).

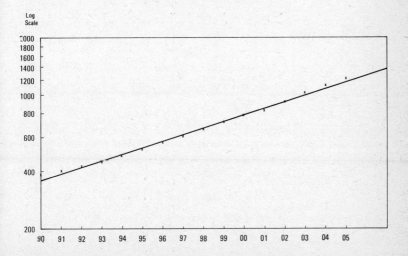

Table 9.3. Personal Income Formation in Unteland $U (Billions)

Year	Coded year (X)	Income (Y)	Absolute year-on-year increase in Y $(Y_X - Y_{X-1})$	y = Log Y	Xy	X^2
1990	$X_1 = 1$	$Y_1 = 384.4$		5.9517	5.9517	1
1991	$X_2 = 2$	$Y_2 = 399.0$	14.6	5.9889	11.9780	4
1992	$X_3 = 3$	$Y_3 = 424.5$	25.5	6.0509	18.1527	9
1993	$X_4 = 4$	$Y_4 = 447.0$	22.5	6.1026	24.4102	16
1994	$X_5 = 5$	$Y_5 = 480.7$	33.7	6.1752	30.8762	25
1995	$X_6 = 6$	$Y_6 = 519.5$	38.8	6.2529	37.5172	36
1996	$X_7 = 7$	$Y_7 = 566.1$	46.6	6.3388	44.3714	49
1997	$X_8 = 8$	$Y_8 = 609.1$	43.0	6.4120	51.2959	65
1998	$X_9 = 9$	$Y_9 = 667.5$	58.4	6.5035	58.5319	81
1999	$X_{10} = 10$	$Y_{10} = 725.8$	58.3	6.5873	65.8727	100
2000	$X_{11} = 11$	$Y_{11} = 780.7$	54.9	6.6602	73.2621	121
2001	$X_{12} = 12$	$Y_{12} = 838.0$	57.3	6.7310	80.7722	144
2002	$X_{13} = 13$	$Y_{13} = 917.3$	79.3	6.8214	88.6786	169
2003	$X_{14} = 14$	$Y_{14} = 1013.5$	96.2	6.9212	96.8963	196
2004	$X_{15} = 15$	$Y_{15} = 1119.1$	105.6	7.0203	105.3042	225
2005	$X_{16} = 16$	$Y_{16} = 1210.2$	91.1	7.0985	113.5766	256
Total	$\Sigma X = 136$			$\Sigma y = 103.6164$	$\Sigma Xy = 907.4480$	$\Sigma X^2 = 1496$

$\bar{X} = 8.5$

$\bar{y} = 6.4760$

Semi-logarithmic paper can be obtained from business stationers and is useful for preparing many forecasts, as changes in the slope of the line signal changes in the growth rate. Be careful, however, about showing graphs on semi-logarithmic paper in final forecasts, as they are not understood by most businessmen.

The Y axis gives log Y directly when plotted on semi-logarithmic paper.

Table 9.3. represents the data plotted in Figure 9.2 and Figure 9.3, with all the calculations needed to determine equation (3). Also shown in the fourth column of the table are the year-on-year growth rates in the income formation. You will notice that they are not constant, but increase over time.

$$n = 16 \qquad \overline{X} = \frac{\Sigma X}{n} = \frac{136}{16} = 8.5$$

$$\overline{y} = \frac{\Sigma y}{n} = \frac{103.6164}{16} = 6.4760$$

α and b of expression (3) are calculated as follows:

$$b = \frac{\Sigma X y = n.\overline{y}.\overline{X}}{X^2 - n.\overline{X}^2} = \frac{907.4480 - 16(6.4760)\,(8.5)}{1.496 - 16(8.5)^2}$$

$$\frac{26.708}{340} = 0.079$$

$$\alpha = \overline{y} - b\overline{X} = 6.4760 - (0.079)\,(8.5) = 5.8083$$

Expression (3) becomes

$$y = \log Y = 5.8083 + 0.079\,X \qquad (4)$$

Taking the antilog of α, we obtain the value of (a),

$$\alpha = \log a = 5.8083 \iff a = e^{\alpha} =$$

$$e^{5.8083} = 2.7183^{5.8083} = 333.058$$

(the value of e is 2.7183).

Relation (2) is now written as

$$Y = 333.058(e)^{0.079\,X}$$

which best fits the data of personal income formation. An immediate forecast for 2006 ($X_{17} = 17$), assuming a constant environment, is given by substituting the value of X_{17} in equation (4),

$$\log Y = 5.8083 + (0.079)\,(17) = 7.1437$$

hence the value of Y, on looking in the logarithm tables, is equal to $U1,266 billion.

Extrapolation with Typical Growth Patterns

The previous example has shown personal income formation growing at a marginally increasing rate over time. In real economic life we are often confronted with products whose sales are characterised by increasing growth rates in the first phase of development followed thereafter by decreasing growth rates. An elongated S curve is extensively used to describe these series, characterised by varying marginal growth rates. Let us look at Example 3.

EXAMPLE 3. FORECASTING THE RATE OF PENETRATION OF COLOUR TELEVISIONS (CTVs) IN UNTELAND
Table 9.4 represents the percentage penetration of CTVs in households in Unteland for the 13-year period from 1977 to 1989. As can be observed in the fourth column of the table, the marginal growth rate rapidly increased up to 1986, characterising the fast penetration of the product during the first ten years of its introduction, and decreased after that.

The data in Table 9.4 can be described by the following curve,

$$Y = e^{a\, -\, b(c)^X} \qquad (5)$$

which shows a point of inflection (this point corresponds to the value of X which annulates the second order derivate of the curve) where

$$X = \log\tfrac{1}{b} / \log c$$

To the left of this point the slope increases with (X); to the right the slope decreases. As (X) approaches infinity, (Y) approaches e^a, which means that as far as we can project into the future, the value of Y can never be higher than e^a. This is quite normal, since we know that the park of consumer durables will never exceed some multiple of the total number of households (e.g. 120 per cent, with all households with one CTV and 20 per cent with two CTVs).

The forecasting problem consists in determining the values of the parameters (a), (b) and (c) so that the resulting curve best fits the data.

The determination of the coefficients (a), (b) and (c) is beyond the scope of our calculations here. But because this type of curve is extremely useful in forecasting and because of its wide use, the reader

Table 9.4. Percentage Penetration of CTVs in Households in Unteland

Year	Coded year (X)	% Penetration (Y)	Absolute year-on-year increase in Y ($Y_X - Y_{X-1}$)	Year-on-year % change in Y	Fitted curve with equation (5)	Fitted curve with equation (6)
1977	1	1			0.660	0.660
1978	2	2	1	+ 100	1.617	1.617
1979	3	3.8	1.8	+ 90	3.393	3.393
1980	4	6.5	2.7	+ 71	6.263	6.263
1981	5	10.3	3.8	+ 58	10.400	10.400
1982	6	15.5	5.2	+ 50	15.821	15.821
1983	7	21.9	6.4	+ 41	22.386	22.386
1984	8	29.9	8.0	+ 37	29.832	29.832
1985	9	37.7	7.8	+ 26	37.831	37.831
1986	10	46.3	8.6	+ 23	46.047	46.047
1987	11	54.6	8.3	+ 18	54.175	54.175
1988	12	62.2	7.6	+ 14	61.974	61.974
1989	13	68.8	6.6	+ 11	69.268	69.268
1990					75.946	75.946
1991					81.955	81.955
1992					87.284	87.284
1993					91.953	91.254
1994					96.004	96.005
1995					99.490	99.491

is invited to familiarise himself with how the calculation is made. In business life he will need to use a computer package.

A computer package is illustrated in Tables 9.5 and 9.6 to show how these coefficients are estimated. First we have to enter starting estimates for the curve's parameters; then through an iterative process (repeated calculations), using non-linear regression, the starting estimates are improved upon until the parameter values that best fit the data are found (i.e. the programme converges). Table 9.5 fits the data of Table 9.4 with equation (4) and the best estimates of the coefficients are given:

$$Y = e^{4.77087 - 6.26893\,(0.82727)X}$$

There is an inflection point where

$$X = \frac{\log 1/b}{\log c} = \frac{\log \dfrac{1}{6.2689}}{\log (0.8273)} = \frac{-1.8356}{-0.1896} = 9.6 \simeq 10$$

i.e in 1986. When (X) approaches ∞, $Y = e^{a} = e^{4.7709} = 188$ per cent, i.e. the rate of penetration will saturate at 118 per cent as we go further and further into the future. This absolute saturation will occur in early 2000, where the growth rate is practically nil. From the marketing point of view, however, we can say the market begins to mature and become difficult after 1986, when the year-on-year increments in sales to first buyers start to be smaller. The high growth rate that has aided the smaller company disappears, the market starts to look for lower and lower prices, novelties appear and the smaller suppliers get squeezed. **Replacement demand** is reflected in these calculations of household penetration, which should really be called 'apparent household penetration', regarding all sales as first-time sales. These replacement sales do not undermine the validity of the household penetration approach—the important fact to hang on to is that once we have passed the turning point in the S curve, we are due for severe fluctuations in growth, with a lower growth rate complicated by postponements of replacement in economic downturn years, later compensated by upturns. It is possible, of course, to build a model of demand where household penetration by the first television is calculated, together with replacement demand, from consumer surveys of ownership of durables. The market analyst often uses several methods like this in order to build up a consistent view of national demand for a product.

Table 9.5. Calculation of Best-fitting Curve for CTV Household % Penetration in Unteland

$$y = e^{4.66087 - 6.26893 (0.82727)^t}$$

FINAL PARAMETER VALUES:

B(1) 4.77087E+00
B(2) 6.26893E+00
B(3) 8.27275E—01

INDEX OF DETERMINATION = 1.000
AVERAGE ABSOLUTE % ERROR = 5.82
MEAN % ERROR = —4.86

SUBCOMMAND? Print

BEGINNING PERIOD, ENDING PERIOD? 1977, 2000

PERIOD	ACTUAL	FITTED	RESIDUAL	% DIFF
1977	1.000	0.660	—0.340	—33.98
1978	2.000	1.617	—0.383	—19.15
1979	3.800	3.393	—0.407	—10.72
1980	6.500	6.263	—0.237	—3.65
1981	10.300	10.400	0.100	0.97
1982	15.500	15.821	0.321	2.07
1983	21.900	22.386	0.486	2.22
1984	29.900	29.832	—0.068	—0.23
1985	37.700	37.831	0.131	0.35
1986	46.300	46.047	—0.253	—0.55
1987	54.600	54.175	—0.425	—0.78
1988	62.200	61.974	—0.226	—0.36
1989	68.800	69.268	0.468	0.68
1990		75.946		
1991		81.955		
1992		87.284		
1993		91.953		
1994		96.004		
1995		99.490		
1996		102.469		
1997		105.001		
1998		107.143		
1999		108.947		
2000		110.464		

By Courtesy of Control Data Corporation

Table 9.6 fits the data with another variant of the curve (4), which we call the **Gompertz curve**. The equation of the Gompertz curve is

$$Y = A.B^{(C)^X} \qquad (5)$$

The best estimates of parameters (A), (B) and (C) calculated via the computer package are given

$$Y = (118.025) (0.001894)^{(0.827278)^X}$$

Table 9.6. Calculation of Best-fitting Curve for CTV Household % Penetration in Unteland, Using a Gompertz Curve

---

$$Y = (118.025) (0.00189446)^{(0.827278)^X}$$

COMMAND? Trend/Gompertz: 0

FINAL PARAMETER VALUES:
   B(1) 1.18025E+02
   B(2) 1.89446E—03
   B(3) 8.27278E—01
INDEX OF DETERMINATION   = 1.000
AVERAGE ABSOLUTE % ERROR = 5.82
MEAN % ERROR   = —4.85

TRE SUBCOMMAND? Print

BEGINNING PERIOD, ENDING PERIOD? 1977, 2000

PERIOD	ACTUAL	FITTED	RESIDUAL	% DIFF
1977	1.000	0.660	—0.340	—33.98
1978	2.000	1.617	—0.383	—19.15
1979	3.800	3.393	—0.407	—10.72
1980	6.500	6.263	—0.237	—3.65
1981	10.300	10.400	0.100	0.97
1982	15.500	15.821	0.321	2.07
1983	21.900	22.386	0.486	2.22
1984	29.900	29.832	—0.068	—0.23
1985	37.700	37.831	0.131	0.35
1986	46.300	46.047	—0.253	—0.55
1987	54.600	54.175	—0.425	—0.78
1988	62.200	61.974	—0.226	—0.36
1989	68.800	69.268	0.468	0.68
1990		75.946		
1991		81.955		
1992		87.284		
1993		91.954		
1994		96.005		
1995		99.491		
1996		102.470		
1997		105.002		
1998		107.144		
1999		108.949		
2000		110.465		

By Courtesy of Control Data Corporation

Taking the logarithm of both sides of relations (4) and (5), we obtain similar expressions,

$$Y = e^{a - b.c^X} \implies \log Y = a - b.c^X \tag{6}$$

$$Y = A.B^{(C)^X} \implies \log Y = \log A + (\log B)(C)^X \tag{7}$$

After substituting all the parameters with their estimated values, equations (6) and (7) become,

$$\log Y = a - b.c^X = 4.77087 - 6.26893 (0.82727)^X$$

$$\log Y = \log A + (\log B)(C)^X =$$

$$\log (118.025) + [\log (0.001894)] (0.827278)^X =$$

$$4.77089 - 6.26882 (0.827278)^X$$

which are in fact two different expressions of the same relation.

Fig. 9.4 shows the fitted curve (an S curve, exactly the same as the Gompertz curve) superimposed, with the dots representing the actual data. Note that to the left of the year 1986 the slope of the curve increases with (X) and that it decreases to the right of 1986.

One last word about the Gompertz curve. You can check whether your data is likely to fit this curve by looking at the year-on-year percentage change in the data (and *not* the year-on-year absolute increase). The year-on-year change should be decreasing over time, as shown in column 5 of Table 9.4. Such data, when plotted on semilog paper, will show the slope of the curve steadily decreasing as X increases. This is illustrated in Fig. 9.5.

Moving Average to Highlight Underlying Movement of a Series

In the previous section the pattern of gradual growth of a data series was described in terms of a mathematical equation. In doing this the assumption was made that the growth pattern of the product forecast would change in a systematic way along the product life cycle. But in real economic life the growth pattern of many products, while following a certain trend, may also show significant deviations, owing to the general movements of the economy as well as to strikes, riots,

Fig. 9.4. CTV penetration rate (per cent) into households in Unteland.

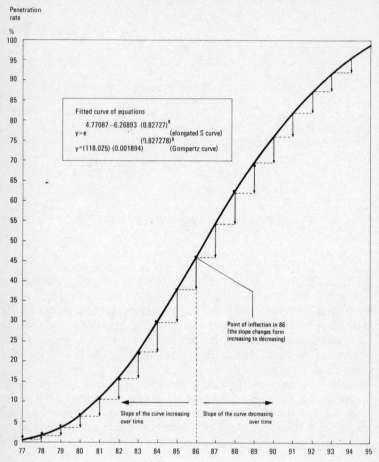

even sports events, etc. To be able to identify the effect of the **cyclical** swings of the economy and of any causative event that has influenced past sales, we need to reconstruct the underlying movement by examining the past history of sales. This will be a powerful aid to understanding and forecasting the shape of the year ahead.

A moving average can be calculated by replacing each value in the data series (e.g. each month) by the average of its value plus some of the values directly preceding and following it. For instance, if the sales values for January, February, March, April and May are respectively

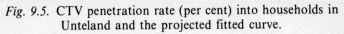

Fig. 9.5. CTV penetration rate (per cent) into households in Unteland and the projected fitted curve.

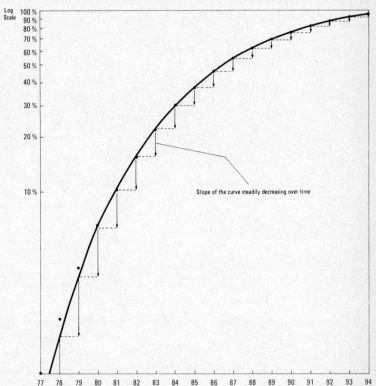

78, 90, 150, 114 and 106, then the three-month moving average for February is obtained by averaging the three values of January, February and March, i.e. $(78 + 90 + 150) \div 3 = 106$. It is worth noting that averaging over an even number of periods, say 4, 6 or 12 months, will generate an initial moving average value falling between successive months. In such cases we bring the moving average value back in line (or centre it) by using the average of the two initial moving averages. For example, the above four-month moving average values between March and April and between April and May are respectively 108 and 115; so the four-month moving average value centred at April is obtained by taking $(108 + 115) \div 2 = 111.5$. This procedure has been applied to calculate the centred 12-month moving average of the car sales data shown in Figs. 9.6 and 9.7.

The purpose of fitting a moving average to a data series is to remove

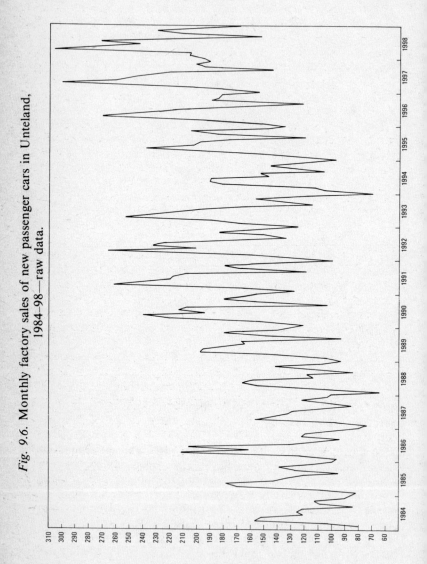

Fig. 9.6. Monthly factory sales of new passenger cars in Unteland, 1984–98—raw data.

(or **smooth out**) the disturbing fluctuations that obscure its underlying movement. The choice of an appropriate period for averaging is critical, and depends mostly on what you want to smooth out. In a series dominated by a strictly uniform seasonal pattern, a 12-month moving average would remove all the seasonal variations. If all business cycles were exactly the same both in duration and amplitude, then a moving average with a period equal to the period of the cycle would remove the cyclical variations. However, strictly periodic uniform cyclical or regular movements do not exist in economic series, so that the moving average process can never completely eliminate certain fluctuations in the series. As illustrated in Fig. 9.7, the centred 12-month moving average describing the underlying movements of car sales in Unteland during the 1984–98 period smooths out the seasonal variations, highlighting the cyclical and the trend components of the series. Cyclical variations are shown to coincide closely with the general business cycles of the Unteland economy up to 1992. Then there occurs an early downturn in car sales, following the threat of war early in 1993. The recessional 1994–5 period is characterised by improvement in car sales, but this is making up for the postponed purchases of 1993.

In general, in a seasonally adjusted series, the underlying movements can be obtained by using a three- or five-month moving average, depending on how much fluctuation is shown in the deseasonalised series. We will return to this question when we tackle the problem of analysing a time series. The 12-month moving average is a rapid method of sorting out the past trend and the cyclical component.

Table 9.7 gives an example of how the moving average is calculated. The table shows you how a 12-month moving average is calculated. The moving average (MA) is centred at the middle of the year to remind the user that it lags behind what is happening in the latest months, as it contains a year's history.

Table 9.7. 12-Month Moving Average Fitted to Sales of Lawnmowers

Year	Sales	12-Month totals	Monthly Average (12)	Centred Average
1974	Jan. 228			
	Feb. 386			
	Mar. 624			
	Ap. 701			
	May 690			
	June 540			

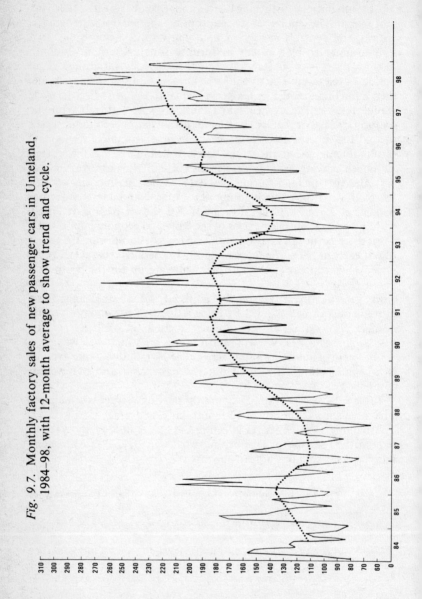

Fig. 9.7. Monthly factory sales of new passenger cars in Unteland, 1984–98, with 12-month average to show trend and cycle.

Year	Sales	12-Month totals	Monthly Average (12)	Centred Average
	July 390			380.7
	Aug. 280			382.1
	Sept. 280			383.5
	Oct. 150			382.3
	Nov. 149			383.9
	Dec. 150	4,568	380.7	384.8
1975	Jan. 245	4,585	382.1	393.1
	Feb. 403	4,602	383.5	393.9
	Mar. 610	4,588	382.3	397.3
	Ap. 720	4,607	383.9	387.3
	May 700	4,617	384.8	387.2
	June 640	4,717	393.1	387.5
	July 400	4,727	393.9	388.7
	Aug. 320	4,767	397.3	387.4
	Sept. 160	4,647	387.2	378.7
	Oct. 149	4,646	387.2	373.7
	Nov. 153	4.650	387.5	367,8
	Dec. 164	4,664	388.7	362.0
1976	Jan. 230	4,649	387.4	361.2
	Feb. 298	4,544	378.7	358.7
	Mar. 550	4,484	373.7	350.9
	Ap. 650	4,414	367.8	355.5
	May 630	4,344	362.0	
	June 630	4,334	361.2	
	July 370	4,304	358.7	
	Aug. 227	4,211	350.9	
	Sept. 215	4,266	355.5	

Seasonal Adjustment

In the previous section the use of a 12-month moving average removed the seasonal effects on sales without quantifying what those effects were.

Seasonal Effects and Reasons for Adjustment

When we look at monthly or quarterly sales data, we usually find that they show a more or less regular pattern within the year, which is repeated in subsequent years. Such a pattern is called the **seasonal pattern** and is explained by consumers' buying habits and even the effects of the weather. For instance, in the automobile market we observe that sales of new cars are affected by positive seasonal influences during spring and early summer (from March to July) and by negative seasonal influences in autumn and winter, in the retail toy market sales are stronger in November/December, ice-cream has a summer peak, and so on.

Because seasonal influences may obscure the basic growth pattern of a series within a year, *seasonal adjustment* of the data is required, especially when we wish to compare the sales achieved in different months in the same year. For example, we might find that an increase of 10 per cent in sales in September over August in a particular year actually represents a decline if the normal seasonal index for September is 20 per cent above the seasonal index for August. In other words, if there is an increase, but not as large as is expected from historical data, then a decrease relative to those expectations has occurred.

There are many ways of measuring seasonal variations. They range from crude approximations based on simple calculations to highly refined techniques involving computer processing. Whatever technique you use, the influence of the season is measured in terms of a **seasonal index** associated with each month of the year. The average for a month in a year will be 100, and the total for the year will be 1200, but each month will vary around the average of 100 in a more or less significant way (e.g. August will often have values of 40 to 60 for many products). The way to work out seasonal factors is set out in full in the Statistical Workshop A (p. 241). Four types of seasonal adjustment are described in full in the workshop, but for the purposes of this chapter it is important first of all to understand what seasonal adjustment achieves.

How Seasonal Adjustment Aids Forecasting

Fig 9.8 shows raw data for CTV Deliveries in Unteland. As you might expect, this graph does not give us much help in forecasting. How can we understand what is going on? Fig. 9.9 shows us the seasonal factors, which are calculated by using the trend-adjusted relative percent method described in full in Statistical Workshop A. Fig. 9.10 then shows us the same data on sales after seasonal effects have been removed by the trend-adjusted relative percent method and a three-month moving average has been applied.

Fig 9.10 gives us a better feel for the way that sales are progressing. As we leave 1990 we know that sales are on a strong upward trend, something we would not have been sure about if we had only looked at the raw data. The picture of sales will be presented to management in the form of Fig. 9.11 (for a similar product), which shows the way that the annual sales achieved was built up.

This type of analysis should normally be applied to cover one

Fig. 9.8. WPU deliveries in Unteland—raw data.

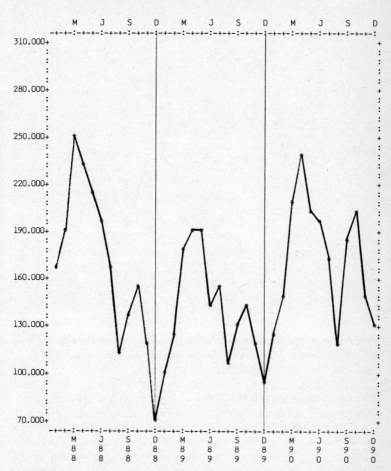

business cycle and, where possible, two. In this way the influence of the economic cycle can be picked up (as it is by the 12-month moving average method), but the individual recurring factors affecting sales can also be seen. Years in which there is a trade fair, for example, may be characterised by a take-off in demand after the fair that produces a particular 'shape' to the year. If one of these events is certain in the following year, the analyst can decide on the shape of the seasonally adjusted year to come and work backwards to calculate actual sales by month with better accuracy than if he had employed the seasonal adjustment factor alone. More information on these methods is given in the Statistical Workshop. The two types of seasonal adjustment

Fig. 9.9. Seasonal factors.

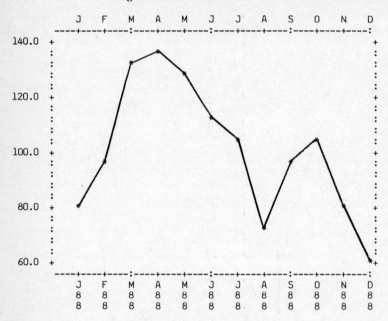

used to show the trend of sales during past years and the current year are called **Trend-Adjusted Relative Percent Method (TARPM)** and **Ratio to Moving Average Method (RMAM).**

TARPM has been used in the example above but both these methods give an excellent feel for whether total market sales in any particular month represent a real increase or decrease compared with any previous month. This information is absolutely vital if the product in question is strongly affected by the economic cycle, for if there is a downturn in progress that is masked by the seasonality, there may be a build-up of inventory (stocks) that may remain unsold for a long time. The sales manager may announce, 'We're having a good spring', as sales take off after the slack winter period, but the reality may be that the underlying trend for sales is flattening or even in decline.

How Seasonal Adjustment Aids Forecast Monitoring

Achieving the year's forecast is the industry's goal, and each month contributes something to that goal. To know whether the contributions of January, February, March and so on are enough, and to

Fig. 9.10. WPU deliveries in Unteland, seasonally adjusted with three-month moving average.

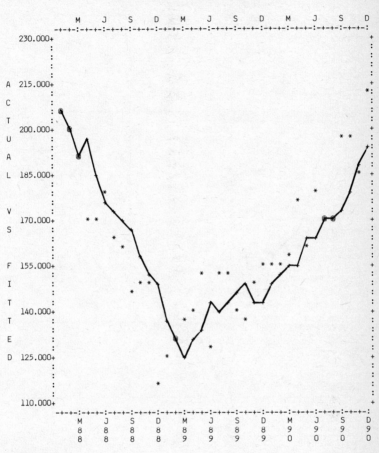

*=ACTUAL
+=FITTED
@=COINCIDING POINTS

know how much they should contribute, it is usually adequate to use two single forms of seasonal adjustment described in full in Statistical Workshop A. They are **Percent of Seasonal Average Method (PSAM)** and **Relative Percent Method (RPM)**. These methods are also useful (because rapid) for markets not subject to much fluctuation from year to year. If the forecast for annual industy sales is, say, 3,720 tonnes of product, the analyst uses the seasonality calculated by the arithmetic-

Fig. 9.11. XKJ deliveries in Unteland, seasonally adjusted with three-month moving average.

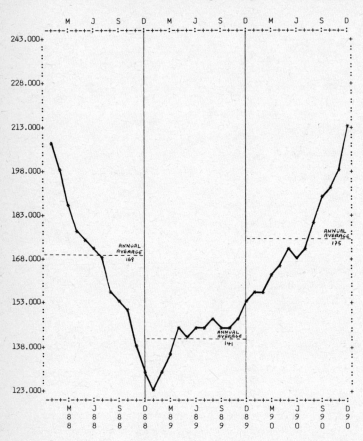

ally simple PSAM or RPM method to work out how much January, February, March and all the other months should contribute. He may also work out how much sales in those months can differ from the calculated seasonality, before the forecast needs to be revised, and use this to monitor the progress of sales during the year, as described in Chapter 10. Table 9.8 exemplifies the use of seasonal adjustment to forecast sales by month.

A final warning is worthwhile. Always use four or five years' data to calculate seasonality, if you can, as this is the only way to take in the effects of the economic cycle. If you are just starting to sell, you will

Table 9.8. Forecast Industry Sales by Month where Annual Sales Equal 3,720 tonnes

	A. Seasonal factors*	B. Forecast average sales per month	Forecast sales per month = A × B
Jan.	80	310	248.0
Feb.	84	310	260.4
Mar.	88	310	272.8
Ap.	110	310	341.0
May	120	310	372.0
June	122	310	378.2
July	120	310	372.0
Aug.	78	310	241.8
Sept.	113	310	350.3
Oct.	104	310	322.4
Nov.	98	310	303.8
Dec.	83	310	257.3
Total	1,200	3,720	3,720.0

*Calculation based on previous four years' sales

not be able to use such data, of course, and you will have to guess the seasonal pattern. If, on the other hand, you are able to sell everything you can produce, all you need is your manufacturing manager to forecast how many can be produced. If that is the case, do not waste your time forecasting demand by just looking at the statistics; get busy investigating future demand for the product by research among customers to see whether an increase in capacity is justified.

Key Concepts

Quantitative Demand Analysis. A method of analysing the effects of direct marketing and environmental forces on sales of a product over time by mathematical techniques.

Extrapolation. Projection onwards into the future of trends visible in past sales.

Mature Markets. Markets for products that have been sold for at least four years, for which new customers are being found at a declining rate if at all, are difficult for new companies to enter, and often move in cycles upwards and downwards with the rate of growth of the economy.

Regression. A mathematical method of showing the influence of one factor (such as personal income) on another (for example, purchases of package holidays) where good available forecasts for one factor are employed to forecast for the related variable.

Correlation. A mathematical measurement of the relation between two variables.

The Park. The total stock of a durable product in use by customers, analogous to 'car park'.

Penetration. The degree to which the total number of places or groupings where a product might be installed is in fact achieved by the product, usually expressed as a percentage. Household penetration is a common measure for consumer goods.

Moving Average. An average calculated for more than one time period, shown as one point, for each period sequentially, in order to smooth out the effects of random fluctuations and seasonality.

Seasonality. The way in which sales go up and down each year under the predictable influence of such factors as weather, holidays, traditional dates for certain activities, payment bonuses, and so on.

Seasonal Adjustment. A method of allowing for the effects of seasonality in order better to understand the underlying trend in sales or to monitor progress in sales versus the annual target.

Sales Forecast Monitoring. The systematic examination of sales, usually on a monthly basis, to find if they are compatible with the year-end forecast.

Exercises

1. The data below shows sales of oriental carpets in Unteland, where a trade fair is held every two years, though not always on the same date. Although he cannot prove it, the Secretary of the Oriental Carpet Importers Association (OCIA) believes that these fairs are followed by a substantial flattening in basic demand. Use the RMAM seasonal adjustment technique outlined in Statistical Workshop A to tell him when the trade fairs occurred and the length of time they affected sales.

Carpet Sales in Units of 1000

	1976	1977	1978	1979
Jan.	17.3	48.5	101.3	132.5
Feb.	23.3	42.2	98.9	117.8
Mar.	60.3	82.2	210.3	232.2
Apr.	54.5	62.1	167.3	174.9
May	79.8	82.3	225.0	227.5
June	54.0	54.0	144.0	144.0
July	60.8	62.4	156.8	158.4
Aug.	42.1	46.5	106.9	111.3
Sept.	113.4	138.9	287.4	312.9
Oct.	60.1	83.5	153.7	177.1
Nov.	134.6	214.6	350.6	430.6
Dec.	82.8	151.8	220.8	289.8
TOTAL	783.0	1,069.0	2,223.0	2,509.0

2. The OCIA Secretary (see previous question) forecasts that 3 million carpets will be sold in Unteland this year. Use the PSAM method to tell him how many carpets he should have sold by June to reach his forecast.

3. Here are annual sales data for garden furniture. Derive a best-fitting trend line for the data and use this to forecast sales for the next two years.

Annual Sales of Garden Furniture—$U million

1994	1995	1996	1997	1998
98	103	104	114	120

How would you modify your forecast if a downturn in the economy like that of 1996 were forecast?

4. Regression analysis has been mentioned in this chapter and the method will be explained in Chapter 10. Before reading Chapter 10, make a list of the factors you would expect to influence the sales of the following products, both positively and adversely, and to be worthy of examination.

Kitchen cabinets	Sprinkler systems
Business textbooks	Skiing holidays
Records	Yachts
Alcoholic beverages	Nuclear power stations
Steel	Cash dispensers and credit cards

10
Forecasting for an Existing Product—the National Market

In this chapter the 'topdown' route towards forecasting for a company's sales of particular products is outlined, and some mathematical methods of computation are explained. The topics covered are:

1. The need to make a global industry forecast before a company forecast.
2. Using industry consensus forecasts.
3. Industry forecasts made on short-term data.
4. Forecasts for an industry on the basis of long-term data (illustrated with an analysis of car sales).
5. Longer-term forecasts.
6. Methods of forecasting employed in the business world.

Why Bother Forecasting for Total Market or Industry?

No matter how small a company is, it always needs to consider what will happen in the total market for its products before it goes on to forecast its own performance. This consideration may, in the case of very rapidly growing small companies in large markets, only require a few seconds' reflection, but for the majority of businesses what is happening in the market-place in total is only too relevant to the future of the products of a particular company.

One of the basic questions with regard to future performance is whether the company can grow at the same rate as the industry in general (hold its **market share**) or actually grow at a more rapid rate (increase its market share). In order to have some feel for how much growth is possible inside the company, it is essential to consider what the total industry sales will be.

Using Existing Market-related Information

The best sort of information concerning markets is historical data referring to the past and recent sales of the product, published by the national government or by trade associations. In some cases there may be indicators highlighting the future behaviour of sales, such as surveys by the CBI of business opinion in the UK, or the series published by the EEC in *European Economy* (Supplement—Series B). With regard to consumer goods, other relevant data may refer to a consumer panel's usage of a particular brand of product, as national data at the required level of disaggregation is not available. Besides all the quantitative data mentioned, the prospects for consumer goods may be affected by current awareness of the product, the relative price of the product versus competition and the volume of advertising for the product and its competitors—all information that will need to be taken into account when making a forecast.

It should be mentioned here that, in the early evolution of some markets, the rate of growth of the total market may be determined to some extent by the amount of advertising expenditure and other promotional effort backing the product. This is true where there is a change of taste in the market that requires people who are unfamiliar with the product in question to sample it for the first time (as, for example, the introduction of fast food to the UK market). In such cases forecasts of how much advertising expenditure is likely to be put behind the new product by the competitors are relevant in arriving at a forecast for the total market and for the company's own products; although, to be fair, this judgement will generally have to be made without the benefit of any statistical methods.

Using Industry Consensus Forecasts

In any large, well organised industry there will be an industry forecast available to each particular forecaster. It is an elementary precaution to compare one's own forecast with the forecast produced by the industry. Wherever the forecaster's view differs significantly from the industry's forecast, he should ask himself whether he is making any special assumptions that are not held by the industry, or whether the industry's forecast is in fact a political statement made to its customers with an in-built bias. These kinds of questions can be settled by examining the forecaster's own record versus that of the industry. Table 10.1 shows the annual forecasts (from 1985 to 1990) of CTV domestic sales made by the Unteland industry and by a company forecaster.

Table 10.1. Forecasts of Domestic CTV Sales in Unteland (1000 units)

Special events		Forecast by industry		Forecast by company		Actual	
		Growth rate (%)	Volume Error (%)	Growth rate (%)	Volume Error (%)	Growth rate (%)	Volume
	1985		1,390 — 7		1,450 — 3		1,488
World Cup	1986	+16	1,731 — 7	+21	1,800 — 3	+24	1,852
Recession	1987	+ 3	1,906 + 9	+ 8	2,000 +14	— 5	1,754
Olympic Games	1988	+ 9	1,911 — 8	+ 8	1,900 — 9	+19	2,082
Price cuts	1989	+ 2	2,120 —10	+ 7	2,230 — 5	+13	2,355
World Cup	1990	+ 2	2,405 + 1	— 3	2,290 — 4	+ 1	2,375

Table 10.1 shows that the following performance of the company is more accurate than the industry's. Except for 1987, a recession year, the industry's forecasts tend to be more pessimistic than the company's, and there is a reason for this. With the heavy cyclical loading of the second half of the year, the cost of holding stocks can be punitive for the industry, and if the wholesaling sector sees that pressure to clear stocks is building up, it can exert strong downward pressure on the price. Thus the industry will tend to understate the total sales achievable in a future year.

Industry Short-term Forecasting by means of Time Series Analysis and Projective Techniques

In order to estimate the contribution of seasonality, trend, cycle and random events, all of which will affect the sales level in the total market, the forecaster needs to apply time series analysis and projective techniques to a few years of past sales history, even when forecasting solely for one year ahead. Undertaking this in a methodical manner is the best way of beginning his analysis.

Plotting the Data

An essential point is to plot the data on a graph so that the stark mass of figures for the sales in a market already have a visual shape. On examining the plot of the raw data, you may find certain questions arising; the answers to these will be relevant to the final forecast. For example, in Fig. 10.1, which represents the raw data for factory sales and imports of domestic CTV sets between 1984 and 1987, we see that in 1986 sales were high in the first half of the year and stayed steady in the second half, against the normal pattern of higher sales at the end of the year. What is the cause of this unusual departure from the seasonal pattern of a lower first half of the year? Is the new pattern for these months likely to recur? Investigation of such unusual factors can reveal indicators for future sales.

Sorting out Seasonality, Trend and Cycle

Because seasonality is linked with short-term periods, and trend and cycle to longer periods, the forecaster has to identify each of these components separately. Fig. 10.1 shows the seasonal factors to be fairly consistent, with a slump in August and high pre-Christmas sales, with the exception of the unusual peak in the first half of 1986. Fig. 10.2 shows the result of removing the seasonal pattern from the raw data. This deseasonalised curve, although retaining its zigzags, gives a good first impression of the basic movement of sales. The smoother curve that is superimposed represents the **trend cycle**, and is obtained by applying the moving average technique to the deseasonalised data. The trend cycle is a combination of the trend and cyclical factors at work for this product. It is worth noting that the differences between this trend cycle line and the deseasonalised data curve represents the irregular (**random**) component the forecaster should always try to remove, measure and understand. Every up-and-down of the trend cycle can be explained by knowledge of specific causative events. In this case the large peak in 1986 is the result of the Soccer World Cup contest in which Unteland was represented. The peak in 1984 is accounted for by the Olympic Games, and the 1985 peak is due to price-cutting, after stocks of CTVs had built up to an unacceptable level. The trough at the end of 1986 and the start of 1987 coincides with a national recession. What is so useful in this breakdown is that the analyst knows that the World Cup will happen again in 1990, and that its impact is likely to be even greater as lower income football-loving households buy a new television set.

Protecting Growth Rate of Trend Cycle

Determining the rate at which the trend cycle is changing and projecting this rate forward over the interval to be forecast is the most challenging job for the forecaster. A plot of the year-on-year variation in the trend cycle, as shown in Fig. 10.3 for cars, can help him to recognise the successive ups-and-downs of the trend cycle. A simple year-on-year growth rate can be adequate to show the cycle in mature

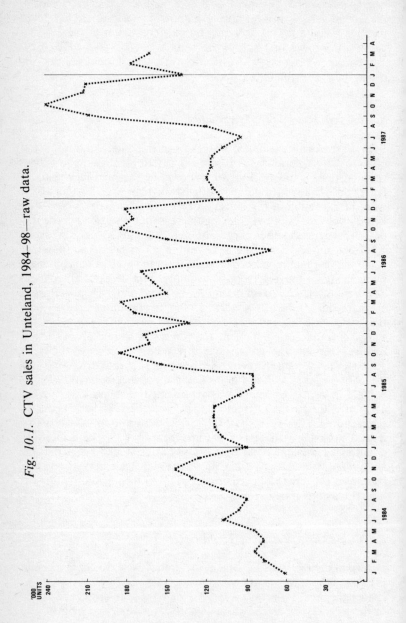

Fig. 10.1. CTV sales in Unteland, 1984–98—raw data.

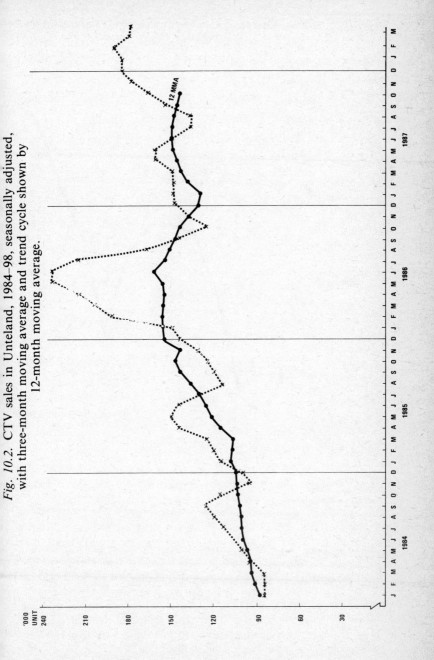

Fig. 10.2. CTV sales in Unteland, 1984–98, seasonally adjusted, with three-month moving average and trend cycle shown by 12-month moving average.

Fig. 10.3. Annual factory sales of new passenger cars in Unteland, 1984–98.

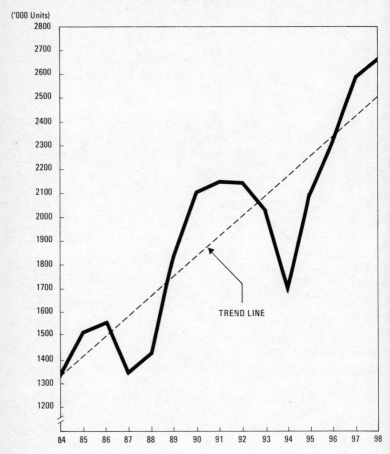

('000 Units)

TREND LINE

markets. Fig. 10.4 shows year-on-year percentage growth rates for CTVs and illustrates the way in which the CTV market matures in Unteland, with the end of high growth and the start of cyclical (up and down) behaviour. To project this forward, the analyst needs the help of indicators of the market and forecasts of the economy, as discussed below. Forecasting based on analysis of the patterns of change in the growth rate reveals more accuracy in predicting turning points than where the trend cycle is used on its own.

Fig. 10.4. Year on year percentage growth rates—Unteland CTV sales.

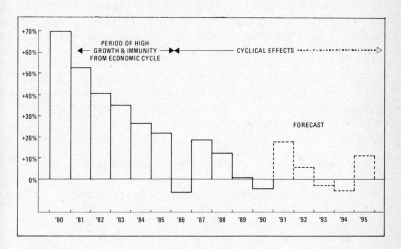

A full example of the use of tend, cycle, seasonality and random components in forecasting of car sales in Unteland is given in Statistical Workshop B.

Longer-term Industry Forecasts

Making forecasts for an industry for periods of five, ten or more years ahead requires judgement on the maturity of the product and can use the concept of market penetration and replacement to identify the mature phase of the market.

Identifying the Product in its Life Cycle

One of the important but difficult tasks of the forecaster is to decide when changes in the slope of the trend of sales are likely to occur as the product enters a later phase of its total life cycle. In our experience, it is extremely difficult to do this because there is an inbuilt tendency (as we have seen for the industry CTV forecast) to be conservative in forecasting the future, as it shields us from the worst effects of a downturn. Methods of deciding whether a market is reaching maturity include comparison with the USA or with other countries more developed than our own. Experience in the telephone market has been that European countries have consistently underestimated strength of demand for the telephone, deciding that the installations of telephones in people's homes were flattening at a point far ahead of the still unreached time when the phone really does begin to slow down.

The identification of a product in its life cycle should ideally permit one to distinguish between short-term downturns (associated with the business cycle) and longer-term trends associated with the maturity of the product. It is worthwhile knowing the concepts, although in practice the confusion of the two sorts of slow-down will be inevitable, as the recession often starts the rot in long-term growth.

Using the 'Park' to Forecast Long-term Market Demand

The demand for a product with reference to any period T, can be regarded as being made up of demand from initial buyers and demand for replacement at this moment in time. In the CTV market as shown in Table 10.2, the total demand is in fact 'apparent consumption', made up by domestic deliveries and imports. The concepts of (*a*) **the park**, i.e. total number of sets in existence or cars in the car park or whatever product, and (*b*) **the initial demand** and **replacement demand**, are extremely useful for forecasting the market.

Apparent consumption, in fact, should be disaggregated to distinguish demand for first sets, second sets and replacement in order to get a good picture of development in sales. Table 10.2 is in fact the result of a great deal of complicated calculation, because a life for CTV sets has to be assumed, spread over a number of years. For example, 5 per cent of sets might be assumed to be replaced when eight years old, 15 per cent at nine years old and so on, and calculating for the whole park is time-consuming. Making a perfect model of what happens is not possible, but the household penetration + park + replacement + second set (if possible) gives valuable information about the future maturing of a market.

As the market evolves, the analyst will give up this model as unnecessarily complicated. The replacement cycle becomes variable and far more important than new sales, so that a straightforward time series of sales is more relevant. However, the household (market) penetration plus replacement model is of particular value until replacements come up to overtake 'first buyers' as most important in the sales mix. Thus this technique is useful as any new product takes off, but must always be cross-referenced to the history of household penetration of similar products, for which typical rates are shown in Fig. 10.5.

Fig. 10.5. Household penetration of selected consumer durables in Unteland—years after full-scale launch.

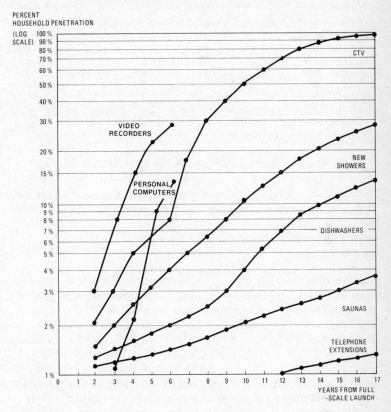

Table 10.2. Sales of CTVs in Unteland, Forecast in 1985, based on Park and Replacement

Actual	Year	Penetration (%)	Total park	Demand from 1st buyers	Replacements	Total Demand —Actual
216,000	1978	1.0	216,000	216,000		216,000
233,000	1979	2.0	449,000	233,000		233,000
396,000	1980	3.8	845,000	396,000		396,000
618,000	1981	6.5	1,463,000	618,000		618,000
874,000	1982	10.3	2,337,000	874,000		874,000
1,118,000	1983	15.5	3,519,000	1,182,000	6,480	1,188,000
1,513,000	1984	22.1	5,010,000	1,491,000	22,110	1,513,000

Actual	Year	Penetration (%)	Total park	Demand from 1st buyers	Replacements	Total Demand —Forecast
1,865,000	1985	29.8	6,871,000	1,861,000	54,110	1,915,000
1,754,000	1986	36.2	8,378,000	1,507,000	113,100	1,620,000
2,082,000	1987	46.0	10,741,000	2,363,000	202,140	2,565,000
2,356,000	1988	54.0	12,700,000	1,959,000	327,740	2,287,000
2,375,000	1989	61.0	14,469,000	1,769,000	491,670	2,261,000
2,269,000	1990	67.0	16,013,000	1,544,000	701,100	2,245,000

The model, developed in 1985, warns that the market will peak in 1987. In fact, peaking occurs in 1988, but the important fact is that the market is fast maturing, and this is signalled by the forecasts.

Methods of Forecasting Employed in the Business World

The would-be analyst might well ask, 'Which of these methods are really used in business?', and here the authors can only speak of their experience of eight companies. The methods are first listed, and then discussed in more detail.

METHOD	COMMENT
Target-setting. Usually an increase	The target becomes the forecast. In well run companies, it is achievable.
Segment/sales area aggregation	Sum total of detailed bottom-up forecasting. Used widely.
Instinct, seat-of-pants	Will often beat statistically based forecasts in well-run businesses because it contains the wisdom of the manager's unconscious numeracy.
Market share plus industry forecast	Percentage share of what the industry is forecasting, with some assumptions as to growth in market share. Very common.
Percentage growth	Extension from past sales on a straight percentage growth basis, often reflecting the industry consensus. Probably the most commonly used method for long-term forecasts.
Statistical methods of all types	Generally used in marketing services departments and staff departments needing to double-check forecasts of doubtful performers.

Notice how much of forecasting is based on what the company wants to achieve. What attitude does the forecaster adopt to targets? Should he not set higher forecasts than he believes are achievable in order to encourage effort by the sales force? Experience teaches that this is a mistake to avoid: always insist that the forecast made takes into account the history of past effort, and represents what is possible. Consistently undershot forecasts are the death knell of any business looking for managerial support. Consistently unrealistic forecasts are the death knell of any market analyst.

Target-setting

This is not forecasting. The analyst can aid target-setting by providing sensible forecasts on which the targets can be based by management, but should resist target-setting as such.

Segment/Sales Area Aggregation

Usually unsatisfactory as a solo method of forecasting and requires to be double-checked against the aggregated total. A method employed in many companies is to get in all the sales area forecasts, analyse them and compare them with the company forecast. The sales managers are then called in to hear the views of the national sales manager, and each area sales manager discusses the way in which his forecast needs revision with the national sales manager. The detailed sales plan that emerges is a very powerful tool for success because everyone is committed to specific targets.

Instinct/Seat-of-Pants

The analyst will encounter many sales managers who 'get it right' year after year, and the only way to recognise them is to look at their forecasting record, because all sales managers, whether good or bad at forecasting, are by definition very plausible.

Market Share plus Industry Forecast

This method is open to industries well served with statistics, including consumer durables, convenience foods and many raw materials. The industry forecast is employed to simplify the task of forecasting, and the market share is generally increased, so that the net result can often be a target. Industry forecasts are often subject to systematic bias, i.e. consistent over- or under-forecasting, and the record should be examined. A key element may be the volume of imports into the market.

Percentage Growth

In many early phases of growth, when annual increases of over 15 per cent are achieved, this is a sensible way of forecasting. 'We will increase sales by 20 per cent next year' is generally a promise that the major constraint will be how much can be produced, not how much people want, and for practical purposes a detailed forecast is not needed. Percentage growth over the next five years is often employed, using compound growth tables or a calculator, and this produces straight-line trends on semi-logarithmic paper.

The analyst will find this a very useful method to employ to work out the basic trend, particularly if extended backwards for at least five years to show the deviation from trend. In making the forward forecast, allowance must be made for cyclical effects (upturns or downturns in the economy) and the analyst often simply plots likely looking figures by hand and reads them off on to the tabulated forecast.

Statistical Methods of All Types

Even the seat-of-pants forecaster will often employ a **seasonal adjustment** method of the simpler type for his annual forecast. Where there is a failure to do this and there is guess work, the end of the year (September to December) usually becomes overloaded with sales, and so it is always worth the analyst's while to double-check the seasonality even if the annual forecast seems sensible.

Moving average and **exponential smoothing** methods of forecasting certainly are used in business, but they have been encountered rarely by the authors of this book. The reason is that these methods are usually highly concerned with the next month, whereas most businesses are looking out at least a year ahead. Secondly, the sorts of changes in trend signalled by these methods can be red-flagged by cumulative sum sales monitoring methods.

Trend projections are very popular with businessmen generally, with straight-line being the most popular. In most cases the straight-line is probably done by eye, using a ruler and, although this may seem shocking, it is usually acceptable.

Cumulative sum sales forecast monitoring by Z charts is moderately popular and deserves to be even more widespread. **Computerised forecast monitoring** by systems such as the Trigg method are used in some large companies, such as Kodak, which offer a wide variety of products to the market. (See D. W. Trigg, 'Monitoring a Forecasting System', *Operational Research Quarterly*, Vol. 15, pp. 271–4, 1964; and Paul F. Bestwick, 'A Forecasting Monitoring and Revision System for Top Management', *Operational Research Quarterly*, Vol. 26, pp. 419–429, 1975.)

Box-Jenkins forecasting is used among some large companies. Because of its dependence on the computer, it will probably be limited in its penetration to these leading companies for some time, despite its excellent record and adaptability to the task of forecasting for any product.

Forecasting using models will also be confined to fairly rare strata of industry. Modelling is of particular interest in industries selling products to the construction industry, where part of demand is related to new buildings started (given in government statistics as starts or permits, depending on country), but there is a significant element of demand related to replacement and/or renovation, which requires explanation in terms of variables such as disposable income.

Despite the fact that so much of the business world is not automatically analytic, marketing analysis as a discipline needs mathematical forecasting techniques, and the aspiring business manager needs to employ them until he has mastered the complexities of the market in which he operates and his faculty of unconscious numeracy takes over (if he has got one—we admit that we do not have one). In the evolution of a marketing career numerical forecasting requires to be mastered early on, if only to avoid being destroyed by unrealisable targets in a badly run business. The basic disciplines, as outlined in this book, will provide most marketing managers with what they need for day-to-day business.

Exercises

1. Imports of 'SN 82s' (an electronic product) are shown in the table below. Forecast the volume of imports in 1998, as well as the total domestic purchases of SN 82s based on the statistics for imports and the industry forecast.

Purchases of SN 82s from All Sources ('000 units)

	1993	1994	1995	1996	1997	1998 (f'cast)
From domestic suppliers	1,021	3,468	7,890	10,095	11,030	n.a
Imports	24	129	701	1,643	2,604	n.a
Total	1,045	3,597	8,591	11,738	13,634	16,500

Look at trends, using straight-line projections and semi-logarithmic paper, and examine the history of the import market share. What research will be necessary to check whether trends are changing?

2. A fast-moving grocery brand achieves statistically significant increases in its market share for one month when it drops its price for promotions of one month's duration, but these do not appear to have any influence on the 12-month moving market share. The marketing director points out that this price activity is nevertheless a component of the market share platform. Construct a series that shows this effect, assuming price-cutting four times a year. What is the correct way of understanding what is going on?

3. Describe strategies to fill seasonal lows for the following products (add others of interest to you): a Scarborough hotel, a racetrack, kennels, a mail-order company, a brewer, a fuel merchant, a construction company, a manufacturer of electronic games.

4. A branded goods manufacturer with $U38 million national sales runs a pilot market promotion in one area, accounting for 8 per cent of national sales. Annual market share in the area was 3 per cent, but it rises to 6 per cent for the duration of the three-month promotion. The promotion has a negative impact on return on sales equivalent to a minus one per cent return on sales for the three-month period. The management team are sure that expenditure at the same level can ensure a similar market share increase anywhere for the same period of time and an increase to 4 per cent for a three-month period is compatible with breaking even. Outline what conclusions should be drawn about use of this technique in attacking a national market divided into 12 fairly similarly sized areas, showing any further information it is desirable to have.

5. Prepare a presentation to a small company that you know to be losing market share to show why the company should buy information on its market share, month by month, as if you were the representative of a company that provides an audit of consumption of products. The small company, your potential client, is unaware that it is losing market share, and it is permissible to let it know this if you feel it will aid your sales case.

11
Forecasting for an Existing Product— the Company

In this chapter the position of the company in the market is examined, with particular reference to **market share**. Many companies, both large and small, have an unclear idea of their market share because of problems of quantifying and defining precisely the national market; but they are still well aware that they are losing or gaining share by a simple test—are they growing more quickly or more slowly than the generally accepted growth rate for the industry as a whole? Where data is available to calculate market share, it should always be included in the methods of forecasting, because it provides a double-check on realism and it enmeshes with the strategy of the company, its strengths and weaknesses, and the way it responds to competition.

Topics that will be covered in this chapter are:

(*a*) the market share of the company,
(*b*) the market share of imports,
(*c*) revising forecasts during the year.

Using Market Share

The company's present market share is a useful tool for forecasting future company sales. If its market share were to persist, then company sales could be directly derived from anticipated industry sales by a straightforward projection. But the market share is not static; its dynamism lies in the fact that the company may lose ground because of increasingly keen competition or gain ground because of imminent company innovations or marketing expenditures. Therefore, the problem of predicting company sales is the same as that of forecasting the probable course of the company's market share.

Market share analysis is of further importance to management because it indicates whether changes in company sales are due to uncontrollable outside forces or to weaknesses in the company's marketing programme. As illustrated in Table 11.1, product B would show, in the absence of any indications of the size of market, a better marketing case with actual sales running at 5 per cent ahead of the forecast against a dramatic shortfall of —20 per cent for product A. But if we consider the size of the market and the company's market share, the scenario is totally different. The shortfall in product A is not as dramatic as long as it is accounted for by outside forces (the **recessional market**). In fact, the market share for product A remains unchanged while it declines for product B.

Table 11.1. Market Share Analysis

Product	Company sales forecast	Industry sales forecast	Market share forecast (%)	Company actual sales	Industry actual sales	Market share (%)
A	1,000	10,000	10	800	8,000	10
B	600	7,500	8	630	12,600	5

If a company's sales fall but its market share remains constant, this implies that the whole industry is affected by similar environmental forces. If management could not maintain its share of the market, the implication is that the company's marketing is at fault.

When is Market Share Forecasting Employed?

Usage of market share information implies the regular collection of reliable statistics on a national scale. Consumer durables such as cars or television sets will have statistics on a monthly basis, whereas data on raw materials such as plastics or metals will be available on a quarterly basis after a long delay. Such information is never up-to-date, but even with a six-month publication delay, it can be useful when considering the forecast for the company for the next year. This is because, although the market share is very volatile, it will not change outside certain limits. The history of the market share over a few years is very useful in establishing what these limits might be.

Dynamism of the Market Share

Fig. 11.1 shows the changes in market share at a large flat-screen CTV supplier called Kjaerco in Unteland in the 1990s. The chart shows the effect of the end-of-year sales surge that Kjaerco makes to achieve its targets. But this up-and-down movement is difficult to understand, for

Fig. 11.1 Kjaerco's quarterly market share of the Unteland flat-screen CTV market.

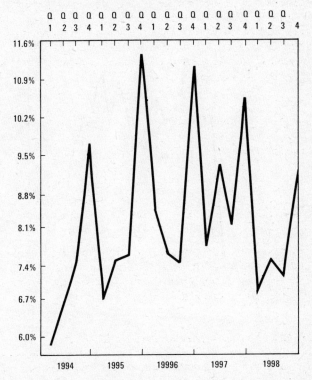

which reason the analyst draws up the 12-month moving market share. This is made by taking the company's sales in each succeeding 12 months, dividing it by the industry sales in the same period, and multiplying by 100 to give a percentage figure. Fig. 11.2 shows the result.

This chart has removed a lot of the volatility of the series, and reveals a striking downturn in market share. With such a precipitous drop revealed, it is clearly indicated that a market share suddenly reverting to 9 per cent is improbable, unless there is something which offers the same market share increase as was achieved in 1995. What was it that gave Kjaerco such a lift in 1995 and 1996, and is there going to be anything like it in 1999?

Questioning the marketing manager reveals that the 1995 increase was acheived by the introduction of the first metre-square flat-screen CTV, and the loss of share in 1998 was entirely due to the competition catching up. The marketing director reveals that there is another 'first'

Fig. 11.2. Kjaerco's 12-month moving market share of the Unteland CTV market.

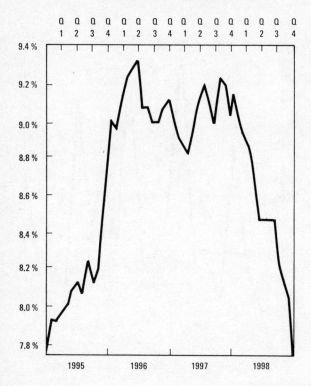

coming up for Kjaerco in 1999—a portable flat-screen CTV that can be supported on any wall surface by just one drawing pin because it is so light. Once again Kjaerco will have a leading product.

The analyst is now in a good position to make judgements with regard to market share. An increase back to the level of 1997 is possible—after all, such a growth in market share was achieved in 1995. The analyst gets a lot more information about the likely importance of the new product in the total mix and discovers that the contribution of the new product will not be so great as the original metre-square product of 1995 because it is severely limited by production. Indeed, talk with the production manager convinces the analyst that sales will not really begin until the third quarter, whereas the metre-square product was available from the second quarter of 1995. The analyst decides that an increase back to 8.5 per cent looks feasible in 1999, and this is fed into his forecast.

Market share forecasting has comprised an analysis of the

company's marketing and innovative skills, its production strengths and the relative strength of the competiion. When extended into future years, it may require an assessment of the company's financial strengths and ability to invest in order to produce the new products (or cost-reduced unchanging products) that will ensure an increase in market share.

Of course, predicting the market share achievable requires an exercise in judgement—but so should all forecasting. The endless projection forward of past trends that statistical forecasting represents in its most mechanical use is brought up slap against reality when the analyst considers market share. He is also brought up against the aspirations and hopes of the whole team that makes and sells the product for which the forecast is made. The only defence against the over-enthusiastic sales manager who swears that this time the portable flat-screen CTV is going to take Kjaerco to an Unteland market share of 10 per cent is a detailed analysis of what was achieved last time the market share surged, how next year will be similar and how it will differ. Market share dynamism also happily can sometimes correct a depressing tendency for statistical forecasts to project an endless decline in a company's fortunes.

However, the history of the market share may show no great changes from the past, even with innovations. The future innovation will be hailed as a 'quantum jump' by the sales manager, and once in a while he or she may be right. The analyst will have to make up his mind. But do not neglect to look at the 'quantum jumps' that were claimed in previous years. Ideally, about eight years' data is needed to establish what is the **market share platform** of the company—the underlying basic share which it can defend and which it can spring up from. In the volatile history of many consumer goods the 'staircase' is seen as often as the 'platform'.

Market Shares of Competitors—Import Data

Data on competitors' market shares are available in the automotive industry but as a general rule this type of information is not freely available across an industry. The exception is of course where imports are significant as a source of competition; import data can be used to derive the market share for imports in apparent consumption of the product in question. The equation employed is,

Apparent consumption = Domestic Production + Imports — Exports.

Import data, like all other sales data, requires to be examined over at least four years to get some feel for what is happening. Imports are subject to variations caused by changes in exchange rates or expectations of such changes, and occasionally by changes in tariffs, so data for one year can be very misleading.

Dynamism in the market share of imports is a frequently seen phenomenon, not only in the UK but in all major open markets. It is useful to plot the 12-month moving average for the market share of imports, just as for the company, in order to have some feel for how far the progression may go. In forecasting for the European market for cars it is useful to take the market share achieved by each country's exports in each other country's markets and then add the effects of non-European countries. Interesting patterns emerge, with the displacement of Italian cars, for example, by Japanese cars outside Italy at one time. This provides one part of the pattern needed to produce a forecast of Italian automobile production.

The Role of Market Share Forecasting in the Total Forecast

A forecast of total national sales (or apparent consumption) of a particular product is necessary if the projected market share for a company is going to be used as a method of forecasting. But, besides using these two forecasts, it is desirable to make company forecasts by the classical decomposition method (see page 250) and then double-check back with the market share that is implicit in the forecasts thrown up by the other methods. It is in this way that the analyst reaches a forecast which can stand up to the criticism to which all forecasts are subject.

Revising Forecasts—Forecast Monitoring

One of the constant duties of the analyst is to revise forecasts during the year in order to keep production at an adequate level, to avoid a build-up of inventories, or simply to give an early signal to management that their profit expectations will have to be changed downwards or upwards. The method employed to do this requires:

(*a*) an annual forecast,
(*b*) monthly forecasts based on past seasonality,
(*c*) a calculation of how much randomness can be expected in sales as they cumulate during the year.

The seasonal adjustment method to be employed should normally be a simple PSAM (percent of seasonal average method) as explained in Statistical Workshop A. The first step to be taken is to calculate the seasonal adjustment factors from at least four years' data. If there is evidence of longer cycles in sales, as, for example, are to be found in car sales in some countries, then this period should be employed as the basis of calculation.

Table 11.2 shows the pattern of mountain tourist revenue in Unteland recorded in terms of how many nights tourists stay in hotels and inns. From the table, we see that the bookings for Unteland

Table 11.2. Thousand Bed–nights in Unteland Mountain Resorts, 1986 to 1989, and Calculated Seasonal Adjustment Factors

	1986	1987	1988	1989	Seasonal adjustment factors*
January	130	185	187	239	129.9
February	143	163	165	212	119.8
March	128	169	176	210	119.8
April	90	133	110	138	82.6
May	108	176	115	178	101.1
June	115	187	121	160	102.2
July	115	152	116	123	88.7
August	116	169	113	128	92.2
September	97	175	99	160	93.1
October	81	101	85	128	69.3
November	85	79	117	118	70.0
December	164	152	217	216	131.3
Total	1,372	1,841	1,621	2,010	1,200.0
Average month	115	153	135	168	

*Based on 1986 to 1989 sales (use relative percent method).

mountain resorts are heavily influenced by the skiing season. The low altitude of Unteland mountains means that Easter skiing is impossible. May and June have picked up slightly thanks to the efforts of the Unteland Tourist Board to promote school mountain weeks, arranged with the cooperation of the Ministry of Education. But the summer is poor, owing to a whole complex of factors, among which unreliable weather is predominant.

The Unteland Tourist Board is proud of its record. In 1987, the year that promotion began, there was a huge upsurge in summer bookings, and the weather was kind. They hope to achieve a large increase in 1990, to 2,350,000 bed–nights. However, they know that their major dependence is on the weather. If there is little snow, as in 1988, an extra large packet of March promotion will be needed to fill the summer beds. Fortunately, the Untelanders do not plan summer holidays until Easter, unlike the rest of us.

The second step in devising the forecast monitoring system is to superimpose the seasonal pattern on the annual sales and calculate how big were the differences between actual sales and how the sales would have behaved if the seasonality were absolutely regular. This idea may seem a little difficult to understand, but if you go through Table 11.3, it will become clear. The meaning of the calculations is explained again after the table. 'Mean' indicates the monthly average sales at the bottom of each column of raw data, and SF means the appropriate seasonal factor for the month.

Table 11.3. Differences between Sales Achieved and Monthly Sales Calculated by Applying Seasonal Factors to Annual Sales

	1986	1987	1988	1989
Actual for month of *January*	130	185	187	239
Calculated value (mean × SF)	148	199	176	218
Difference	—18	—14	+11	+21
Actual for month of *February*	143	163	165	212
Calculated value (mean × SF)	137	184	162	201
Difference	+6	—21	+3	+11
Actual for month of *March*	128	169	176	210
Calculated value (mean × SF)	137	184	162	210
Difference	—9	—15	+14	+9
Actual for month of *April*	90	133	110	138
Calculated value (mean × SF)	94	127	112	138
Difference	—4	+6	—2	0
Actual for month of *May*	108	176	115	178
Calculated value (mean × SF)	116	155	137	169
Difference	—8	+21	—22	+9
Actual for month of *June*	115	187	121	160
Calculated value (mean × SF)	117	157	138	171
Difference	—2	+30	—17	—11
Actual for month of *July*	115	152	116	123
Calculated value (mean × SF)	101	136	120	149
Difference	+14	+16	—4	—26
Actual for month of *August*	116	169	113	128
Calculated value (mean × SF)	105	141	125	154
Difference	+11	+28	—12	—26
Actual for month of *September*	97	175	99	160
Calculated value (mean × SF)	106	143	126	156
Difference	—9	+32	—27	+4
Actual for month of *October*	81	101	85	128
Calculated value (mean × SF)	79	106	94	116
Difference	+2	—5	—9	+12
Actual for month of *November*	85	79	117	118
Calculated value (mean × SF)	80	107	95	117
Difference	+5	—28	+22	+1
Actual for month of *December*	164	152	217	216
Calculated value (mean × SF)	150	201	177	220
Difference	+14	—49	+40	—4

This table shows a whole variety of particular errors in most months, which we can describe as arising from random or irregular factors—as was seen in Chapter 10 (page 168). The next step in understanding how far sales can vary from the seasonal pattern is to take the squares of the errors and calculate the standard deviation. This is done in Table 11.4.

Table 11.4. Squared Residual Errors of Seasonal Adjustment Calculations

	1986	1987	1988	1989
January	324	196	121	441
February	36	441	9	121
March	81	225	196	81
April	16	36	4	0
May	64	441	484	81
June	4	900	289	121
July	196	256	16	676
August	121	784	144	676
September	81	1,024	729	16
October	4	25	81	144
November	25	784	484	1
December	196	2,401	1,600	16
Totals	1,148	7,513	4,157	2,374
Grand Total	15,192			

Standard deviation* $= \sqrt{\frac{15,192}{47}} = \sqrt{323} = 17.97$

Two standard deviations $= 35.94$ (i.e. 2×17.97)

*Because the errors for seasonal adjustment calculations must approximate to zero, this formula can be substituted for the full formula for a standard deviation.

The two standard deviations calculated as about 36 tell us that for any particular month the amount of error (or randomness) to be expected in 95 per cent of cases is no more than plus or minus 36,000 bed–nights. This can then be applied to the forecasts for the year in order to find out how far the actual performance can differ from the forecast for the month before the year's forecast needs revision. This is shown in Table 11.5.

In Table 11.5 the year-end forecast of 2,350,000 bed–nights is taken and the seasonal adjustment factors are applied to it. The tolerances calculated, i.e. two standard deviations of the errors, apply to any one month's figure. If you add the months to produce cumulative totals, it is not necessary to multiply by the number of months, but by the square root of the number of months. This, which is shown in the column called 'multiplier', has the effect of tightening the tolerances as the year goes through. The tolerances calculated are called 'warning limits' in the table, because they warn that 19 times out of 20 a result like this is not compatible with the whole year's forecast.

Table 11.5. Forecast Monitoring for 1990—Monthly Performance Required for 2,350,000 Target Bed–nights in Unteland Mountain Resorts—'000 Bed–nights

Month	Mean (M)	SF	Monthly forecast M×SF 100	Cumu- lative	Two SD	Multi- plier	2SDx mult.	Cumulative warning limits Lower	Upper
Jan	195.83	129.9	254	254	36	1.000	±36	218	290
Feb	195.83	119.8	234.5	489	36	1.414	±51	438	540
Mar	195.83	119.8	234.5	723	36	1.732	±62	661	785
Apr	195.83	82.6	162	885	36	2.000	±72	813	957
May	195.83	101.1	198	1,083	36	2.236	±80	1,003	1,163
Jun	195.83	102.2	200	1,283	36	2.449	±88	1,195	1,371
Jul	195.83	88.7	174	1,457	36	2.645	±95	1,362	1,552
Aug	195.83	92.2	181	1,638	36	2.828	±102	1,536	1,740
Sep	195.83	93.1	182	1,820	36	3.000	±108	1,712	1,928
Oct	195.83	69.3	136	1,956	36	3.162	±114	1,842	2,070
Nov	195.83	70.0	137	2,093	36	3.317	±119	1,974	2,212
Dec	195.83	131.3	257	2,350	36				
Total	2,350.00 (rounded)	1,200.0	2,350						

The marketing director of the Unteland Tourist Board is shown Table 11.5, and it is explained that if there is an exceptionally good January to March it may even be possible, by looking at the upper warning limits, to decide that promotional expenditure can be saved this year because of the buoyancy of demand. This, unfortunately, appears unlikely, as the budget has been set very high to match all the recent hotel building.

In the event, bed–nights (equivalent to sales) reach 240,000 in January, 450,000 in January and February, and a total of 650,000 in the first three months. There is a clear signal that the year-end target will not be reached, and the promotional package is brought into play.

Fig. 11.3 shows a full-scale usage of the same method in graphical form. The charts are called **Z charts** because of their shape. Notice the use of the 12-month moving average at the top of the chart, which signals the trend of sales. Dropping out of the confidence limits at the top of the chart gives reassurance that the trend of sales is declining and that it is not just a question of freak seasonality.

Fig. 11.3.

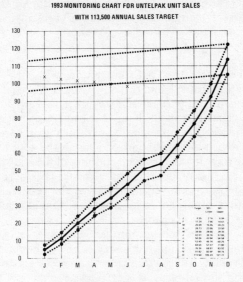

**1993 MONITORING CHART FOR UNTELPAK UNIT SALES
WITH 113,500 ANNUAL SALES TARGET**

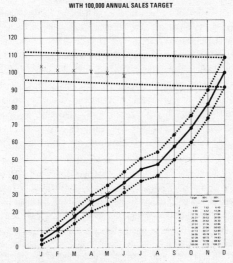

**1993 MONITORING CHART FOR UNTELPAK UNIT SALES
WITH 100,000 ANNUAL SALES TARGET**

Usage of Sales Monitoring Methods

Besides the simple sales monitoring method outlined above, some more elaborate methods exist for keeping track of the development of sales, some designed, like the Trigg method, to look at a lot of products using computer services, and some amenable to calculation for each product. (See D. W. Trigg, 'Monitoring a Forecasting System', *Operational Research Quarterly*, Vol. 15, pp. 271–4, 1964; and Paul F. Bestwick, 'A Forecast Monitoring and Revision System for Top Management', *Operational Research Quarterly*, Vol. 26, pp. 419–29, 1975.)

The analyst needs to avoid some pitfalls with all these methods. First, they are statistical, and can only work on past data. The future can differ from the past—a sudden order, a new dynamism, the addition of capacity, can all change the way the company behaves in the market-place. So double-checks on the real world are needed, and statements about the likelihood of making the forecast should be framed in a way that makes the neutrality of the statistics clear, e.g. 'Based on seasonality and random effects in sales over the past few years, the statistical odds against making the year-end forecast are now more than twenty to one'. The analyst should recommend both upward and downward changes in the forecast when he has acquired a feel for how the sales behave—probably in his second year, when he will be willing to advise on changes. Of course, if the performance falls well outside the warning limits, it will be necessary to advise on a change; but if this happens, it is often clear to most of management that a revision of the forecast is required anyway.

A second pitfall is the issuing of warnings far too late. In many businesses large inventories are needed early on in the year, and the analyst must find out what is the inventory exposure and when it arises. There is no point in giving late warnings.

The third pitfall is that the warning system is not infallible, and the analyst will make some mistakes. In the ten years' experience of the authors of using these methods, warnings were proved unjustified in 3 out of 36 cases—that is, an error rate of about 8 per cent, not far different from the 5 per cent error you might expect (that is what 95 per cent confidence levels mean). For many reasons these errors are always very painful, re-emphasising the need to double-check made above. But the specific pitfall to be avoided is making justifications for the error—it is one method, to be used with judgement, and it includes a chance of failure. Even an analyst must know how to take a risk. One thing to look out for is the way that sales can show an acceleration or deceleration, which makes a dramatic move within the confidence limits. If that occurs for two months, there is often some new dynamism at work (a new product, say, or a competitor losing market share), signalling a change that is sustainable for a few months.

Summary

This chapter has emphasised that, where market share data exists, it should be used in forecasting. A market share is defined, not only by the size of the total market and the size of sales by the company into it, but also by the length of time to which it refers. Analysts should always check just what is being claimed about market share by referring to the period of time concerned: clearly a large market share achieved in one quarter of the year can be lost in the other three. For this reason, a 12-month moving market share is to be employed for looking at all market share data, including that for imports.

Finally, a method of checking whether revision of sales forecasts is required was outlined, and its limitations explained. This chapter reinforces the message that statistics are just a reflection of the real world, and that the contribution of the analyst in an active company must derive from a thorough knowledge of how his company competes, how it has achieved its success (both shown in market share history), an awareness of when sales revisions need to be signalled (because of inventory problems or labour constraints), and a willingness to exercise judgement in using the tools of statistical analysis. The route to forecasting for the company has now been defined:

(*a*) the industry forecast,
(*b*) the company forecast, based on market share,
(*c*) the sales monitoring system, keeping the forecast up-to-date.

The analyst will often have a role in aiding the various business managers in making their forecasts, and will be required to make decisions about the timing of the upturn or downturn in the business cycle before the business manager. This makes the task more difficult and liable to error than the business manager's own forecast—but how much more hangs on the business's final forecast! Remember that the analyst offers a service to the entrepreneur which reduces his risk but does not remove it. If you find the only risk you have to take in your career is being wrong in a forecast, think yourself lucky. At the end of the day, it is the buying and selling of better produced merchandise that pays the analyst's salary, and the entrepreneurs who achieve that are the ones who will have the greatest rewards. An important (but not the sole) component of business success is the achievement of riches through taking risks, and the role of the analyst is to assist the entrepreneur in the successful company. The unsuccessful company does not have an analyst. Who wants a forecast of disaster?

Key Concepts

Twelve-month moving market share. The market share of a product expressed as own sales divided by national sales times 100, calculated for successive 12 month periods (e.g. January to December, February to January, March to February and so on).

Market Share Dynamism. Tendency for the market share to increase or decrease rapidly in fast-moving consumer goods for periods of more than three months, once a change begins.

Market Share Inertia. Tendency for the market share to remain exactly the same in raw material markets constrained by inadequate capacity to meet demand or affected by special controls (e.g. cartels in Germany).

Market Share Platform. The lower limit on market share in the forecasting period, even if there is some market share loss, usually calculated by looking at long-term trends.

Z Charts. Charts that show the sales forecast as a cumulative sum over the year, together with a running 12-month total for sales.

Exercises

1. Fig. 11.3 shows the progress in the year-to-date of sales of units of Untelpak. Sales decline in July and August to reach a total of 40,000 units in the year to date. What advice should the analyst give to management about the likely year-end performance?

2. Seasonal factors for sales of a consumer good are shown below. The annual sales target is 25,000 tonnes. Calculate the sales forecast by month, using the seasonal factors. What further data would be required to monitor performance versus the target, and is it likely to be difficult to obtain?

SEASONAL FACTORS

Jan.	Feb.	Mar.	Apr.	May.	June	July	Aug.	Sept.	Oct.	Nov.	Dec.
47.41	80.62	103.88	73.34	78.31	87.36	88.43	76.35	130.33	130.16	130.69	173.19

3. The data below show the moving annual market share of a consumer goods manufacturer. Plot it and decide what is the market share platform. What are your forecasts for the next 12 months?

1987	16.2, 16.3, 15.8, 15.6, 15.7, 15.5, 15.2, 15.0, 15.0, 15.2, 15.2, 15.6
1988	15.6, 15.4, 15.2, 15.0, 15.2, 15.3, 15.5, 15.3, 15.1, 15.0, 15.2, 15.0
1989	15.0, 15.2, 15.3, 15.4, 15.6, 15.6, 15.5, 15.4, 15.0, 14.8, 14.6, 15.2
1990	16.0, 16.1, 16.1, 16.2, 16.3, 16.5, 16.3, 16.1, 16.5, 16.4, 16.3, 16.1
1991	16.2, 16.3, 16.0, 16.0, 15.9, 15.8, 15.6, 15.7, 15.8, 15.8, 15.4, 15.2
1992	15.0, 14.9, 14.8, 14.6, 14.7, 14.7, 14.8, 14.9, 14.7, 14.9, 14.9, 15.0
1993	15.0, 14.9, 14.8, 14.7, 14.9, 14.8, 14.6, 14.0, 14.2, 14.3, 14.3, 14.4
1994	14.6, 14.7, 15.0, 15.1, 15.3, 15.5, 15.7, 15.9, 16.0, 15.9, 15.8, 15.9

4. The following represent sales of an electronic component. Prepare a monitoring chart for 1996.

SALES OF COMPONENT RK77

	1991	1992	1993	1994	1995
Jan	5,032	5,536	6,088	6,696	7,360
Feb	5,940	6,534	7,191	7,911	8,694
Mar	7,623	8,382	9,229	10,153	11,154
Apr	10,192	11,200	12,334	13,566	14,910
May	9,932	10,920	12,025	13,221	14,534
Jun	6,416	7,056	7,768	8.544	9.392
Jul	6,736	7,408	8,152	8,968	9,864
Aug	4,420	4,860	5,350	5,885	6,470
Sep	6,496	7,147	7,861	8,652	9.513
Oct	12,662	13,936	15,327	16,874	18,551
Nov	15,345	16,890	18,570	20,445	22,470
Dec	9,666	10,638	11,700	12,879	14,157

12
Presenting the Report—Making Marketing Analysis Actionable

The goal of marketing analysis is the provision of information to the manager about evolving customer needs and satisfactions, in order that the enterprise may organise itself to serve them at a profit. A key task as the analysis is completed is to ensure that the entrepreneurial team 'gets the message', in terms of understanding what happens in the market-place and also how best to serve user needs. This chapter is therefore one of the most important in the book. Written from the viewpoint of a business career in marketing, its emphasis is on getting the main thrust of a message over to people who are pressed for time and used to rapid evaluations by means of face-to-face contact.

In this chapter the business of communicating the information obtained is explained in terms of a 'report'. The most common forms of report are verbal, ranging from such simple pieces of information as 'We've won the Block 4 contract' to the sales manager's long explanations of all he knows about prospects in a certain market. There is nothing reprehensible or feeble about the spoken word; the written word becomes necessary only in the following instances:

(*a*) the subject is complicated,
(*b*) the information has to be widely circulated,
(*c*) the information needs to be acceptable as trustworthy and thus requires to be supported by documentation.

Reports from a consultant, agency or department may also be necessary when the report represents part of an agreement and is the visible proof that the agreement is fulfilled.

The good report writer writes to communicate something other than his love of report writing. Writing a long report can be a dreadful waste of time if the information obtained indicates that a certain line of action, e.g. launching a particular new product, should not be carried out. So long as those responsible accept the analyst's verbal report, because of his repeated ability and intelligence, why bother with long written reports?

Although some written reports are unnecessary, obviously some reports must survive. But even when the report is written, verbal communication of the result is always more important than what is written on the page; for if the report is actionable, it will enter the world of speech in which managers discuss what action should follow from its conclusions. It is usually at one such discussion that the analyst is asked to present his findings to the decision-making body. The best report in the world, if badly presented, may fail to result in the appropriate action, since the management loses faith in the researcher. So skills of explanation, using the spoken word and the chart, are the primary skills required in business for market analysts. In this chapter, three topics will be covered:

(*a*) personal presentation of report findings,
(*b*) some general rules for written reports,
(*c*) why recommendations are worthwhile.

Personal Presentation of Report Findings

The meeting at which report findings are presented is called, appropriately, a **presentation**. The goals of those listening to a presentation are,

1. To learn rapidly what the presenter knows, without the need to read the report.
2. To satisfy themselves that the work is reliable by asking telling questions.
3. To apply the facts to increasing the profit of the company.

The presenter should have the same goals and must avoid giving long details of how the problem posed by the research was solved—something on which he may congratulate himself, but which is irrelevant to the purpose of the meeting unless it is the subject of a question.

Tools of Presentation

Written material of a very abbreviated type is essential for a good presentation. It can consist of slides, transparencies or flip-charts for large meetings, or stiff white board of A4 size for across-the-desk personal presentation to the entrepreneur/director. The first chart (Fig. 12.1) will provide the name of the study, the date and the name of the presenter, and the next chart will usually state the objective of the analysis or research carried out. Fig. 12.2 is a typical example.

Fig. 12.1.

```
SUNGLASSES STUDY




Prepared By:
Ronald A. Roland                August 1992
```

Fig. 12.2.

```
SUNGLASSES STUDY


OBJECTIVE: TO DETERMINE WHETHER

PARTICIPATION IN THE UNTELAND

SUNGLASSES MARKET BY ACQUISITION

IS WORTHWHILE
```

The wording of Fig. 12.2 might vary in companies that prefer familiar jargon: for example, it could be expanded to 'To determine whether an acquisition strategy in the European sunglasses market might represent a profit-engendering action which is fully compatible with company strategy'. But to do this would be wrong. Much better would be: 'Should we acquire a sunglasses company?'

The exhibit should be as brief as possible, and as the management look at it the presenter can fill in any nuances to do with strategy and so on. The presenter should not read the contents of the exhibit aloud, but he might say: 'This was our objective. We have tried to find out what the profit prospects are like and whether the market requires the sort of skills that we have in our company, making it strategic sense to expand in this market'.

The presenter then goes on to his main findings.

The presenter might say, 'This is essentially a saturated market, with over 60 per cent of the total population, children included, possessing a pair of sunglasses. It is a market in which 82 per cent of a sample could not recall what brand of sunglasses they were wearing. Some recent improvements, such as the super lightweight plastics, just like the improvements in anti-glare properties of the 1960s and 1970s, are

Fig. 12.3.

MAIN FINDINGS

- STATIC MARKET
- FAR-EAST IMPORTS TAKE GROWING SHARE IN LOW-PRICE MARKET SECTOR
- RECENT TOP-SECTOR INCREASES IN UNIT VALUE ARE SHORT-TERM
- UNTELAND PRODUCTION IS DECLINING
- UNTELAND MARKETING REQUIRES HIGH ADVERTISING EXPENDITURE AT THIS TIME
- RISKY MARKET TO ENTER

---

already available to the Far East producers. Over 30 hand operations are necessary in producing sunglasses and prospects of mechanising these are negligible. Imports based on low labour costs will continue to grow and Unteland producers are becoming sellers of these. Advertising expenditure is growing.'

The presenter then shows the next slide, showing the market (Fig. 12.4). Graphics are preferred by the marketing fraternity but in some companies there is a preference for the raw figures. The presentation must be arranged, of course, to suit the preferences of the audience.

The presenter might continue: 'The market is documented in government statistics. It is essentially static but affected by the summer weather, which you see produced the upturn of 1990. Imports

Fig. 12.4. Production, domestic sales, exports and imports of sunglasses in Unteland, 1987–91 ($U millions).

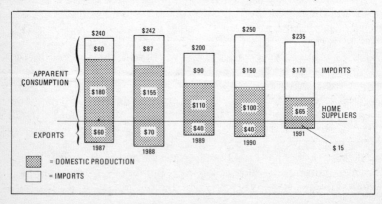

have grown from 20 per cent to 81 per cent of the market over the last five years. Data on volume of production is unavailable but would certainly show that in number terms the number of home-produced sunglasses is even lower in terms of market share. The decline of the Unteland production is opening the market to classic reselling marketing operators like Forensic. Advertising has risen from less than $1/2$ per cent of sales to almost 2 per cent, according to media expenditure surveys, and the advertisers have increased from 8 to 11. Forensic have come up from nothing but it has cost them 6 million Unteland dollars over four years. Limited details indicate a profit squeeze'.

Table 12.1 Profit and Loss in the Unteland Sunglasses Industry

Companies Quoted	Estimated number of Employees, 1991		Total sales ($U million)		Return on sales (%)	
	Manu-facturing	Other	1990	1991	1990	1991
Regard	120	40	50	46	(2.3)	(4.1)
Turn On	60	80	57	51	1.0	1.3
Ponty	—	30	5	5	1.0.	(0.5)
Other						
Sea Cool	120	40	38	35	Loss	Loss
Forensic	—	120	38	54	Breakeven?	

'This is a low margin market with significant losses over the past two years. The numbers employed in manufacturing have in fact been halved in Unteland over the past three years and it looks as if they will continue to decline.' See Table 12.1.

Table 12.2. Estimated Sales of Higher Cost Sunglasses—1987 and 1991 ($U Million)

	1987	1991
Sporting Personality (Konishi, Bill Menlow etc.)	3.0	3.0
New technology		
Ultra lightweight plastic	3.0	3.2
Electronic	0.4	0.1

'Attempts to hold up the value of sales by special marketing efforts are not doing well and the innovations have already reached the Far

Eastern suppliers, who can provide ULP glasses at very low prices.'
See Table 12.2.

Table 12.3. Options for Entry by Acquisition

Company	Strengths	Weaknesses
Regard	Old-established	Need to restructure, low morale, losses
Sea Cool	Old-established	Need to restructure, low morale, losses
Turn On	Growing market share Good morale	Still needs to reduce headcount, Low margins

'These are the prime candidates for acquisition (Table 12.3). Forensic is unlikely to be available in the next three years, because the owners, Nelsons, take a long view on market entry and profit. Two of the largest companies, Regard and Turn On, will have high costs as they are forced to close their factories. None of the small companies is suitable because of the distribution structure.'

Fig. 12.5

> Shares of sunglasses sales by retail outlets (%)
>
> 3 MASS MERCHANDISERS (THE BIG 3)
> (GRANDCASH, PHARMADRUG AND
> TILLRING)............................. 62
> 2,000 OPTICIANS 14
> 4,300 INDEPENDENT PHARMACIES 16
> ±7,000 ALL OTHER OUTLETS 8
> ——
> 100

'As you see, the grip of the big three on the market is strong (Fig. 12.5). Sales to the other outlets are simply too expensive for an operation like our own. The secret of the market is to get into the big three, and you cannot do it without pull-through advertising. In the case of Pharmadrug, as well, the manufacturer is obliged to provide rack-fillers (persons paid to fill display stands with sunglasses) to keep the stands full of the product.'
'So finally our conclusions about the desirability of entering the market are that it is not advisable to enter at the present time (Fig.

Fig 12.6

```
                  ACQUISITIONS
CRITERIA                    SUNGLASSES
* SUCCESSFUL BUSINESSES
  AVAILABLE                 NO
* MATCH TO OUR SKILLS       YES
* RETURN ON SALES OVER 5%   NO
RECOMMEND: KEEP OUT
```

12.6). The market may settle down later but at the moment the chances are that margins will stay generally depressed for some time.'

So the presentation concludes. There may be a dozen back-up slides designed to handle questions, only one or two of which will probably be shown. If the conclusion of market analysis is negative, no one wants to make a meal out of finding out if the conclusions are fully validated, unless there is a patron for the scheme. If there is such a person and he is ranked above everyone else present, there will be a battle. For this reason the analyst presents his research in an objective manner, avoids the word 'I' and tries to let the facts speak for themselves.

At the start of his career, the market analyst may find that feedback from management about his work is non-existent. There is only one way to avoid this—go to the person requesting the research and ask them to let the analyst present the findings rapidly. It may only take five minutes for simple exercises, but the analyst will have the satisfaction of knowing that his or her contribution has been digested—it may even be corrected. It is also a painful fact that many reports are never read, even by the people that requested them. Projects that are essential for the future growth of the company get forgotten in the rush of daily production and sales, but the future still depends on the work that the analyst has completed. The manager may not have the time to progress things, but a good presentation of a real opportunity can show the hard-pressed manager the potential for a new product or service that he is interested in, and a person who might aid in its development at the same time. A thick report will not achieve that.

Presentations use up a lot of adrenalin. They are the best way of finding out what exactly the entrepreneur is after, because, however good the briefing, it is the reaction to the analyst's answers that reveals the personality and preoccupations of the manager. Presentations leave no opportunity for fudging the issue—they force the analyst to be committed to one course of action or another. If the result of analysis is an indication that some line of action would be unprofitable, it may take courage to state it, but the statement should be made, not as a challenge but in a low-key inoffensive manner. Probably 19 out of 20 presentations wave red flags—'Look out, this market is not for us!'—inside a company. The analyses behind the presentations will save a great deal of money that would otherwise be wasted on unsuccessful schemes. If a positive opportunity turns up, and it will do, the analyst's credibility will be aided by the determination to state the truth at any odds that he has shown with products that will not fly.

Coping with Adverse Reactions

Presentations can occasionally be argumentative occasions, through no fault of the analyst. Because someone does not want to believe the findings of the analyst, a whole series of defence mechanisms can come into play, and the analyst may find his report dismissed as irrelevant, over-academic, subject to error and personal bias, naïve and lacking in imagination.

All these represent faults of some analysts, but the fact is that when research happens to confirm the hunch of the entrepreneur, he sees it as central, correct, good value for money and very pragmatic. In companies with a strong innovatory tendency, or with market leadership, the work of the analyst market researcher is highly valued and the standards of work are high because so much research is carried out (most of which will be negative, once again). The analyst should be prepared to be considered as one more input to the management information service.

If incorrect attitudes exist towards data that come from the market-place, it will take some time to cure them. Be philosophic: time will tell. One of the commonest of these attitudes in small consumer goods companies is the *managing director's wife's syndrome*. Research on a particular product, say a biscuit, may have established a market slot at a particular price, targeted at a certain income group. The managing director may still test the product on his wife and reject it if she does not like it. Such rejections do not always spring from an unconscious strategy (e.g. 'Everything we produce must be good enough for my wife to eat') but can represent a confusion as to what really is the market and what is the best way to maximise profits. If the views of one woman are given precedence over a test with 200 consumers. there is only one thing to do: recruit the managing director's wife to assist in the field tests. Only if she is confronted first-hand with the consumer will she start to acquire a sense of the compromises that have to be made to create a product that will sell profitably.

Getting Presentations to the Shop Floor

If he can get to him or her, the analyst will find that the worker on the shop floor is very interested in the results of most marketing analysis. Some research findings will have implications for the factory worker, particularly those to do with the image of the company, delays in delivery and product quality. If commissioned image research or direct export research reveals problems on these scores, it is worthwhile making a presentation to the factory workers—if the analyst can get to them.

Such presentations can be aided by tape-recordings of comments from buyers, made with their permission. Great care has to be exercised in encouraging the respondents to talk clearly and slowly to get their points across, and it will usually be necessary to use an agency to conduct this research because only thus can the 'politeness effect' be avoided. In many cases it will be necessary for someone else to speak the words spoken by respondents in order to achieve anonymity.

It may be a revelation to the workforce that some potential customers regard their product as poor, from tests they have carried out, or that some existing customers are so pleased with the product they buy. If the basic problem of the product is that other companies are producing similar products that are better value for money and/or are delivered in time, whom better to inform than the workforce? There is no need to make a theatrical performance out of it—the working woman or man can assess the facts as intelligently as the management. If marketing analysis is to precede action in the market, the presentation of information to the workforce is very useful.

General Rules for Written Reports

Every week reports land on the desk of busy managers, and they are not read with excitement and very seldom read from cover to cover. The report may have the chance to receive 30 seconds' scrutiny. If its findings impress the manager concerned, he will attend their presentation to learn more. The report will rely on its summary to get its message across, and on its logic and clarity to educate the manager; it will depend on its authenticity to convince the manager, and on the way it is edited to simplify the task of scanning its pages. The four marks of the good report are the following:

(*a*) brevity,
(*b*) logic and clarity,
(*c*) authenticity, .
(*d*) the way it is broken up,

for which the acronym BLAB can be employed.

Mr Harold Geneen, when President of ITT, summarised the requirement for a report summary in a memorandum entitled 'Facts'. He wrote:

> In short, a professional report must start with a brief summary that gives in CLEAR factual language (1) the problems; (2) the action recommended; (3) the reasoning behind the recommendation in terms of its relation to the problem; and (4) the position taken by the writer of the report or memorandum. Evasive language at this point is a sign of poor preparation or poor sense of responsibility. I want every report specifically, directly and bluntly to state at the beginning a summary containing the following facts in this order:
>
> 1. A brief summary of what the problem really is.
> 2. A clear short statement of the action recommended.
> 3. The reasoning and the figures where necessary for clarity and perspective, to understand the basis of the reasoning and judgement areas leading to this recommendation.
> 4. A brief personal statement by the writer expressing any further personal opinion, his degree of confidence and any other questions that he has in this respect.

Mr Geneen, in the same article, pointed to the need for the truth about the market that is the goal of the marketing analyst. He wrote: 'The highest art of professional management requires the literal ability to "smell" a *real fact* from all others—and moreover to have the temerity, intellectual curiosity, guts and/or plain impoliteness, if necessary, to be *sure* that what you do have is indeed what we call an *unshakeable fact*'.

Brevity Above All in the Management Summary

The art of writing brief summaries has to some extent disappeared at market research agencies because of the photocopier. Making and circulating copies of published reports is illegal, and, to prevent this happening, agencies that sell multi-client reports have taken to producing very thick reports without decent management summaries, making the effort of circulating the information they contain very burdensome in terms of photocopying effort, so ensuring that photocopying does not take place. Within the company the example of the thick agency report should not be followed. All the results of a report should be condensed on to one page at the start of the report. The paper need not be a different colour to the rest of the report (one study has shown that this does not assist the reader) but the summary page should be right at the start of the report, before or after the title page and even somtimes reproduced additionally as an attachment outside the report—anything to ensure that it is read. Let us consider the example of the report on sunglasses in Unteland—a detailed work of 60 single-spaced pages based on over 100 interviews and packed with data. How is this to be reduced to its bare bones? Below we show the management summary, which, not surprisingly, is almost exactly the same in form as the presentation.

MANAGEMENT SUMMARY—THE MARKET FOR SUNGLASSES IN UNTELAND

Objective. To determine whether participation in the Unteland sunglasses market by acquisition is worthwhile.

Recommendation. Neither entry to the market by acquisition of an Unteland producer nor creating a marketing operation for imported sunglasses is recommended at this time.

Main Findings. Home producers are suffering declining sales of sunglasses in both the home and export markets, and this will continue because of Far East labour cost advantages.

Supply to the Unteland Home and Export Market ($U millions in prices of year)

	1987	1988	1989	1990	1991	Average annual change 87-91 (%)	1996 (Forecast)
Home production	240	225	150	140	80	—32	40
+ Imports	60	87	90	150	170	+30	205
— Exports	60	70	40	40	15	—41	10
= Apparent consumption	240	242	200	250	235	—0.5	235

Demand. The market is essentially saturated and static, with large fluctuations depending on summer sunshine. New technologies and marketing methods are forecast to continue to make no difference to growth.

High Advertising Expenditure. The price of visibility at market entry is at least $U1.5 million in year, as paid by Forensic, a recent entrant.

Unteland Advertising Expenditure and Market Share—Sunglasses, a Volatile Open Market with High Advertising Expenditure

Brands	Market share (%)		Advertising expenditure ($U000)	
	1987	1991	1987	1991
Regard	38	19	200	1,200
Sea Cool	26	15	320	360
Turn On	16	21	200	1,390

Brands	Market share (%)		Advertising expenditure ($U000)	
	1987	1991	1987	1991
Forensic	—	23	—	1,110
4 others	20	—	—	—
7 others	—	22	300	120
Total	100	100	$U1,020	$U4,180

Profitability. The Unteland sunglasses industry, which achieved 5 per cent ROS in the 1980s is forecast to continue to make losses until 1995.
Distribution. Three retail chains—Grandcash, Pharmadrug and Tillring—account for 62 per cent of sunglasses sales in Unteland.

Logic and Clarity

Reports cannot always follow the same format, as they depend for their logic on the logic of the problem being attacked. However, it will often prove possible to see the following structure in a report:

Demand for the Product
1. Demand for the product class to which the product belongs (past 5 years' data).
2. Demand for the product (past 5 years' data).
3. Determinants of demand.
4. Purchasers by segment.
5. Forecast demand.

Supply of the Product
1. Major suppliers and market shares.
2. How products are marketed.
3. Characteristics of distribution.
4. Forecast changes in supply.

Demand for the Product by Specification
1. Requirements of purchasers.
2. Comparative competitive offers.

If demand is distinguished from supply, it becomes much easier to organise information. Five years' statistics are always given if possible, and the product should be situated in the market (product class) in which it belongs before considering the product itself. For example, if the analyst is looking at the market for a building product, he must look at the prospects for building generally in order to understand the product's prospects.

Determinants of demand will often refer to how much income is available to buy it (e.g. Government military budgets for arms purchases), or to changes in fashion or other factors affecting demand for a product. It is at this point that the need satisfied by the product can be examined. A profile of market segments will be included.

'Supply' is a picture of what is happening to those who provide the product and a snapshot of how they go about their marketing. It is here that the analyst might note, for example, that although the second telephone can be regarded as another electronic consumer durable, it is not marketed like this by a particular telephone administration (this is not a reference to British Telecom, who are the leading European marketers of telephones). The supply section will consider profitability, productivity where it is available and other characteristics of supply. Once again the rule of trying to have information about five years will apply. The analyst will note trends in supply and forecast changes. Demand for the product by specification is not always required, but if a company is interested in entering a market, it may be necessary to show exactly what is on the market and what is required in terms of price, mechanical and performance characteristics, appearance, delivery and so on.

The logic of a particular problem often requires a special layout, of course. If the question is, 'Will the brewer accept this new package for retailed beer?', the report may be a very brief statement of what the brewer requires from a retail package—compatibility with the existing filling system, a shelf-life of x weeks, a good surface for labelling, a good appearance, greater consumer acceptability than cans or glass, a price equal to existing packaging materials, and so on.

Clarity must ride with logic. If masterly logic dictates that the analyst examine first the public market and then the private market, he should take care that someone reading the report does not confuse the two sectors because they are placed next to each other. It might be better, even if more lengthy, to report on demand for the public sector product followed by supply to the public sector, rather than to lump demand for both the public and private market together, followed by supply to both the public and the private market. Then no one will be confused. Get someone to read a report in draft to ensure clarity.

Authenticity

A report should be a self-authenticating document. Every table should give the source of information clearly. If it is a question of 'guesstimation', the report should clearly state 'guesstimate'. Facts are sacred, estimates can be useful, and guesses based on estimates are also very useful if it is explained how they are reached.

Self-authentication means that there must be no loose ends, no errors and no contradictions. An authentic report will explain how a forecast is derived and not simply drop numbers on the page without explanation. The summary has to rely on the report behind it for its validity and credibility. Making a report authentic may tend to make it thicker—there should be a play-off between authenticity and brevity, and circumstances will dictate which one will win. Remember, a report can have appendices into which a lot of the detail can be packed.

It should be noted that authenticity sometimes requires the use of a special language. Economic forecasts, for example, which ought to be paraphrasable in simple terms like 'more money in the buyer's pocket', seem to require phrases like 'disposable income will increase in real terms', in many companies. Consider the needs of the audience: a report on a high technology product for a board with no engineers must be written differently from a report on the same topic addressed to the head of an engineering consultancy.

Break-up

Finally, each page of a report should be looked at carefully to see whether it is possible to use sub-headings to guide the reader through the report more easily. Four pages, even two pages of densely typed report, without any headings on the content can be difficult to read. Everything should be done to help the reader to find the information he is seeking in the report. Charts and illustrations also help the reader to remember where a particular piece of information is written in the report, and they make the report much more interesting in appearance.

This chapter has shown that the primary skill of human communication is by person-to-person contact and that report writing is an aid to that contact where more complicated information is required to be recorded and distributed to a group of people. The analyst should aim to make a personal presentation of his findings his main target and ensure that reports, which are usually required as back-up, are easily read documents that inspire confidence. Figure 12.7 provides a check-list of what a report and presentation should contain.

Fig. 12.7

REPORT CHECKLIST

Objective stated	Logical
Actionable recommendations	Findings Validated
Readership listed	Consistent
Appearance required	Sources stated
Businesslike	Unshakeable facts
Impressive	Adequate samples
For special readers	Forecast method explained
or for general readers	Forecast confidence limits
Easy to read	Delivered on time
Summary provided	Value for money
Brief as possible	Man–days
	Cost

PRESENTATION CHECKLIST

Clear visual aids	Voice-over script
Brief as possible	Main findings stated
Businesslike	Recommendations stated

Why Recommendations Are Worthwhile

The closer that analysis gets to the strategic considerations of the company, the more important it is to have the recommendations of the analyst. Of course, summaries describing an industry generally require no recommendations, but the answer to such a question as 'Should we enter this market or sell this product?' deserves the recommendation of the analyst. The analyst may represent the person with most experience of the market needs that have been investigated, and his judgement should be exercised. Of course, it is possible that the judgements are incorrect or naïve, but judgements made on guesswork rather than by looking at the market are even more likely to be wrong. There is a second reason for recommendations: it is only by exercising judgement that the faculty of judgement becomes strong and canny, through the experience of mistakes as well as successes. Finally, the analyst's recommendations are no more than that, their rejection or acceptance depending on all sorts of factors. The analysts are not running industry. Nor will they ever be.

Key Concepts

Presentation. An occasion when information is conveyed in person to one or more people, using flip-charts, slides or other aids.

Exercises

---

1. Take the latest *Financial Times* special supplement and summarise its contents in one page. Envisage the board of directors as your target audience and highlight facts and figures in your summary.

2. Prepare your *curriculum vitae* (your career summary) as a presentation for your colleagues, with your target to persuade them to employ you as a member of a marketing team. Make the presentation to them, using flip-charts, transparencies or slides.

3. Choose one of the lectures in a week's curriculum and make a one-page summary of its contents.

13
Agency or In-house Research

Using a market research agency or employing a consultant to give information about a market is something that thousands of companies are doing every day, and by and large most of them are very satisfied with the services they receive. In the career of a marketer, and the history of a growing company, there must always be a first time that these outside services are employed, and this chapter is designed to help make this task of selecting, briefing and working with an agency as rewarding as possible. The purpose of using agency research, as of all analysis, is to provide management with a view of the market's needs that has clarity and conviction.

These questions will be addressed:

1. When should an agency be used?
2. How do you find an agency?
3. How do you choose an agency?
4. How can you get the best from an agency?

At the end of the chapter there is a very lengthy exercise that was originally designed by a leading agency for presentation to a group of professional market researchers within a large company. The researchers were divided into different 'agencies' and prepared proposals for the imaginary client on how they would undertake the research. This exercise, if undertaken by at least two groups, will provide a good idea of the constraints that an agency works under. Any agency is limited by the quality and number of its staff, the past work it has undertaken, the particular skills it has developed, the size of its order book, its ability to convey its ideas well and its sheer need to make money. It can never be stressed enough: good information and advice cost a lot of money.

Why Employ an Agency?

There are a number of compelling occasions when an agency will need to be approached:

1. If the company lacks adequate personnel resources.
2. If there is a need for anonymity in approaching a market.
3. If disagreements within the company on the potential of a market make an independent assessment desirable.
4. If speed in getting information is critical.

The lack of internal personnel resource may not be absolute: it may just be that there is no one with adequate experience of some particular technology in a very complicated or closed market (e.g. to outsiders electronic components may appear bafflingly technical, and the oil industry may seem to be a market where finding the right contacts appears dauntingly difficult). The need for anonymity arises particularly with potential acquisitions or new or existing products to be offered to markets new to the company. It is also relevant to studies of the **image** of a company, where respondents have to be approached by a neutral source in order to avoid the receipt of information distorted by politeness or the wish to grumble about deliveries or prices. One common motive for using an outside agency is the need to settle some internal argument between an entrepreneur and someone acting as a restraint.

In these cases the agency should be provided with plenty of information about the company's position, in order to aid their assessment. Some of the best agencies will provide a very straight picture of the potential, but it is probably fair to say that they will have a tendency to lean towards optimism on behalf of their client. This is partly a result of their relation to an existing and potentially longer-term client, but also to their valuable experience of having seen successful and unsuccessful innovators in the market in question. An agency does not need as much imagination as the internal market researcher when forecasting success, and has much less to lose if the project is an ultimate failure. So if an agency signals a red light, it should be taken very seriously. If an **image study** shows a negative image, agencies will have no bias in reporting it, and probably will be able to suggest how to counter it. The agency will be in a much better position to comment adversely than the internal market research department, as the top management of a company does not like what appears to it as criticism coming from inside the organisation.

Finally, speed in fieldwork may make the use of an agency desirable. Table 13.1 lists this and the other requirements mentioned.

Finding Agencies

The best way to find an agency is by word-of-mouth recommendation from someone with first-hand experience of several agencies' performances. Always approach more than one agency, even where a

Table 13.1. Requirements Prompting the Choice of an Agency or In-house Research

Agency	In-house
Cost	Cost
Anonymity	Need to build-up detailed contacts/
Independence	expertise for the future
Speed	Speed
International expertise	Flexibility in revising targets
Other special expertise	

personal recommendation is made, because it makes better sense to shop around for the best package available. In each visit to an agency or by an agency to your offices there will be a lengthy dialogue of question and answer, which constitutes the briefing for the research and the analyst's probing of the experience and competence of the agency. This briefing cannot really be too long. A full day will usually need to be put aside for each agency, and if there is a high technical content, visits to the relevant company expert may need to be arranged. These briefings are by no means one-way flows of information. The agency will already be teaching the analyst about the realities of the market-place and the constraints on finding the information sought.

Agencies are listed in the *International Research Directory of Market Research Organisations*, published by the Market Research Society and the British Overseas Trade Board. The areas of expertise of each agency are indicated in this directory. (The names of four large consultants that do not include themselves in these lists are provided in Appendix 1.)

One of the jokes about agencies is that their objective at the briefing is to find out what recommendations the client wants in order to give them to him. That is of course a slander, but it draws attention to the purpose of the whole activity: to exchange information for money. How much you are willing to pay for information depends on how much you need it as well as how much money you have in your budget. Not all the information supplied by the agency can be costed exactly; although visits to respondents for industrial market research can bear an exact charge or interviews with the public a definite price, there will usually be a great deal of information held in an agency's collective memory that bears no exact value. Once the agency has given you that information, it cannot be sold to you again. Therefore the company buying research must seek at least two suppliers if it wants to be certain to avoid paying a monopoly price for information. Provided this rule is borne in mind, some of the least expensive research in Europe can be bought in the United Kingdom, representing excellent value for money. British agencies can also carry out good research on European countries at a lower price than if continental agencies are employed.

Briefing Agencies

Agencies work on a professional code that protects any information from a client or prospective client from being disclosed to any other party, and this is adhered to with absolute fidelity. There is therefore no reason why each briefing should not be as frank and open as possible.

Choosing the Agency

After the briefing meeting an agency will normally address a letter to its prospective client setting out its proposal and costs for doing research. This document will lay down the objectives of the research, how the agency understands the questions that the research is designed to solve, the methods to be employed to obtain the information, the cost and method of payment, the way the results will be presented and the timing of research. The analyst will normally be receiving proposals from two or more agencies, and will be able to compare the agencies' proposals on the basis of their comprehension of the problem and efficiency in solving it, as well as on the other factors listed in the checklist. Attention should be directed particularly to the number of interviews that are promised in the research, as this is a critical factor with regard to the confidence one can give to the results. Provision should be made for liaison meetings with the agency before research is completed, as part of the contract, and the project leader should always be present at these meetings.

Figure 13.1. CHECKLIST FOR COMPARING CONSULTANTS

Recommended by ....
Relevant qualifications of staff
Previous clients/markets expertise
Quality of proposal

    Understanding of needs
    Relevance
    Methods
    Cost effectiveness

Project leader ....
Skills of agency in verbal presentation
Timing

The cost of the research is of course of vital importance. Some of the money for research will have to be paid at the time the survey is commissioned. Note the proposals for presenting the results. Will there be a presentation to management, as requested, included as part of the cost? The timing can be a problem, as delays may make the research an unusable waste of resources (e.g. a potential acquisition is only kept on the hot list for two months and the date of the next meeting must be met) and advice should be sought from the legal department about this. At least one body offering market research in Europe has a poor record of delivery on time, but the fact that most agencies deliver on time all the time has more than once caught the customers of the inefficient report-producer off their guard. If delivery on time is vital, take advice from a lawyer before signing any acceptance with contractual force. In addition, find out whether expenses are to be paid by the client or are included in the cost of the research: the expenses for research in Saudi Arabia can be astronomical and need to be regularised before the contract is signed.

How to Get the Best from an Agency

Everything in the information and analysis business depends on the competence and goodwill of the researcher, and the prime requisite for successful cooperation is to ensure that you know who is responsible for the work at the agency from the very outset. Make sure that the agency knows that you want this personal attention, and do not work with an agency you distrust. Literate, numerate but inexperienced researchers are sometimes entrusted with all the preparation and writing of reports on highly complicated markets, and occasionally their lack of experience is evident in internal inconsistencies in their reports. There is no harm in using all levels of competence in research: the young woman who gets a telephone interview with a managing director about his attitude to hotels used for conferences is using her particular competence to get past a secretary to a very busy man in order to elicit his views on something his secretary would regard as trivial. Willingness to listen and not lead a discussion will be part of the competence of the recent graduate probably starting his career at the agency. But the client has the right to expect that an experienced and knowledgeable expert should direct, oversee and write the main part of the report compiled for him, and make appropriate recommendations.

Make sure that you keep in contact with the agency as research progresses. Visits every week at a specified time, which are made by some users of outside research, reassure the client and can prevent nasty surprises.

The agency should not be asked to do things that are outside its charter. Detailed notes on interviews with named individuals in named companies on behalf of an anonymous enquirer cannot be specified as part of the contract, because agencies are not in the business of industrial espionage. Any information brought back from specified persons can only be given with their permission. There are many ways of obtaining information, and a good agency will be able to advise the analyst on roads that are open and avoid those that are as closed to it as to anyone else.

The point at which the agency will give you most help is when the results of its research are presented to its client. Arrangements should be made for this to take place no later than a week after the report is received. All recipients of the report should be invited to a presentation (a debriefing meeting) given by the agency while its enthusiasm is still hot and the interviewers still retain strong impressions of the market-place. This will give everyone a chance to ask the difficult questions, and if there is disappointment in the findings, the agency will bear the brunt of this directly rather than through the painful cushion of the analyst. Feelings at such meetings can run deep, but the professionalism and lack of emotionalism of a good agency presentation will defuse the atmosphere and remove any grounds for reproach. Such meetings are very good for long-term agency relationships, as well, because the researchers are much more strongly motivated to aid in any further research if they meet the persons who are receiving their information, and who are using it to direct their commercial strategy.

Multi-client Surveys and Audits

In some cases an agency will approach your company to be a sponsor. If a market is new to you or evolving very fast, the information can be very useful even though you will share it with many potential competitors. Included under this heading are the audits of consumption of packaged groceries offered by A. C. Nielsen and the surveys of office equipment usage sold by INDAL (Comtec) in the United Kingdom. The sheer size of the samples needed to monitor developments in the office equipment market make the use of such continuing audits of consumption mandatory for companies with budget limitations.

Summary

Outside agencies should be employed for work on large geographically spread samples for which no adequate labour exists inside the company. They are valuable for explorations of markets about which the company lacks definite knowledge and can be used to obtain information very rapidly.

Invitations to quote for research should usually be made to more than one agency and each agency should be briefed fully on why the need for information exists.

Word of mouth recommendations with reference to agencies are the best way to make a short-list.

Clear arrangements should be specified with regard to expenses associated with field research and presentation of results.

After selecting an agency on the basis of its recommendations, price and timing, as set out in its offer, maintain regular liaison with the team doing the research.

A presentation of results to the company management should be arranged about a week after the report is delivered.

Key Concepts

Image Study. A study of the way that buyers of a company's products or investors and potential investors in its stocks perceive the company in terms of characteristics that the buyers rate as important for their purchasing decision.

Multi-Client Study. A survey of a market available to any subscriber.

Exercise

Based on a simulation originally provided at ITTE to 36 market research managers by Mr Colin Walpole of BIS Marketing Research Ltd, this exercise can be carried out by an individual but is more rewarding if undertaken by competing teams. It consists of a briefing, some background data, information about the profile of each agency and a score sheet for the proposals made by the different 'agencies'. The data about the agency is *not* typical of market research agencies in the 1980s and 1990s but has been arranged to highlight the constraints under which agencies compete. Allow about three hours for the whole exercise. If carrying it out alone, write a proposal to Vanco covering your appreciation of their problem, the objectives of the research, the methods to be employed, the cost in your local currency, and the timing and the proposals with regard to presenting the results of the research. In team working the proposals should be presented by the team leader on flip-charts before a panel of judges.

BRIEFING

'My name is David Spondo, Vice-President of International Division of a Vancouver BC Company engaged in Ship chartering—Vanco of Canada. Vanco has several ships of its own and many long-term contracts which assure the Company's long-term profits of at least $5 million per annum but our growth rate in profits of the 1980s and 1990s has not been maintained because of the over-supply of cargo space brought about by the huge shipbuilding boom of 1985–7. Vanco is becoming increasingly interested in making a series of acquisitions in going concerns in less vulnerable fields.

'Because we are in the transport business, we have decided to broaden our operations within this basic philosophy, and packaging manufacturing has been selected as one of the areas to investigate. Also, we like the look of Europe because packaging is not as intensively used there as it is in North America. We have just heard from one of our shipping agents that a French corrugated case company may soon be for sale because the family which owns it has to pay a large death duty bill. Now, this news reached me only a day or two ago at the Hilton hotel here in Perlindome. Unfortunately I have to fly back to Vancouver later today and can spend less than one hour briefing you on our interest. Your proposal has to be ready in 48 hours and needs to be presented to our Vice-President of Finance who will be in Perlindome on other business. Neither I, nor our Vide-President of Finance, know much about the corrugated industry or about Unteland, so we will rely heavily on your investigation to show whether or not we should approach Untel-Pak SA, with a provisional offer to buy control. The investigation must be completed within six weeks from now because we have reason to believe Untel-Pak will by then be actively approaching companies to see if they are interested in investing in their company.

'The Vanco corporate finance staff will be used to prepare a report on Untel-Pak SA's financial returns. We know that detailed work will be undertaken with Untel-Pak's financial people to get the real truth if we make an approach, so do not concern yourselves with this aspect of the evaluation. I got the name of your company from the EVAF directory of research agencies and selected you and some other agencies because in the directory you mention "packaging" as one of the industries in which you have worked. During the past 36 hours, I have had our Agent dig out some information about the Unteland corrugated case market and industry and I will hand this to you when I have explained what we are looking for in the investigation and I will then try to answer any questions you may have.

'Because I am a "shipping man", I cannot give you a detailed briefing and nor can anyone else in Vanco because investment overseas and investment in manufacturing are new to us. All I can do is to outline our interests and leave it to you to interpret them into a proposal and costing—after all, you guys are the experts.

'Our main interest at this stage is to get an overview of the future for corrugated cases in Unteland and an assessment of how Untel-Pak looks from the standpoints of its locations, its marketing and its overall competence. I guess we want to know how the corrugated market in Unteland has grown over the past few years and how things look in the longer term. In the shipping business we try to keep good relations with customers in several different industries in different parts of the world so that we are not too dependent on one area or one type of industrial customer. This kind of information would be useful if you can get it on Untel-Pak's customer and geographical spread.

'As I mentioned earlier, our main business is suffering because of over-capacity of cargo space and in Vancouver we are all very sensitive on this point, so please be sure to cover this same point in your report on Untel-Pak. My grandfather, David Spondo I, used to say "Companies are as good as the guys running them". We believe sincerely in good management, especially if we are going to spend several million dollars in an industry we do not know in a country five or six thousand miles away from home. Can you help us get a good feel of Untel-Pak's status as a supplier?

'Back home we see corrugated being used more and more in new applications and dropping out from some others because new techniques, like plastic film packaging, are displacing it. Can you give us a view about Untel-Pak's involvement in growth and non-growth markets and assess the threat to corrugated coming from competitive packaging methods?

'Bearing in mind we want steady long-term growth in our business, together with a good measure of security, I guess we are especially interested in an acquisition that is integrated into its customers or into its suppliers, so please give us a rundown on this aspect of Untel-Pak. If the company has not made such a move, we would not be keen to provide the funds because the cost would probably be too big to make now. My father, David Spondo II, is president of Vanco and he has always said, "Our customers pay a cent or two per tonne extra because we look after them really well". So, we are keener to invest in companies which really look after their customers well when times are good because it pays off when times are bad. Now, we are over in Vancouver and want to be sure that Untel-Pak won't let us down when the market gets tough, so do they go for the last cent at good times and cut their prices when the market turns down?

'This report we want you to prepare must be confidential and nobody is to be told that Vanco is your client, so clearly you can't visit Untel-Pak itself, nor do we want you to indulge in any unethical practises, so in your proposal explain to us how you would approach any organisations you visit. Naturally, we would like you to give verbatim answers to your questions, together with who made the remarks. This would add greatly to the confidence we have in the report. I guess this is OK? Would it be possible for you to give us a fairly close idea of the percentage profit on sales that a good case maker in Unteland should make at average times? Also, my wife's cousin had a two-week holiday in Unteland last month and told us that things are going really well there at the moment, so can you check this and give a few pages on the economy from, say, 1985 to 1995?

'If we do get talking to Untel-Pak, we want to be able to discuss their industry and its markets in detail so that is clear to them we have taken trouble to understand them. My son, David Spondo IV, is in the military and told me his commanding officer once said, "Time spent in preparation is seldom wasted", and I feel the same way! We must not have our approach to Untel-Pak rejected because we have failed to do our preparation. Also, we want to be able to volunteer some positive suggestions to help Untel-Pak grow; we can't supply any management, so if we invest, we want to give them your report to help them with their own planning and marketing policies. So please ensure that you collect information of use to Untel-Pak if we decide to invest and they accept our offer.

'Let me now give you the data sheet I have got our shipping sales agent to put together. I will now try to answer your questions for the next five minutes before I leave for the airport.'

(The attached data sheet is all you could get yourselves at short notice. So you

can devote your time to preparing the proposal. Also attached is a data sheet about your own company.)

DATA SHEET
The Unteland Corrugated Case Industry and Market

Supplied by David Spondo to market research agencies preparing proposals for Vanco.

1. For some reason it seems that demand for corrugated is 20–30 per cent down in the first half of 1995 compared with the first half of 1994. Stock changes may account for part of this, or it may be caused by an increase in the use of competitive packaging materials.

2. In 1994 Unteland used 1.5 million tonnes of corrugated. This figure was obtained from the Unteland Case Makers Assocation, which seems helpful.

3. In 1993 and early 1994 Unteland case makers are believed to have suffered from a scarcity of materials, which are largely imported from North American and the Nordic countries. Domestic mills became very busy at that time, but the situation has now changed, with imports freely available.

4. There seems to be a relationship between GDP and corrugated demand.

5. There seems to have been a swing towards the lower quality case-making materials during the shortages of high-quality foreign supplies. This could be a permanent downgrading.

6. Recent press articles indicate that there is a surplus of corrugating capacity, particularly in some regions of Unteland.

7. Corrugated cases are folded flat to users and can travel economically within a radius of 75 km.

8. The Unteland Case Makers Association has given the following analysis of case markets for 1994, the first and only year this information has been collected and distributed. There are no plans to repeat the exercise in future.

Corrugated Board: 1994	*Consumption '000 Tonnes*
Canned and bottled foods	48
Fresh fruit and vegetables	57
Fresh meat, poultry and fish	42
Milk and milk products	126
Wines and spirits	104
Beer and soft drinks	60
Other foods	176
Soaps, detergents and cosmetics	67
Paper products	52
Electrical and domestic appliances	62
Light engineering	60
China pottery and glass	93
Clothing, textiles and footwear	113
Other non-foods	425
TOTAL	1,485

9. Since 1992 about 10 new corrugators of 30,000 tonnes capacity each have been installed.

10. In Unteland, there are 30 companies making corrugated cases, and they

own a total of 100 corrugators situated at 50 different locations. There are 15 mills making case-making materials in Unteland and 10 overseas mills represented by sales offices or agents.

Information on Untel-Pak SA

1. Owns two corrugators producing 50,000 tonnes per annum of corrugated cases. One factory is at Loso, the other is 15 km south of Scoss. The Loso factory was opened in 1992.

2. The company owns a small mill making low-quality case-making materials; production in 1994 was 80,000 tonnes.

3. The company is wholly owned by the Clifton family, and all the five directors are Cliftons.

Information about Your Research Agency

1. You know very little about the packaging industry and your entry in the market research directory (which mentioned your earlier work in packaging) referred to an expert you had on your staff in 1992, but he left to join an Unteland plastics manufacturer as marketing director.

2. You have three staff only available for this assignment because your other 20 staff are all fully occupied. One man is a good 24-year-old economist who has worked for you for three years in industrial research, the other is a director who has been with your company for six years and has good experience in this type of work. Their salaries are $U12,500 and $U20,000 per annum and, because of overheads, holidays, illness etc., their costs to you are three times this, without profit. You can buy good industrial interviewing at $80 per interview and this includes travel expenses and analysis of the questionnaires.

3. Your company prides itself on the clarity and detail of its proposals and you always work for a set fee. You always prepare a detailed job costing sheet and for the purpose of this assignment you seek to make your normal profit margin. The cost of preparing the proposal is included in your costing and will not be refunded unless you are given the assignment.

SCORING GRID FOR AGENCY PROPOSALS

	Maximum out of 10 points
Clarity and depth of understanding of the client's total real needs as opposed to his requests.	
Correctness of balance in proposal between important parts of the client's requests for information	
Sampling and cost-effectiveness of methods to be used for collecting market information	

Sampling and methods to be used for
collecting information on Untel-Pak SA

Insurances to be used for safeguarding:

(*a*) Confidentiality
(*b*) Not relying on only one type of source
of information

Cost of report

Verbal *presentation* of proposal

TOTAL

The 'Scoring Grid for Agency Proposals' given above provides a handy form
for assessing the relative performance of competing agencies in making their
proposals. Each heading covers an important criterion to be applied to their
agency's proposal, and the score is put on the right. Scores can be weighted
according to each factor's relative importance: for example 10 points as
maximum for the cost of the report, but only 8 points concerning the
sampling method as a maximum if considered less important; or all given
equal weight. The marketing professionals who adjudicated at the original
conference where this case study was employed created this list of criteria for
judging the proposals of different agencies.

14
Market Analysis and Business Strategies

Steven E. Permut, in an article called 'Marketing Research: The European View' (*European Research*, Vol. 6 Number 2, March 1978), contrasted the views of European and American executives on this function, and found that European management regarded market research activity most favourably when results were 'actionable' and clearly presented. The European managers in Permut's sample liked simple techniques of research rather than esoteric ones, and wanted communication to be less pontifical and more effective. Also important was that market research should provide deeper, clearer analysis. To provide that sort of actionable clear input to management, the analyst must put on the manager's hat and become a strategist in order to see what information is required to improve the company's products and market share, and launch new ventures. It requires an ability to see beyond the figures and what they project to the realities of the world of which the statistics are shadows, and a determination to change the world by offering it something it will want to buy.

'The people in the company who are least afraid are the few in our small Market Research Department', wrote Joseph Heller in *Something Happened* (Corgi Books, 1975). He explained that they were not afraid partly because their salaries and budgets were small. He continued: 'People in the Market Research Department are never held to blame for conditions they discover outside the company that place us at a competitive disadvantage. What is, is—and they are not expected to change reality but merely to find it if they can and suggest ingenious ways to disguise it'.

Unless the marketing analysts or the market researchers can take part in changing reality in the company, they will have nothing to fear except small salaries and small responsibilities. Marketing analysis must be the servant of the entrepreneur—the analyst needs to enter the entrepreneurial mind, resolve contradictions, and be at the service of a comprehensible strategy. Like everyone else in the company, he is able to suggest improvements in the strategy and better ways of implementing it. In fact, he is at an advantage. Analysis must be the servant of enterprise. This chapter will show how an actual market strategy could engender marketing analysis, and will refer to many of the methods outlined in the course of this book.

Packaging Strategy Case Study

To illustrate the way that marketing analysis serves marketing strategy and is itself driven by strategy, let us consider an example of a new product destined to be launched in Unteland by a packaging manufacturer. The product, called New Pack, is already available in the USA. It consists of a laminate of cardboard, various plastic films and aluminium foil; is intended for any beverage (including fizzy drinks); and has a type of ring-pull opening that provides a good spout for pouring. It takes up little space and has no protrusions that might make storage difficult. It is reclosable and disposable, and stands up well. The New Pack can be handled on existing filling systems for bottles or cans, although at slightly lower rates because of the slower closing of the product than is achieved by systems for putting on can lids or bottle caps. But if a bottler or canner decided to go over entirely to the New Pack, it would be possible to install new filling lines that would in fact be as fast as any existing technology.

There are one or two more snags with New Pack—there are nearly always some for any new product. For one thing, it is more expensive than any existing competitive packaging medium, by a factor of 50 per cent. This will in fact eventually be reduced to make the product much cheaper than bottles or cans, but the volume required to achieve this will be very large, equivalent to 30 per cent of all Unteland packaged beverages, including milk.

Secondly, the advantages it may offer—lightness, the ability to be packed into a smaller place—could be unimportant to the final user, and this is so far unknown. Untel-Pak has not made up its mind about the new product, but it feels it must keep abreast of this new technology in case its competitors, especially Remplicase, decide to enter the market, when the product would threaten Untel-Pak's sales of cartons. Untel-Pak gives the responsibility for marketing the new product to a bright but relatively junior product manager, with the knowledge that the young PM will regard this as an opportunity for ultimate promotion. The PM writes a draft strategy and a timetable, which he calls a road map, and he develops a plan for market research with the aid of the analyst.

Product Strategy in Outline

The summary of the strategy, in accordance with company policy, takes two pages and is reproduced below. Much of the information is really guesswork, but it is the best guesswork available at this moment.

DRAFT STRATEGY FOR NEW PACK IN UNTELAND
Relation to Company Strategy. New Pack offers an opportunity to enter new markets and reduce dependence on the Unteland Milk Cooperatives (45 per cent of sales).
End-User Market. The market for soft drinks, mineral water, alcoholic and other packaged beverages is stable, overall, with growth for certain beverages compensated by declines elsewhere. Consumers appear slow to accept changes in packaging and recent innovations have not swept the market.
Drink Suppliers, Bottlers and Canners. All manufacturers are very slow to take up any new packaging technology, and extensive tests are an essential part of any new product launch. Changes in packaging have not been the focus of competition in recent years.

Competing Packaging for Cold Beverages, Unteland

	Bottle	Can	Plastic Bottle	Carton	New Pack
Reclosable	Yes	No	Yes	No	Yes
Market sectors excluded	None	Milk	Spirits	Carbonated beverages, spirits, beer	Spirits
Sizes excluded	Over 2 litres	None	Less than ½ litre	Over 1 litre	Over 2 litres
Index of cost per unit—on existing lines	100	120	na	25	180
—on new lines	100	120	na	na	30 to 120
Shelf life	1 year	3 years?	11 months?	11 months	8 months
Pluses	Familiar, attractive, rigid	Easy opening, light, familiar	Non-returnable, light	Compact, light	As for can, plastic bottle and carton
Minuses	Heavy, fragile	Expensive	Fragile	Bad pourer	Unfamiliar, expensive
Major producers	Glaspak	Boitel	Remplicase	Untel-Pak	None

	Bottle	Can	Plastic Bottle	Carton	New Pack
Future New Pack suppliers?	No	No	Very probably	Possibly, if others introduce	—

Untel-Pak Profile. Untel-Pak is a major carton manufacturer with an excellent reputation for milk and fruit juice packaging. It has no experience of other beverages. Introduction of the New Pack by a competitor would reduce Untel-Pak's sales of cartons by 20 per cent.

Objectives

1. To be ready to offer a market-adapted product if an adequate market exists and a competitor invests in New Pack equipment and enters the market.
2. In the event of entry, to achieve a 25 per cent market share in order to be capable of offering a product at a competitive price.

Strategies   *(for objective 1)*

1. Establish market requirements, price tolerance and volume.
2. Maintain an intelligence programme on competitive activity.
          (for objective 2)
1. Sell to key innovative accounts capable of achieving over 25 per cent of the total volume of beverages sold in New Pack.

Programmes (for objective 1)

1. Consumer research with New Pack (deadline May 1991).
2. Industry research with prospective customers (deadline May 1991).
3. Competitive intelligence programme (continuous).
4. Short-list of major prospective accounts (May 1991).
5. Product launch plan and capital authorisation case (September 1991).

The Market Analysis Input—Company Strategy

At the top of the draft strategy document is a reference to the company's dependence on one existing customer. Part of the job of analysis in many companies is an examination of the degree to which a company is dependent on a handful of key customers. A customer screening programme establishes the percentage of sales and profits accounted for by the top ten customers, analyses the associated marketing costs, establishes which customers are so important that they should be served directly by the managing director, marketing director or president, coordinates the sales approach, calculates the vulnerability of the company from possible changes in buying policy at the key customers, and serves as an input to strategic goals for reducing dependence on some particular customers if that should seem desirable. In this case the main objective is to widen the customer base away from fruit juice and milk, but not, of course, in any way that threatens profit. As has been seen, Untel-Pak does not want to enter this market unless some other company does so first, and mainly as a defensive measure.

End-user markets

The strategy is a draft, so far, and the PM is not absolutely certain of the facts put down about consumer conservatism. The packaging manufacturer is always required to know a lot about the final user of a packaging product, but finds himself up against the conservatism of his direct customers (i.e. the bottlers, canners or packers). This is described as **downstream marketing myopia**. In many markets the immediate supplier can be a poor marketer of his product, and his packaging provider may in fact have a better concept of how to market the final product to the end-user. Heaven help him if this aptitude should become apparent to his customer!

The Prime Customers

The packaging manufacturer has to discover the innovators in the market who are willing to try the New Pack, but only large customers are really desired. The worst situation is to launch the New Pack with a small company hoping to use the pack as a marketing plus, because a defeat for the small company (which might be due to all sorts of factors, from the taste of their beverage to the smallness of their advertising budget) will be construed as a defeat for the new package.

Competitive Intelligence

The table of competitive products is a mixture of fact and guesswork, for no one in Untel-Pak really knows the cost of bottling or canning beverages, and the data have been taken from old studies and press articles. Getting this information in detail will be the job of the market analyst, and he will do it with the aid of the sales force and their contacts in the beverage industry, from direct industrial market research with canners and bottlers, and possibly by the use of outside agencies or consultants if there is insufficient information from the other sources. The question of the plans of other packaging suppliers to enter the market will also require some intelligence work, and this will use the sales force, once again, and lots of contact with the

American supplier of New Pack machinery. The New Pack machinery supplier may or may not let Untel-Pak know about competitors' activity in Unteland, depending on the agreement reached with any existing customer and how much spare capacity he has for producing the equipment. The sales force will be a good source for contacts, but like to send their hottest information to persons very high in the company hierarchy (i.e. they bypass the analyst). As long as this is understood, they are a good source of intelligence.

End-user Research

The PM envisages that good consumer research may aid Untel-Pak to sell New Pack to brewers, and avoid the ultimate fiasco of poor consumer acceptance. The brewing sector looks as if it will be most important in terms of volume potential, followed by soft drinks. The analyst runs two separate discussions (see page 112) with housewives and married men, each with eight persons present. From the discussions it emerges that wives do buy some beer for their husbands, but they will be reluctant to sample new packaging unless offered at a very low price or after extensive advertising. They fear that beer or lemonade in the New Pack will taste of cardboard, that it will go off rapidly, and that the package will look like fruit juice or milk. The men like the idea of a light pack, and suggest that distinctive labelling like that on beer cans might avoid the problem of confusion with fruit juice. They are also sceptical about the shelf-life of the product and how fresh it will keep after being opened and reclosed.

The analyst is by now developing some hypotheses. In the first place, the product which most resembles (see p. 20) the New Pack from the consumer point of view is seen to be the carton, while a resemblance to a can would be more beneficial in suggesting no hint of a taste of cardboard, and also enjoy the halo effect of general acceptance of beer in cans. What is the volume of canned and bottled beer sales in Unteland? A call to the National Federation of Unteland Brewers establishes the volume and the rate of growth for cans and bottles. The analyst uses the data supplied for the past five years to project growth (see page 139) and tests the industry forecast against that which is suggested by trend-projection. The fact that sales are very seasonal is noted, but there is a second high season at Christmas that is not enjoyed by fruit juice or milk. This will be of benefit to Untel-Pak.

Now the analyst and the PM look at the problem of possible consumer acceptance of the product. The analyst is insistent that only a test with the actual product versus other packaging will give results in which it is possible to have any confidence. He would like to have a proper store test at a realistic price, but the cost of arranging this is prohibitive, equipment leased from the USA being needed. The question of how to carry out the consumer research is left unsolved for the present as the analyst begins the industrial research stage (see p. 84). If brewers are interested in the new product, they will have suggestions on how to conduct the consumer research. The analyst writes **draft terms of reference** for the industrial market research (see p. 37), which follows the broad pattern laid out below.

Industrial Market Research

Like Germany and the United States, Unteland has many brewers, from mammoths down to one-county producers. Carbonated soft drinks are, however, highly concentrated in the hands of only seven companies. Working on the minimum rule of thumb of at least 25 interviews (see p. 81), the analyst decides to see the top ten brewers, all the seven soft-drink bottlers, and finish off with eight small brewers chosen at random. This plan is agreed with the PM. He sees smaller companies first and works up to the largest companies. With only one exception, they want no new packaging for beer.

The brewers are indeed extremely conservative. They supply some data on the cost of bottling and canning beer, which allow the analyst to sharpen up the picture of competition between the different sorts of packaging. The relative size of the different brewers is established, and everything needed for directing the sales effort to the right customers is obtained in the industrial research. One brewer is very helpful with data on filling rates, and this data is put into the competitive picture.

But at the end of the day, the brewers believe, it is the taste of the beer that counts and the container will not sway consumers away from existing choices. There are no advantages in their making contracts to buy untried packaging. In fact, they believe that, given a choice, beer drinkers would opt for bottles or cans rather than New Packs. What if the New Pack were cheaper? It could be, of course, provided that all brewers convert to it, after which economies of scale will be significant. The answer is—there will be no such conversions unless the New Pack is the successful focus of competition between brewers. What sort of demonstration would impress the brewers? If there were a significant preference for the New Pack at a cost equal to that of a bottle, then the brewers might be willing to think again.

Registering the reactions of the brewers as negative, with the exception of the small Jungsla brewery, the analyst now directs his attention to the soft drinks industry. Smaller in potential than the giant Unteland brewing industry, it proves to be more open to the idea of new packaging. However, like the brewers, the bottlers explain that it is increasing their profits that is their main goal, and they like to see definite economies in using a product rather than problematic increases in market share. It appears that a discussion with teenagers (the group that leads carbonated soft drink consumption) would be useful to obtain some handle on how they talk and think about the new packaging. A discussion is held, and at the same time some artwork for very colourful New Packs is presented. The response is very encouraging.

Taking Stock

At this point, the PM and the analyst compare notes and evaluate progress to date. The PM accepts that the total ultimate market (see p. 23) for beer will be substitution for about half the cans sold. Cans have made only small progress over the past 30 years—the traditional bottle looks set to continue to dominate because of consumer inertia. If a New Pack can be made to look as much like a can as possible, this will aid sales. It might be worth testing such a product with a brewery at various prices to see what would be acceptable to the beer-drinking public. But total potential will probably not be large enough. The best potential is now seen to be in carbonated soft drinks. This is the market that must be explored. It could prove to be sufficient to justify the New Pack, always assuming that another packaging company decides to enter the market.

At this point Untel-Pak learn that Remplicase is also researching the market. The Untel-Pak analyst meets the Remplicase analyst at a professional conference, and some highly confusing information is given. Whatever the truth is, he decides, it is in neither company's interest to share it, so the information is ignored (see p. 56).

The entrepreneur and analyst now make an interim presentation (see p. 196) to management, summarising progress and further plans on one transparency. Copies of an interim report on the market for New Pack in Unteland are issued to back up the presentation (Table 14.1).

Management accepts the report on progress to date and advise the PM that his budget will be extended to $U50,000 to pay for all costs associated with research, even leasing New Pack equipment if that should be necessary. Feigning delight, the PM retires with the analyst to consider what can be done with such a low budget—he had hoped for more.

Budget Considerations

The low budget for market research and trials is a very common feature of commercial life, which has to be lived with. Consumer

Table 14.1 New Pack Programme Summary

Completed	Results	Outstanding questions	Action
Request to sales force for competitor info.	Remplicase is evaluating new pack	Will Remplicase invest?	Continue monitoring
Interviews with seven soft drink companies	Some prospects	Can sufficient volume be reached to offer economies?	Check USA consumer research and loop back
Interviews with 18 brewers	Poor prospects	Could it be focus of competition?	Liaise with Jungsla if soft drink usage flies
Three consumer discussions	Need can image for beer	Will it sell at lower prices?	Consumer market research—test price sensitivity versus can for beer
	Probably acceptable for carbonated soft drinks	What price will the user pay?	Consumer research

research will probably have to be bought in, so it is decided that the market research agencies approached will need to be informed of the budget restraints that apply. Accordingly the analyst approaches three agencies (see p. 213) and asks for their proposals against broadly indicated budget limits. The analyst learns something from each agency. Scrutins & Wavy, an old-established but small house, advises them that Untel-Pak is wasting its time unless it invites the soft-drink manufacturers to join the briefing because, in the end, the results must impress the soft-drink bottler, if the product is to be launched. It advises that Untel-Pak go back to the most friendly/most enterprising soft-drink manufacturer and try to interest them. Do not expect them to agree that any particular results will commit them to even being interested in New Pack, but agree that the results of the test should be quotable to others in the event of no contract being forthcoming at a certain date. The analyst explains that Untel-Pak only wants to launch New Pack if someone else does so, so this is ruled out as an approach.

In fact, Untel-Pak will have to rely on the expertise of Scrutins & Wavy (or whatever agency is chosen) in being capable of saying, 'New Pack will fly for soft drinks', without the benefit of the direct soft-drink manufacturers' yea or nay. Scrutins & Wavy stress that they can do this, and advise that they have had three of the top soft-drink manufacturers as past clients. A method of soft-drink assessment they have employed has used a particular youth club, and they are sure that at least one of the bottlers will respect their results if it should ever prove to be necessary to quote them, because someone else had entered the market. Why not save money, anyway, if Untel-Pak will only enter the market in second place? What is the logic in all this? The analyst replies that the price to be charged for the package to the bottler is crucial. But surely, the agency says, that price will be defined by the competition? Yes, but the only way of knowing what the competitor will charge will be to assume that he also is intelligent and will find out what the market will bear. Untel-Pak needs the data to work out if the enterprise will be profitable.

The second agency visited, Transnational Interpond, stresses the need for a proper store-test over at least 13 weeks. It has facilities to do this in a provincial city where results can be compared with a matching control store, can advise on how many samples will be required, and has good experience of translating the results into sales forecasts. The New Pack must contain a well known soft drink such as Gran Cola, and must be sold next to cans or bottles of Gran Cola. The analyst explains that Untel-Pak does not want to approach the soft-drink manufacturer. Transnational Interpond are polite but firm: unless Untel-Pak uses real recognisable products, they say, they are wasting their time, and so the agency refuses to quote.

Finally, they go to the famous consultant Brendonk Mory. He listens to all the problems, and promises to provide a documented 'opinion' (rather like a legal opinion) on whether the product will be successful, based on 30 years of evaluating packaging and extensive experience of the United States. Here at least is a definite answer to Untel-Pak's problem.

Appraisal of Proposals

Written proposals are received from the three agencies consulted. The content is summarised in Table 14.2.

The analyst discusses these findings with the PM, who rejects the Brendonk Mory approach at once; any experience Mory has cannot be superior to the collective experience of the packaging industry, in which one thing is known—it is the customer that counts. If you took the New Pack to Gran Cola and said, 'Brendonk Mory says it's going to be a winner', they would ask you 'How much did that opinion cost?'

Thinking about the advice from Transnational Interpond, the PM has to admit the sense of the agency's argument. Clearly, it will not be possible to be second in the market after all—Untel-Pak should either go for pioneering the pack or hold back from any research at all. In the

Table 14.2. Competing Proposals for New Pack Research

Agency	Method	Reputation/ experience	Cost ($U)	Special factors
Scrutins & Wavy	Youth-club bar	Top three bottlers: competent	13,000	Proposal requires creating a spoof soft drink for tests
Transnational Interpond	Store test	High reputation, very wide expertise	15,000	No quote: reject spoof soft drink approach. Suggest revise strategy
Brendonk Mory	Opinion	Very wide	16,000	Solves problems of spoof drinks

latter case it will need to simply to follow the price leadership of the first entrant, but there will be no way of predicting whether that will mean profit or loss because it will not know what price will be asked. It has to be mentioned that Unteland has a history of the purchase of new equipment that never recovers its cost, because of the pricing policy of new entrants, hoping (without success) to freeze out followers. Transnational Interpond suggests that there is nothing to say that this practice will stop. Of course, it might be possible to arrange something with a soft-drink producer by which they test-market the New Pack together. But if, afterwards, Untel-Pak said it was not going to sell the product even though it looked as if it would be successful, there would be very bad feeling—not something Untel-Pak would permit.

So the PM goes back to the managing director and explains why he thinks that a following strategy is impossible. He is heard kindly and, after much argument, it is agreed that pioneering looks necessary. However, only successful pioneering will be tolerated, so look out! It should be noted here that each company's basic strategy could affect the progress of the new product. If one particular company regards itself as a leader in innovation, it might well go hell for leather for launching the New Pack, and this would be predictable.

The PM's air fare is paid so that he can look at the progress of the New Pack at first hand in the USA, but a skiing accident causes the task to be shifted to the analyst.

The US Market

Preparing almost as if for export market research (see p. 126), the analyst draws up an interview list based on the clients claimed by the

New Pack equipment producers. The results are encouraging but inconclusive: New Pack is the focus of competition at four small soft-drink companies, but the companies claim to be picking up market share selling at prices equal to the large brands, rather than at prices above it. Interestingly, one is a fruit-juice manufacturer using New Pack to diversify into carbonated drinks. It is difficult to translate all this into the Unteland situation, where all the brands' shares are of much the same size, and the New Pack would need to be offered at a higher price to retain margins. Consumer enthusiasm for the pack in the USA is mixed—it has become a new sort of missile to join the gallery of soft tomatoes and eggs thrown at public meetings. But at the New Pack plant, it is clear that the company producing the manufacturing equipment for the New Pack has many orders and will not be able to deliver equipment within a year. The sales manager says that he cannot guarantee to let Untel-Pak know if anyone else decides to invest in the $U1,300,000 New Pack equipment.

The Market Research Decision

One of the carbonated soft-drink manufacturers approached by Untel-Pak proves to be interested in market research. Spin! Co. will not make any commitment to action on the result of research, but has experience of assessing new products. Spin! Co. is interested in running the New Pack through the same research routine. If 30 per cent of those sampled in three areas normally surveyed by Spin! Co. (see p. 111) state that they will definitely purchase Spin! in the New Pack, that will be an adequate level to justify a market test, based on Spin! Co.'s experience of many similar tests. The test is conducted with 200 specially fitted packs, using Transpond International, and the New Pack is poorly received. The conclusion is reached that the new product is not likely to be a good investment for carbonated drinks by either Spin! Co. or Untel-Pak at the moment.

Appraisal of Marketing Research Carried Out

The result of all the effort for the New Pack has been a sudden collapse of its prospects because of one test. Is this good research? In one sense, no. A proper test in a supermarket over a reasonable period of time would make prospects much clearer, and there might be a chance for consumers to get used to the pack and make repeat purchases. But the main point about research is to reduce the risk of losing money. Unless the product is remarkable, a great deal of risk must attach to it. It is the company that markets what is contained in the packaging that must decide whether New Pack is so remarkably attractive to the consumer that it should be purchased. Spin! Co. has now answered that question definitively in the negative. Company strategies are illustrated in Table 14.3.

Table 14.3. Strategies of Companies Involved in the New Pack Decision

Product	Sold by	Suitable for	Strategy with New Pack
Plant for manufacturing the New Pack	New Pack Inc., USA	Carbonated and still drinks of all types (beer, coke, juices)	Capacity confined: sell at price to give delivery in two years
Cartons	Untel-Pak, Remplicase, Several others	Still beverages only	Extend customer base by buying New Pack machinery if investment can pay off
Bottle manufacturers	Eight companies	Mainly carbonated beverages, beer	Resistance: counter-arguments
Can manufacturers	Three companies	Mainly carbonated beverages, beer	Resistance: counter-arguments
Fruit juice manufacturers	Many companies	—	Examine New Pack for any cost or competitive advantages
Carbonated soft-drink manufacturers	Seven equal-sized companies	—	Examine New Pack for any cost or competitive advantages

So the strategy is left on 'Hold', i.e., if another company enters the market, Untel-Pak may follow. The analyst is fairly happy with this, because he completely understands the strategy. Intelligence from the sales force and the market-place is maintained at a steady level, seeking any information available on competitors' activities with the product. Remplicase, for example, after experiments with Gran Cola, retreats into silence on its plans, which may mean that the New Pack machinery is being purchased or may not. Some discreet questioning establishes that the likelihood of a launch is low.

Meanwhile, the American market is watched carefully, with occasional phone calls and despatches of information on the European market to the contacts established there, including New Pack Inc. Much market analysis and development work is like this in commerce, with re-examinations of the prospects for particular products as the market-place changes, e.g. competitive products change in price, the leading national market gives signals that other national markets are open, consumer disposable income increases, there is a change in the public's attitude, and so on. Every strategy and every piece of work will be different, because the motivation of demand, the forces of competition and the logic of each product will always be different. The New Pack example, which is roughly based on reality, is an example of the normal cul-de-sacs and false starts of product development.

Common Elements in Strategy/Analysis Interface

The checklist below shows the way that market strategy and market analysis work together.

PRODUCT STRATEGY CHECKLIST

Place in overall strategy
How does this product or group of products relate to the total company strategy?

Is there an adequate portfolio of products/new products of which this product is a member?

Market definition and size
How is the product's market defined by area and product functions? What is the current size of the available market and the market to be served?

Segmentation
How is the market best segmented for strategic purposes? By categories of buyers/end-users, geographical areas; by purchasing power/by general or special needs served; by motivation to purchase; by parameters of choice; by distribution outlets, including captive use?

Technology
How will technology change and what effects will this have on the prices paid for the product and the structure of supply and demand?

Market forecast
Three scenarios—low, central and high—for market growth by segment.

Competitive analysis
What is the place of the company in the market? What is its market share, strengths and weaknesses?

What scope exists to increase its market share?

What is the competitive environment? Is the market easy to enter, how significant are technical standards and reputation, how vulnerable is the market to price competition?

Who are the competitors, what are their strengths and weaknesses?

What will be the reaction of competitors to the new product? What strategic options are open to them?

What is the five- and ten-year competitive scenario in terms of the regulatory and economic background and competitive activity?

The new product	How should the new product or product group be positioned in the market in terms of technical characteristics, price and segments addressed? What are the requirements for success, and how can the company ensure that it has them?
Resources required	What resources are required to launch the new product? What particular resources are required for market analysis/research?
Strategy recommended	What alternatives exist? What choice is recommended among them? What critical risks exist? Does a fail-safe strategy exist?
	Actions recommended, expected results.

This checklist tries to cover all the main elements of a product strategy and should be regarded as a sort of aide-memoire. All the topics listed will come out, in some sort of order, if two or three managers in the company sit down to talk about strategy. All the elements will be known to the whole management team, and there will be complete clarity with regard to the future strategy. There is absolutely no point in writing a document about the strategy in such a case—in fact, it would represent a bad personal strategy. But in many large, technologically complicated, successful companies, the sheer volume of information and the number of alternatives canvassed will make an analysis worthwhile.

Decisions are always about alternatives, and the job of the strategic analyst is to show what the alternatives may be, or if they are non-existent. The more imagination the analyst has, in thinking of ways of coping with the challenge of the market-place, the better he will be at doing his job. Marketing should ideally serve the task of testing hypotheses about the alternative ways that the company seeks to increase sales by offering some particular product or service. The good analyst and market researcher can be inventive, not only in finding rapid ways of testing the hypothesis, but also in putting forward ideas to be tested.

Throughout this book the point has been made again and again that analysis is a service to the entrepreneur. Marketing analysis belongs to the descriptive sciences, but it must get as close to being prescriptive as possible. Certain conclusions follow from these views about the career of the analyst. First, he or she has no place in the static or unsuccessful company. Secondly, he or she should never hesitate to make the recommendations that follow from a thorough examination of the market-place. Thirdly, most career development moves from low responsibility and low comprehension of the market towards high responsibility decisions and a greater understanding of the market-place. The world of commerce is not academic. When you enter it, you too will want to be an entrepreneur.

Exercises

1. A new business school, open to graduates without business experience and to persons with at least two years in commerce, is to be set up in Newcastle-on-Tyne. The board of the new enterprise is anxious that the school should exploit some gap in the market for business schools, and talks about finding a 'special market niche' for it. The principal is invited to outline his strategy for the school, and is informed that the board will finance research up to a reasonable sum on any information he needs to complete the strategy. Present his draft strategy with any associated marketing research requirement judged to exist.

2. Coilback Co., a supplier of a plastic compound to over 80 customers, experiences a loss of its larger customers when they reach over 20 tonnes usage per annum, as the customers change to own production. Departure of larger customers takes place irregularly, in economic upturns and is not fully compensated by new entrants to the market. Coilback Co. is backed up by the large funds of its father company Jobsson, which has an excellent profit record. What strategy is advisable for Coilback?

3. Jean Melliau has established a business managing the advertising and promotional contracts for a number of professional sportsmen, including such items as an agreement to wear hats in public by Jos Stallard, the professional boxer (negotiated with the Unteland Hat Promotion Council), another for a ballet dancer for television advertising, and so on. Jean Melliau is afraid both of being overstretched and of drifting downwards (as his clients age) towards an ultimate inability to earn promotional money. He decides to devise a strategy that will be used as a guideline for the business and will aid in impressing the bank when any loans may need to be negotiated. Suggest a strategy.

4. An entrepreneur wishes to introduce a new retail chain that is to imitate the merchandising of chains such as Mothercare, Habitat, Next or even older established retail chains, in any country in Europe. Write a strategy for this 'look-alike', 'me-too' retailer.

5. An erstwhile successful supplier of jeans has already had a strategy of diversification into a wide number of enterprises associated with leisure, mainly in tourism, holiday camps, sailboards, dinghies and camping equipment. The diversified activities now account for 15 per cent of sales and 8 per cent of assets. As a result of the loss of profits in jeans, most of these newer assets are now to be sold. In the course of a boardroom meeting, the managing director claims that these sales are a vindication of the previous acquisition strategy. What could his argument be? Is it valid?

6. A manufacturer of filing cabinets has had his attention drawn to the threat of computerised file retrieval systems in the 'paperless office of the future'. Sales have declined recently, but this may be due to loss of market share or a general business downturn. He asks his analyst to outline a plan for inexpensive research to settle whether there is any threat to the existing business, and develop appropriate strategies. What strategy and plan for research should be suggested?

Statistical Workshop A
Seasonal Adjustment

This section shows four methods of calculating seasonal effects and makes recommendations for their use. The methods are the following:

1. **Percent of seasonal average.** For checking if sales are on target during the year. Markets subject to little fluctuation.
2. **Relative percent.** When the analyst requires 'quick-and-dirty' rather than fine-mesh calculation.
3. **Trend adjusted relative percent.** For analysing the underlying trends in many years.
4. **Ratio to moving average** (XII). Markets subject to significant fluctuations and/or with irregular seasonal patterns. Rapidly growing markets.

The raw data in Table A.1 is used to illustrate the seasonal adjustment calculations.

Table A.1. Monthly Household Consumption of Electricity (million kwh) in Unteland (Raw Data)

	1985	1986	1987	1988
Jan.	150	196	239	286
Feb.	142	184	224	266
Mar.	140	179	219	259
Apr.	122	157	191	225
May	116	149	181	217
June	89	115	140	166
July	80	104	126	152
Aug.	82	107	131	156
Sept.	128	165	200	239
Oct.	136	174	213	252
Nov.	137	176	214	256
Dec.	166	214	262	310
Total	1,488	1,920	2,340	2,784
Average	124	160	195	232

Percent of Seasonal Average Method (PSAM)

This method assumes that the values for different months in a year would be the same if there were no seasonal pattern. It calculates the seasonal indices by dividing each value in the series by the seasonal average of the year. The ratios corresponding to the same period in each season are then averaged over all seasons, to arrive at a final seasonal factor for that period. For example, in Table A.1 the seasonal averages for 1985, 1986, 1987 and 1988 are respectively 124, 160, 195 and 232. The January ratios for the same years are therefore,

$$\frac{150}{1.24} = 120.97 \qquad \frac{196}{1.6} = 122.50 \qquad \frac{239}{1.95} = 122.56 \qquad \frac{286}{2.32} = 123.28$$

The final seasonal factor for January is thus the average of all January's ratios (Table A.2),

$$\frac{120.97 + 122.50 + 122.56 + 123.28}{4} = 122.33$$

Table A.2. Worksheet of Seasonal Factors Calculated by PSAM

| | Percent of seasonal average | | | | Final seasonal factors |
	1985	1986	1987	1988	
Jan.	120.97	122.50	122.56	123.28	122.33
Feb.	114.52	115.00	114.87	114.66	114.76
Mar.	112.90	111.87	112.31	111.64	112.18
Apr.	98.39	98.12	97.95	96.98	97.86
May	93.55	93.13	92.82	93.53	93.25
June	71.77	71.88	71.79	71.55	71.75
July	65.42	65.00	64.62	65.52	64.92
Aug.	66.13	66.88	67.18	67.24	66.86
Sept.	103.23	103.12	102.56	103.02	102.98
Oct.	109.68	108.75	109.23	108.62	109.07
Nov.	110.48	110.00	109.74	110.34	110.14
Dec.	133.87	133.75	134.36	133.62	133.90
	1,200	1,200	1,200	1,200	1,200

Rounding errors cause the sums to differ by negligible fractions from 1,200.

Relative Percent Method (RPM)

This is similar to the Percent of Seasonal Average Method, but uses the overall average instead of the seasonal average in calculating each seasonal factor. For example, in Table A.1, the overall average is 177.75

$$\frac{(124 + 160 + 195 + 232)}{4}$$

In Table A.3 the January ratios for 1985 to 1988 are 84.39, 110.27, 134.46 and 160.90 (each value of January is divided by 1.7775). The average of 84.39, 110.27, 134.46 and 160.90 is the final seasonal factor for January, which equals 122.50.

Table A.3. Worksheet of Seasonal Factors Calculated by RPM

| | Percent relative to the overall average | | | | Final seasonal factors |
	1985	1986	1987	1988	
Jan.	84.39	110.27	134.46	160.90	122.50
Feb.	79.89	103.52	126.02	149.65	114.77
Mar.	78.76	100.70	123.21	145.71	112.10
Apr.	68.64	88.33	107.45	126.58	97.75
May	65.26	83.83	101.83	122.08	93.25
June	60.07	64.70	78.76	93.39	71.73
July	45.01	58.51	70.88	85.51	64.98
Aug.	46.13	60.20	73.70	87.76	66.95
Sept.	72.01	92.83	112.52	134.46	102.95
Oct.	76.51	97.89	119.83	141.77	109.00
Nov.	77.07	99.01	120.39	144.02	110.12
Dec.	93.39	120.39	147.40	174.40	133.90
	837.13	1,080.17	1,316.46	1,566.24	1,200

The seasonal factors in this case are very close to that obtained by the Percent of Seasonal Average Method. It is worth noting that in a strictly uniform seasonal series, the two methods will give the same seasonal factors.

Trend Adjusted Relative Percent Method (TARM)

This method calculates the **long-term linear trend** as a first step and removes it from the data. Having done this, it then uses the Relative Percent Method in calculating the seasonal factors. The trend equation for the annual data of household consumption of electricity in Table A.1 is calculated as follows

Year	X	Y	XY	X^2
1985	0	1,488	0	0
1986	1	1,920	1,920	1
1987	2	2,340	4,680	4
1988	3	2,784	8,352	9
Totals	$\Sigma X = 6$	$\Sigma Y = 8532$	$\Sigma XY = 14952$	$\Sigma X^2 = 14$

$$\overline{X} = \frac{\Sigma X}{n} = \frac{6}{4} = 1.5 \qquad \overline{Y} = \frac{\Sigma Y}{n} = \frac{8532}{4} = 2133$$

$$b = \frac{\Sigma XY - n\overline{X}.\overline{Y}}{\Sigma X^2 - n\overline{X}^2} = \frac{14,952 - 4(1.5)\,(2133)}{14 - 4(1.5)^2} = \frac{2154}{5} = 430.8$$

$$a = \overline{Y} - b\overline{X} = 2133 - 430.8\,(1.5) = 1486.8$$

Therefore $Y_{(\text{annual})} = a + bX = 1486.8 + 430.8X$

The modified equation for projecting monthly trend values for which the base month is January 1985 is obtained as follows (see p. 254 for stepping down the annual trend equation to the monthly trend equation):

$$Y_{(\text{monthly})} = \frac{a}{12} - (5.5)\frac{(b)}{(144)} + \frac{b}{144}.X$$

$$= \frac{1486.8}{12} - 5.5\,\frac{(430.8)}{144} + \frac{430.8\,X}{144} = 107.4\dot{4}6 + 2.992X$$

Table A.4 presents the monthly trend values for January 1985 to December 1988 derived from the above equation. The column entitled *Raw/trend* is the trend-adjusted raw data obtained by dividing the raw data by the trend and multiplying by 100.

Table A.5 completes the calculation of the seasonal factors. The overall average of the trend-adjusted data is calculated,

$$\frac{1,210.56 + 1,207.38 + 1,119.55 + 1,204.79}{4 \times 12} = 100.464$$

The monthly trend-adjusted values of Table A.4 are then divided by the overall average of 100.464 and are shown in Table A.5. The resulting seasonal factors are obtained by averaging all the values for a particular month over the 4 years.

Ratio to Moving Average Method (RMAM)/XII

The ratio to moving average method uses various moving average techniques to smooth the data before calculating seasonality. The

Table A.4. Worksheet of Seasonal Factors by TARM (Part 1)

Date	Time (X)	Raw data	Trend value	Raw/ trend	Date	Time (X)	Raw data	Trend value	Raw/ trend
1985					*1987*				
Jan.	0	150	107.44	130.61	Jan.	24	239	179.25	133.33
Feb.	1	142	110.44	128.58	Feb.	25	224	182.25	122.91
Mar.	2	140	113.43	123.42	Mar.	26	219	185.24	118.23
Apr.	3	122	116.42	104.79	Apr.	27	191	188.23	101.47
May	4	116	119.41	97.14	May	28	181	191.22	94.66
June	5	89	122.41	72.71	June	29	140	194.21	72.09
July	6	80	125.40	63.80	July	30	126	197.21	63.89
Aug.	7	82	128.39	63.87	Aug.	31	131	200.20	65.43
Sept.	8	128	131.38	97.43	Sept.	32	200	203.19	98.43
Oct.	9	136	134.37	101.21	Oct.	33	213	206.18	103.31
Nov.	10	137	137.37	99.73	Nov.	34	214	209.17	102.31
Dec.	11	166	140.36	118.27	Dec.	35	262	212.27	123.49
Total		1,488		1,210.56			2,340		1,199.55
1986					*1988*				
Jan.	12	196	143.35	136.73	Jan.	36	286	215.16	132.92
Feb.	13	184	146.34	125.73	Feb.	37	266	218.15	121.93
Mar.	14	179	149.33	119.87	Mar.	38	259	221.14	117.12
Apr.	15	157	152.33	103.07	Apr.	39	225	224.13	100.39
May	16	149	155.32	95.93	May	40	217	227.13	95.54
June	17	115	158.31	72.64	June	41	166	230.12	72.14
July	18	104	161.30	64.48	July	42	152	233.11	65.21
Aug.	19	107	164.29	65.13	Aug.	43	156	236.10	66.07
Sept.	20	165	167.29	98.63	Sept.	44	239	239.09	99.96
Oct.	21	174	170.28	102.18	Oct.	45	252	242.09	104.09
Nov.	22	176	173.27	101.58	Nov.	46	256	245.08	104.46
Dec.	23	214	176.26	121.41	Dec.	47	310	248.07	124.96
Total		1,920		1,207.38			2,784		1,204.79

resultant smoothed data represent the trend cycle and are removed from the raw data before calculating the seasonal factors.

This type of exercise, like the Trend Adjusted Relative Method, shows up the long-term trend when a series is seasonally adjusted. The **X11 (X eleven) method** developed by the US Bureau of the Census includes further refinements in the ratio to moving average technique.

Table A.6 is concerned with the first step in the ratio to moving average method, that of computing the ratio of each monthly value to the 12-month moving average centred at that month. The 12-month moving totals are centred between the sixth and seventh month of the moving period. For example, the first listed total of 1488 is the total of

Table A.5. Percent Relative to the Overall Average of the Trend-Adjusted Data (Part 2)

	1985	1986	1987	1988	Seasonal factors
Jan.	138.96	136.10	132.71	132.30	135.01
Feb.	127.99	125.15	122.34	121.37	124.21
Mar.	122.85	119.32	117.68	116.58	119.10
Apr.	104.30	102.59	101.00	99.93	101.95
May	96.69	95.49	94.22	95.10	95.37
June	72.37	72.30	71.76	71.80	72.06
July	63.51	64.18	63.59	64.91	64.05
Aug.	63.58	64.83	65.13	65.76	64.82
Sept.	96.98	98.17	97.98	99.50	98.16
Oct.	100.74	101.71	102.83	103.61	102.22
Nov.	99.27	101.11	101.84	103.98	101.55
Dec.	117.72	120.85	122.92	124.38	121.47
					1,200 (rounded)

January to December 1985 values and is centred between June and July.

Because it is more convenient for the moving average to be centred on a month instead of half-way between two months, the two-year centred moving total is calculated. Thus, the first listed total of 3022 includes the January to December 1985 total of 1488 plus the February 1985 to January 1986 total of 1534.

The 12-month centred moving average in the fifth column is simply the two-year centred moving total divided by 24.

Finally, the ratio to moving average in the last column of Table A.6 is the ratio of column 2 (monthly raw value) to the 12-month centred moving average for that month. The ratio is presented as a percentage.

Table A.7 shows the next step in determining the seasonal indices. The modified mean for each month is the mean of the ratios to moving average for each month after elimination of the highest and lowest values. The modified means are then divided by the sum of monthly means (1,198.22) and multiplied by 1,200 to obtain the final seasonal factors.

The seasonal factors by the four methods are shown in comparison in Table A.8. It is worthwhile noting that the seasonal factors for the six first months are lower in the first two types (PSAM and RPM) than in the last two (TARM and RMAM) and it is quite the reverse for the six last months. This is due to the removal of the trend in TARM and RMAM prior to calculating the seasonal factors.

Table A.6. Worksheet for Computing the Seasonal Factors by RMAM (Part 1)

Date	Raw data	Twelve-month centred moving total	Two-year centred moving total	Twelve-month centred moving average	Ratio to moving average (%)
85 Jan.	150				
Feb.	142				
Mar.	140				
Apr.	122				
May	116				
June	89	1,488			
July	80	1,534	3,022	125.92	63.53
Aug.	82	1,576	3,110	129.58	63.28
Sept.	128	1,615	3,191	132.96	96.27
Oct.	136	1,650	3,265	136.04	99.97
Nov.	137	1,683	3,333	138.87	98.65
Dec.	166	1,709	3,392	141.33	117.45

Date	Raw data	Twelve-month centred moving total	Two-year centred moving total	Twelve-month centred moving average	Ratio to moving average (%)
87 Jan.	239	2,156	4,290	178.75	133.71
Feb.	224	2,180	4,336	180.67	123.99
Mar.	219	2,215	4,395	183.12	119.59
Apr.	191	2,254	4,469	186.21	102.57
May	181	2,292	4,546	189.42	95.56
June	140	2,340	4,632	193.00	72.54
July	126	2,387	4,727	196.96	63.97
Aug.	131	2,429	4,816	200.67	65.28
Sept.	200	2,469	4,898	204.08	98.00
Oct.	213	2,503	4,972	207.17	102.82
Nov.	214	2,539	5,042	210.08	101.86
Dec.	262	2,565	5,104	212.67	123.20

continued

Date	Raw data	Twelve-month centred moving total	Two-year centred moving total	Twelve-month centred moving average	Ratio to moving average (%)
86 Jan.	196	1,733	3,442	143.42	136.66
Feb.	184	1,758	3,491	145.46	126.50
Mar.	179	1,795	3,553	148.04	120.91
Apr.	159	1,833	3,628	151.17	105.18
May	149	1,872	3,705	154.37	96.52
June	115	1,920	3,792	158.00	72.78
July	104	1,963	3,883	161.79	64.28
Aug.	107	2,003	3,966	165.3	64.75
Sept.	165	2,043	4,046	168.58	97.87
Oct.	174	2,077	4,120	171.67	101.36
Nov.	176	2,109	4,186	174.42	100.91
Dec.	214	2,134	4,243	176.79	121.05

Date	Raw date	Twelve-month centred moving total	Two-year centred moving total	Twelve-month centred moving average	Ratio to moving average (%)
88 Jan.	286	2,591	5,156	214.83	133.13
Feb.	266	2,616	5,207	216.96	122.60
Mar.	259	2,655	5,271	219.62	117.93
Apr.	225	2,694	5,349	222.87	100.95
May	217	2,736	5,430	226.25	95.91
June	166	2,784	5,520	230.00	72.17
July	152				
Aug.	156				
Sept.	239				
Oct.	252				
Nov.	256				
Dec.	310				

Table A.7. Calculation of Seasonal Factors by the RMAM (Part 2)

	1985	1986	1987	1988	Modified mean	Seasonal factors
Jan.		136.66	133.71	133.13	133.71	133.91
Feb.		126.50	123.99	122.60	123.99	124.17
Mar.		120.91	119.59	117.93	119.59	119.77
Apr.		105.18	102.57	100.95	102.57	102.72
May		96.52	95.56	95.91	95.91	96.05
June		72.78	72.54	72.17	72.54	72.65
July	63.53	64.28	63.97		63.97	64.06
Aug.	63.28	64.75	65.28		64.75	64.85
Sept.	96.27	97.87	98.00		97.87	98.02
Oct.	99.97	101.36	102.82		101.91	101.51
Nov.	98.65	100.91	101.86		100.91	101.06
Dec.	117.45	121.05	123.20		121.05	121.23
					1,198.22*	1,200

* *Note:* This total has been calculated without rounding to the two decimal points shown, and is thus slightly different from the total of the twelve numbers shown (which make 1,198.77).

Table A.8. Seasonal Factors of the Monthly Consumption of Electricity Obtained by the Four Types

	Percent seasonal (PSAM)	Relative (RPM)	Trend (TARM)	Ratio to moving average (RMAM)
Jan.	122.33	122.50	134.04	133.91
Feb.	114.76	114.77	123.48	124.17
Mar.	112.18	112.10	118.58	119.77
Apr.	97.86	97.75	101.97	102.72
May	93.25	93.25	95.23	96.05
June	71.75	71.73	72.04	72.65
July	64.92	64.98	64.11	64.06
Aug.	66.86	66.95	64.98	64.85
Sept.	102.98	102.95	98.49	98.02
Oct.	109.07	109.00	102.68	101.51
Nov.	110.14	110.12	102.12	101.06
Dec.	133.90	133.90	122.28	121.23
	1,200	1,200	1,200	1,200

Statistical Workshop B
Applying the Concepts of Time Series Analysis to Forecasts of National Car Sales, Using Long-term Data

This section summarises the methods of classical time series analysis as it examines data on car sales in Unteland, using,

(*a*) the trend,
(*b*) the cycle,
(*c*) seasonality.

as the means of understanding and forecasting sales.

Principles of Classical Time Series Analysis to be Applied

Sales of most products vary in a mainly systematic way. The most frequent pattern of sales results from three interacting systematic forces: the **trend**, the **cycle** and the **season**.

The *trend* is the basic long-term movement of the series which we understand in terms of a straight line or a gradual growth curve. It results from a growth in population, income, consumption per head, extension of market, or other basic characteristics of the market-place. Identifying the trend is essential to long-term forecasting.

The *cycle*, which causes the wavelike movement of sales, is the direct result of economic upturns or downturns. Isolation of this cyclical component can be useful in medium-range forecasting (over two to four years) and is still relevant for even short-term forecasting. Business cycles are irregular, both in amplitude and duration, which makes the cyclical part of the forecast the most difficult.

The *season* (or seasonal pattern) refers to a consistent pattern of sales movements within the year. Knowledge of the seasonal pattern is useful for short-term forecasting.

Besides these three dominant forces, sales can also reflect the effects of irregular factors, most of which will not be explicable. Among the irregular factors, however, there may be significant non-recurrent or erratic events, the most usual being a strike or the threat of a strike, and the forecaster must talk to someone with knowledge of the industry in order to isolate these particular incidents, which may otherwise obscure the effect of the more systematic forces.

The most common model use for classical time series analysis assumes that the cyclical (C) and seasonal effects (S) move proportionally with the trend level (T) of sales, and that a multiplicative relation best describes the series,

$$Y = T \times C \times S \times I.$$

T is expressed in absolute value while C, S and I (the irregular factor) are stated as percentages or indices.

The classical approach to time series analysis is to identify each of these components, which make up the general pattern of a series. Once identified, they can be used for forecasting quite straightforwardly. The procedure consists first in removing the seasonal effect from the raw data by an appropriate seasonal adjustment method—**X11** (the X-eleven method) is so far the most appropriate for dealing with series with complex patterns. The resulting data, called the seasonally adjusted or deseasonalised data, are then treated by a moving average process to smooth out the irregular effect. The resulting seasonally adjusted and smoothed series describes the underlying movement of the data and reflects the effects of the trend and the cycle, plus major specific causative events, if any, which can be explained. This underlying movement is often called the trend cycle. In X11 the moving average used to estimate the trend cycle component is selected on the basis of the size of irregular variations in the data relative to the size of long-term systematic variations. The trend component can also be obtained by using a linear time regression on the data (generally a least-squares calculation using a calculator) to determine the trend values. Let us now see an application of the procedure to a concrete case of forecasting.

Analysing the Factory Car Sales Data

The plot of annual domestic sales of new passenger cars in Unteland for the 15-year period from 1984 to 1998 is given in Fig. 9.6. Although annual sales are on an uprising trend, there are clear troughs in sales in 1987 and 1994 and peaks in 1986 and 1992 before the respective troughs.

Analysing the Trend

The long-term direction of the series can be determined by a regression trend line using annual data. The use of a trend line rather than any other trend curve for analysing the long-term direction of a series is generally due to the fact that growth in population, income and consumption per head is fairly regular over a long period of time. Straight lines are also easy to understand and project.

As previously explained (p. 250), the least-squares method is used here for determining the trend component. Table B.1 shows the annual car sales data plotted in Fig. 9.6 and includes all the calculations needed to determine the trend equation. This equation can be used as a starting point for forecasting. The slope of the equation indicates that, as a long-term trend, there has been an average increase of 84,528 units sales per year. The trend line is shown superimposed with the actual annual sales in Fig. 10.3.

Table B.1. Annual Factory Sales of New Passenger Cars in Unteland and the Trend Values (1984–98)

Year	Coded year (X)	Sales (000 units) (Y)	XY	X2
1984	1	1,341	1,341	1
1985	2	1,516	3,032	4
1986	3	1,561	4,683	9
1987	4	1,352	5,408	16
1988	5	1,424	7,120	25
1989	6	1,839	11,034	36
1990	7	2,106	14,742	49
1991	8	2,151	17,208	64
1992	9	2,143	19,287	81
1993	10	2,030	20,300	100
1994	11	1,692	18,612	121
1995	12	2,102	25,224	144
1996	13	2,315	30,095	169
1997	14	2,585	36,190	196
1998	15	2,664	39,960	225
Totals	120	28,821	25,436	1,240
Averages	8	1921.4	1695.7	

$$b = \frac{\sum XY - n\bar{X}\bar{Y}}{X^2 - n\bar{X}^2} = \frac{254,236 - 15\,(8)\,(1,921.4)}{1,240 - 15\,(8)^2} = 84.5286$$

$$\bar{X} = \frac{\sum X}{n} = \frac{120}{15} = 8 \qquad \bar{Y} = \frac{\sum Y}{n} = \frac{28,821}{15} = 1,921.4$$

$$a = \bar{Y} - b\bar{X} = 1921.4 - (84.5286)\,(8) = 1245.1714$$
$$Y = a + bX = 1245.1714 + 84.5286\,(X)$$

The data in Table B.1 are used to calculate the components of the equation for the trend line. This equation is $Y = a + bX$.

The components of the equation are shown below the table. The sign Σ means the sum of a number of observations, so it refers to the figure shown in the table above as 'Total'. A letter with a line over it, like $\overline{X}$, refers to the average (or mean), and so is found in the table where the averages are shown. There are 15 observations, so n (the number) equals 15. In these and other calculations multiplication signs are usually not shown, so that (4.2)(2) means 4.2 times 2, which equals 8.4.

Using the calculations, we go back to the data and derive the trend. For the first value we substitue in the equation $Y = a + bX$.

$$Y = 1,245.1714 + 84.5286 (X)$$

The first calculation refers to the first year, which was coded as 1. So we have to substitute 1 for X in the equation,

$$Y = 1,245.1714 + 84.5286 (1) = 1,329.7$$

The second value will be,

$$Y = 1,245.1714 + 84.5286 (2)$$

which equals $1,245.1714 + 169.0572 = 1,414.2286$.

The results are shown in Table B.2.

Table B.2. Calculated Trend of Sales

Year	Fitted trend values
1984	1,329.7
1985	1,414.2
1986	1,498.8
1987	1,583.3
1988	1,667.8
1989	1,752.3
1990	1,836.9
1991	1,921.4
1992	2,005.9
1993	2,090.5
1994	2,175.0
1995	2,259.5
1996	2,344.0
1997	2,428.6
1998	2,513.1

Applying Annual Trend Equation to Derive Monthly Trend Values

The trend equation calculated from the annual car sales data can be 'stepped down' to derive the monthly trend values. This can be done by first dividing the slope of the annual equation (b) by 144 and its intercept (a) by 12:

$$Y_{year} = a + bX_{year} => Y_{month} = \frac{a}{12} + \frac{b}{144} X_{month}$$

So the monthly equation of the car sales data becomes, after substituting the parameters a and b by their respective values given in the equation $Y = a + bX$ in Table B.1,

$$Y_{month} = \frac{1,245.1714}{12} + \frac{84.5286}{144} X_{month}$$

$$Y_{month} = 103.7643 + 0.5870 X_{month}$$

Since the equation $Y = a + bX$ in Table B.1 has its origin ($X = 0$) in the middle of 1983 (end June 1983), the derived equation just given also has the same origin. We have to shift forward the origin of the derived equation to the middle of December 1983 by adding to the intercept of the equation the amount of (0.5870×5.5 months), i.e.

$$Y_{month} = 103.7643 + (0.5870 \times 5.5) + 0.5870 X_{month} \quad \text{or}$$

$$Y_{month} = 106.9928 + 0.5870 X_{month}$$

This last equation now has its origin in the middle of December 1983. Substituting X by 1 for January 1984, 2 for February 1984 etc., we can calculate the montly trend values. These are shown in Table B.3, which gives the actual data of monthly car sales in Unteland during the whole period, and Table B.4, which presents the monthly trend values as derived from the equation above.

The trend equation obtained from directly using the monthly data would generate different trend values than those obtained from 'stepping down' the annual trend equation. Because it is more convenient to have the monthly trend values consistent with the yearly trend, it is recommended to use the procedure of 'stepping down' the annual trend equation to derive the monthly trend values.

Measuring Seasonal Pattern

As previously explained (p. 161), the ratio to moving average method

Table *B.3*. Monthly Factory Sales of New Passenger Cars in Unteland—Raw Data

	1984	1985	1986	1987	1988	1989	1990	1991	1992	1993	1994	1995	1996	1997	1998
Jan.	80	81	96	74	65	104	122	128	139	167	105	129	160	181	206
Feb.	102	111	123	97	101	132	153	166	160	193	124	153	195	210	205
Mar.	157	170	212	157	155	198	215	262	267	254	181	207	271	300	306
Apr.	152	179	161	143	167	196	240	237	201	234	191	238	256	260	271
May	121	143	207	133	158	182	194	220	233	216	190	203	228	250	243
June	126	134	132	128	114	165	214	218	224	199	147	199	210	238	272
July	122	122	115	101	119	168	208	209	171	166	154	176	163	221	216
Aug.	82	94	93	85	84	93	103	119	134	115	106	120	122	144	153
Sept.	108	127	123	107	116	149	158	168	151	137	133	186	190	193	211
Oct.	113	140	119	123	143	181	180	180	184	157	146	206	184	202	231
Nov.	91	115	99	104	109	141	165	144	154	122	118	150	182	190	195
Dec.	87	100	81	100	93	130	154	100	125	70	97	135	154	196	155
Total	1,341	1,516	1,561	1,352	1,424	1,839	2,106	2,151	2,143	2,030	1,692	2,102	2,315	2,585	2,664

Table B.4. Monthly Factory Sales of New Passenger Cars in Unteland—Trend Values

	1984	1985	1986	1987	1988	1989	1990	1991	1992	1993	1994	1995	1996	1997	1998
Jan.	107.6	114.6	121.7	128.7	135.8	142.8	149.8	156.9	163.9	171.0	178.6	185.1	192.1	199.2	206.2
Feb.	108.2	115.2	122.3	129.3	136.3	143.4	150.4	157.5	164.5	171.6	178.6	185.7	192.7	199.7	206.8
Mar.	108.8	115.8	122.8	129.9	136.9	144.0	151.0	158.1	165.1	172.1	179.2	186.2	193.3	200.3	207.4
Apr.	109.3	116.4	123.4	130.5	137.5	144.6	151.6	158.6	165.7	172.7	179.8	186.8	193.9	200.9	208.0
May	109.9	117.0	124.0	131.1	138.1	145.1	152.2	159.2	166.3	173.3	180.4	187.4	194.5	201.5	208.5
June	110.5	117.6	124.6	131.6	138.7	145.7	152.8	159.8	166.9	173.9	181.0	188.0	195.0	202.1	209.1
July	111.1	118.1	125.2	132.2	139.3	146.3	153.4	160.4	167.5	174.5	181.5	188.6	195.6	202.7	209.7
Aug.	111.7	118.7	125.8	132.8	139.9	146.9	154.0	161.0	168.0	175.1	182.1	189.2	196.2	203.3	210.3
Sept.	112.3	110.3	126.4	133.4	140.5	147.5	154.5	161.6	168.6	175.7	182.7	189.8	196.8	203.8	210.9
Oct.	112.9	119.9	127.0	134.0	141.0	148.1	155.1	162.2	169.2	176.3	183.3	190.3	197.4	204.4	211.5
Nov.	113.4	120.5	127.5	134.6	141.6	148.7	155.7	162.8	169.8	176.8	183.9	190.9	198.0	205.0	212.1
Dec.	114.0	121.1	128.1	135.2	142.2	149.3	156.3	163.3	170.4	177.4	184.5	191.5	198.6	205.6	212.7
Total	1,329.7	1,414.2	1,498.8	1,583.3	1,667.8	1,752.3	1,836.9	1,921.4	2,005.9	2,090.5	2,175.0	2,259.5	2,344.0	2,428.6	2,513.1

Note: Totals have been calculated to three decimal points, but compressed here to one decimal point. As a result the totals of January to December will differ from the (more accurate) total given, due to rounding errors.

is more appropriate for analysing the seasonal pattern of a series in which complex patterns of sales are in evidence. The seasonal factors of the car sales data shown in Table B.5 are obtained through the X11 computerised package, including further refinements of the basic ratio to moving average. From this table, we notice that the month with the highest positive seasonal influence is March, with car sales 40 per cent higher than the average typical month; the lowest negative seasonal influence occurs in August, with car sales only 70 per cent of the average month. Car sales are stronger in spring and early summer than in the rest of the year.

Table B.5. Monthly Factory Sales of New Passenger Cars in Unteland—Seasonal Factors by X11 for the 1984–98 Period

Period	Seasonal factors
Jan.	76.646
Feb.	93.513
Mar.	140.094
Apr.	132.292
May	120.712
June	113.596
July	101.070
Aug.	69.830
Sept.	93.411
Oct.	103.018
Nov.	84.752
Dec.	71.066

Applying Seasonal Factors to Deseasonalise Data

The process of removing the seasonal component from the data is called **seasonal adjustment**, or *deseasonalisation*. The monthly values of the raw (original) series are seasonally adjusted by dividing each monthly value by the corresponding seasonal factor for that month. The resulting seasonally adjusted series still contains the trend, cyclical and irregular components,

$$\frac{\text{Original data}}{\text{Seasonal}} = \frac{Y}{S} = \frac{T \times C \times S \times I}{S} = T \times C \times I$$

The usefulness of seasonal adjustment is evident when we compare the raw data in Table B.3 with the seasonally adjusted data in Table B.6. For instance, we can observe that actual car sales dropped from 216,000 units to 153,000 from July to August 1998. However, on a seasonally adjusted basis, car sales effectively increased from 213,700

Table B.6. Monthly Factory Sales of New Passenger Cars in Unteland—Seasonally Adjusted Values

	1984	1985	1986	1987	1988	1989	1990	1991	1992	1993	1994	1995	1996	1997	1998
Jan.	104.4	105.7	125.3	96.5	84.8	135.7	159.2	167.0	181.4	217.9	137.0	168.3	208.8	236.2	268.8
Feb.	109.1	118.7	131.5	103.7	108.0	141.2	163.6	177.5	171.1	206.4	132.6	163.6	208.5	224.6	219.2
Mar.	112.1	121.3	151.3	112.2	120.6	141.3	153.5	187.0	190.6	181.3	129.2	147.8	193.4	214.2	218.4
Apr.	114.9	135.3	121.7	108.1	126.2	148.2	181.4	179.1	151.9	176.9	144.4	179.9	193.5	196.5	204.8
May	100.2	118.5	171.5	110.2	130.9	150.8	160.7	182.3	193.0	178.9	157.4	168.2	188.9	207.1	201.3
June	110.9	118.0	116.2	112.7	100.4	145.3	188.4	191.9	197.2	175.2	129.4	175.2	184.9	209.5	239.4
July	120.7	120.7	113.8	99.9	117.7	166.2	205.8	206.8	169.2	164.2	152.4	174.1	161.3	218.7	213.7
Aug.	117.4	134.6	133.2	121.7	120.3	133.2	147.5	170.4	191.9	164.7	151.8	171.8	174.7	206.2	219.1
Sept.	115.6	136.0	131.7	114.5	124.2	159.5	169.1	179.9	161.7	146.7	142.4	199.1	203.4	206.6	225.9
Oct.	109.7	135.9	115.5	119.4	138.8	175.7	174.7	174.7	178.6	152.4	141.7	200.0	178.6	196.1	224.2
Nov.	107.4	135.7	116.8	122.7	128.6	166.4	194.7	169.9	181.7	143.9	139.2	177.0	214.7	224.2	230.1
Dec.	122.4	140.7	114.0	140.7	130.9	182.9	216.7	140.7	175.9	98.5	136.5	190.0	216.7	275.8	218.1

Fig. B.1. Monthly factory sales of new passenger cars in Unteland, 1984–98, with seasonally adjusted data and centred, four-months moving average to show underlying movement of car sales.

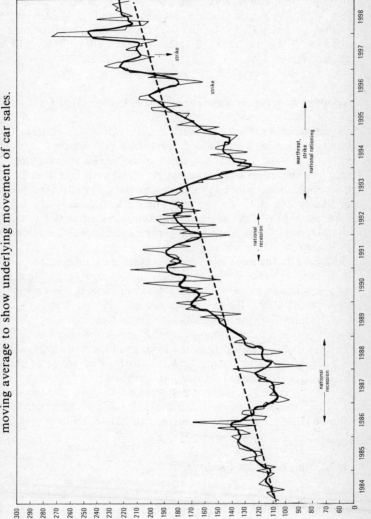

to 219,100 units. Thus, even though an actual decrease occurred, it was not as large a decrease as would be expected on average for August, reassuring us that the market is still going on growing.

Each monthly value of Table B.6 is calculated by dividing the corresponding monthly value in Table B.3 by the seasonal index for that month shown in Table B.5 and then multiplying by 100. For example, the adjusted value of 104.4 for January 1984 is obtained by dividing 80 (from Table B.3) by 76.646 (from Table B.5) and multiplying by 100.

Applying Moving Average Process to Deseasonalised Data

The deseasonalised car sales series, representing the influence of the trend, cyclical and irregular components, is smoothed through a moving average process to remove the irregular influence. The resulting **smoothed series** is called the **trend cycle** and describes that basic movement underlying the original data. Usually a three-, four- or five-month-moving average is applied to the seasonally adjusted data, according to the degree of volatility the data shows. In the X11 computerised package the trend cycle is determined through various sophisticated moving averages.

In this case the trend cycle of the car sales data has been obtained by using the centred four-month moving average of the seasonally adjusted data from Table B.6, and shown in Table B.7. It is also shown superimposed with the deseasonalised data in Fig. B.1.

Each four-month moving average value is located half-way between the second and third month of the moving period. For example, the first listed value of 110.12 is the average of the seasonally adjusted values from January to April 1984 in Table B.6 and is situated between February and March. The four-month moving average centred on a month is obtained by averaging two successive halfway values in table B.7. For example the 4-month moving value of 109.6 centred on March 1984 is obtained by averaging 110.12 and 109.08 in that Table.

Measuring Irregular Component

The irregular indices shown in Table B.9 are obtained by dividing the seasonally adjusted data (Table B.6) by the trend cycle data (Table B.8):

$$\frac{\text{Seasonally adjusted data}}{\text{Trend cycle}} = \frac{T \times C \times I}{T \times C} = I$$

Table B.7. Four-month Factory Sales of New Passenger Cars in Unteland—Smoothed Deseasonalised Data, using Four-month Moving Average of Seasonally Adjusted Data

	1984	1985	1986	1987	1988	1989	1990	1991	1992	1993	1994	1995	1996	1997	1998
Jan.		117.02	137.20	106.58	111.02	137.28	164.80	187.05	170.95	195.38	124.32	154.05	200.18	222.90	245.55
Feb.	110.12	120.25	132.45	105.10	107.40	141.60	164.42	177.65	173.75	195.62	135.80	164.90	201.05	217.85	227.80
Mar.	109.80	123.45	144.0	108.52	118.92	145.38	164.80	171.48	176.65	185.88	140.90	164.88	196.08	210.58	210.92
Apr.	109.52	123.28	140.18	110.78	117.02	146.40	171.0	185.08	183.18	178.08	140.10	167.78	190.18	206.80	215.98
May	111.68	123.12	130.80	107.72	118.80	152.62	181.08	190.02	177.82	173.80	145.90	174.35	182.15	207.95	214.80
June	112.30	122.95	133.68	111.13	117.30	148.88	175.60	187.85	187.82	170.75	147.75	172.32	177.45	210.38	218.38
July	116.15	127.32	123.72	112.20	115.65	151.05	177.70	187.25	180.0	162.70	144.0	180.05	181.08	210.25	224.52
Aug.	115.85	131.80	123.55	113.88	125.25	158.65	174.28	182.95	175.35	157.0	147.08	186.25	179.50	206.90	220.73
Sept.	112.52	135.55	124.30	119.58	129.98	158.70	171.50	173.72	178.48	151.92	143.78	186.98	192.85	208.28	224.82
Oct.	113.78	137.08	119.50	124.32	130.62	171.12	188.80	166.30	174.48	135.38	139.95	191.52	203.35	225.67	224.58
Nov.	111.30	134.40	110.70	116.90	133.50	171.05	188.27	166.68	188.52	132.95	146.42	193.95	211.55	241.22	
Dec.	113.55	133.30	107.75	114.05	134.10	168.02	188.98	165.78	195.48	128.0	151.90	196.08	223.05	247.0	

Table B.8. Centred Four-month Moving Average of Seasonally Adjusted Data

	1984	1985	1986	1987	1988	1989	1990	1991	1992	1993	1994	1995	1996	1997	1998
Jan.		115.3	135.2	107.2	112.5	135.7	166.4	188.0	168.4	195.4	126.2	153.0	198.1	223.0	246.3
Feb.		118.6	134.8	105.8	109.2	139.4	164.6	182.4	172.4	195.5	130.1	159.5	200.6	220.4	236.7
Mar.	109.6	121.8	138.2	106.8	113.2	143.5	164.6	179.6	175.2	190.7	138.4	164.9	198.6	214.2	219.4
Apr.	109.3	123.4	142.1	109.6	118.0	145.9	167.9	183.3	179.9	182.0	140.5	166.3	193.1	208.7	213.5
May	110.6	123.2	135.5	109.3	117.9	149.5	177.5	187.5	180.5	175.9	143.0	171.1	186.2	207.4	215.4
June	112.0	123.0	132.2	109.4	118.1	150.7	179.8	188.9	182.8	172.3	146.8	173.3	179.8	209.2	216.6
July	114.2	125.1	128.7	111.7	116.5	150.0	176.6	187.5	183.9	166.7	145.9	176.2	179.3	210.3	221.5
Aug.	116.0	129.6	123.6	113.0	126.6	154.8	176.0	185.1	177.7	159.8	145.5	183.1	180.3	208.6	222.6
Sept.	114.2	133.7	123.9	116.7	129.3	158.7	172.9	178.3	176.9	154.5	145.4	186.6	186.2	207.6	222.8
Oct.	113.2	136.3	121.9	122.0	132.1	164.9	180.1	170.0	176.5	143.6	141.9	189.2	198.1	217.0	224.7
Nov.	112.5	135.7	115.1	120.6	132.1	171.1	188.5	166.5	181.5	134.2	143.2	192.7	207.5	233.5	
Dec.	112.4	133.8	109.2	115.5	133.8	169.5	188.6	166.2	192.0	130.5	149.2	195.0	217.3	244.1	

Large variations (from 100) can generally be explained by knowledge of specific causative events. For example, the war threat of December 1993 resulted in a substantial reduction in car sales during this month. Strikes in October/November 1997 resulted in the drop of sales during these months and the settlement of these labour disputes was followed by an unusual increase in sales in December 1997 and January 1998.

The indices in Table B.9 are determined by dividing the values of Table B.6 (T × C × I) by the corresponding values in Table B.8. For example the index of 102.3 for March 1984 is obtained by dividing the March 1984 value of 112.1 in Table B.6 by the value of 109.6 corresponding to that month in Table B.8 and then multiplying by 100.

Measuring Cyclical Component

The trend cycle obtained by applying the moving average process to the deseasonalised data is then adjusted by the trend to isolate the cyclical influence,

$$\frac{\text{Trend cycle}}{\text{Trend}} = \frac{T \times C}{T} = C$$

This is done by dividing the values of Table B.8 (the trend cycle) by the values of Table B.4 (the trend).

The cyclical indices for car sales data are shown in Table B.10. In reviewing these indices, which should be looked at in conjunction with Fig. 10.3 we can observe that the years during which substantial negative influence associated with the cyclical component dominates are 1987 and 1994. The depressed level of 1987 coincides with a national recession, while the car sales in 1994 coincide both with the war threat and a national recession. The years during which positive cyclical influence is visible are 1990 to 1992, which followed recovery from the 1987–8 recession and preceded the war threat crisis. The upsurge in the early months of 1993 is attributable to the fact that in the inflationary context of 1993 many car sales were stimulated by anticipation of higher prices to be charged for 1994 models. The depressed level of 1996 is caused by a strike and the upsurge in early 1997 by the settlement of the labour dispute.

The indices in Table B.10 are determined by dividing the values in Table B.8 (T × C) by the corresponding values in Table B.4(T). For example, the index of 100.7 for March 1984 is obtained by dividing the March 1984 value of 109.6 in Table B.8 by the value of 108.8 corresponding to that month in Table B.4, and then multiplying by 100.

Table B.9. Monthly Factory Sales of New Passenger Cars in Unteland—Percentage Variations Attributable to the Irregular Component

	1984	1985	1986	1987	1988	1989	1990	1991	1992	1993	1994	1995	1996	1997	1998
Jan.		91.7	92.7	90.0	75.4	100.0	95.7	88.8	107.7	111.5	108.6	110.0	105.4	105.9	109.1
Feb.		100.1	97.6	98.0	98.9	101.3	99.4	97.3	99.2	105.6	101.9	102.6	103.9	101.9	92.6
Mar.	102.3	99.6	109.5	105.0	97.7	98.5	93.3	104.1	108.8	95.1	93.4	89.6	97.4	100.0	99.5
Apr.	105.1	109.6	85.6	98.6	106.9	101.6	108.0	97.7	84.4	97.2	102.8	108.2	100.2	94.2	95.9
May	90.6	96.2	126.6	100.8	111.0	100.9	90.5	97.2	106.9	101.7	110.1	98.3	101.5	99.9	93.5
June	99.0	95.9	87.9	103.0	85.0	96.4	104.8	101.6	107.9	101.7	88.2	101.1	102.8	100.1	110.5
July	105.7	96.5	88.4	89.4	101.0	110.8	116.5	110.3	92.0	98.5	104.5	98.8	90.0	104.0	96.5
Aug.	101.2	103.9	107.8	107.7	99.8	86.0	83.8	92.1	108.0	103.1	104.3	93.8	96.9	98.8	98.4
Sept.	101.2	101.7	106.3	98.1	98.1	106.5	97.8	100.9	91.4	95.0	97.9	106.7	109.2	99.5	101.4
Oct.	96.9	99.7	94.7	97.9	107.3	106.5	97.0	102.8	101.2	106.1	99.9	105.7	90.1	90.4	99.8
Nov.	95.5	100.0	101.5	101.7	97.4	97.3	103.3	102.0	100.1	107.2	97.2	91.9	103.5	96.0	
Dec.	108.9	105.2	104.4	121.8	97.8	107.9	114.9	84.7	91.6	75.5	91.5	97.4	99.7	113.0	

Table B.10 Monthly Factory Sales of New Passenger Cars in Unteland—Percentage Variations Attributable to the Cyclical Component

	1984	1985	1986	1987	1988	1989	1990	1991	1992	1993	1994	1995	1996	1997	1998
Jan.		100.6	111.1	83.3	82.8	95.0	111.1	119.8	102.7	114.3	70.9	82.7	103.1	111.9	119.4
Feb.		103.0	110.2	81.8	80.1	97.2	109.4	115.8	104.8	113.9	72.8	85.9	104.1	110.4	114.5
Mar.	100.7	105.2	112.5	82.2	82.7	99.7	109.0	113.6	106.1	110.8	77.2	88.6	102.7	106.9	105.8
Apr.	100.0	106.0	115.2	84.0	85.8	100.9	110.8	115.6	108.6	105.4	78.1	89.0	99.6	103.9	102.6
May	100.6	105.3	109.3	83.4	85.4	103.0	116.6	117.8	108.5	101.5	79.3	91.3	95.7	102.9	103.3
June	101.4	104.6	106.1	83.1	85.1	103.4	117.7	118.2	109.5	99.1	81.1	92.2	92.2	103.5	103.6
July	102.8	105.9	102.2	84.5	83.6	102.5	115.1	116.9	109.8	95.5	80.4	93.4	91.7	103.7	105.6
Aug.	103.8	109.2	98.3	85.1	86.1	105.4	114.3	115.0	105.8	91.3	79.9	96.8	91.9	102.6	105.8
Sept.	101.7	112.1	98.0	87.5	90.1	107.6	111.9	110.3	104.9	87.9	79.5	98.3	94.6	101.9	105.6
Oct.	100.3	113.7	96.0	91.0	91.7	111.3	116.1	104.8	104.3	81.5	77.4	99.4	100.4	106.2	106.2
Nov.	99.2	112.6	90.3	89.6	93.3	115.1	121.1	102.3	106.9	75.9	77.9	100.9	104.8	113.9	
Dec.	98.6	110.5	85.2	85.4	94.1	113.5	120.7	101.8	112.7	73.6	80.9	101.8	109.4	118.7	

Forecasting Based on Knowledge of Each Component of Time Series

Table B.11 shows the original sales data (for 1998) *decomposed* into its four basic components: the trend, the cyclical, the seasonal and the irregular. Suppose you want to forecast for the year ahead (say 1999). A good starting point is to project the trend component by using the equation for one month

$$Y_{month} = 106.9928 + 0.5870 X_{month}$$

with $X = 181$ for January, 182 for February 1999, etc. (remember that the initial value of X is 1 for January 1984). The total trend values for 1999 is 2597.6. In the absence of any change in the consumer's habits, the seasonal factors are assumed to remain unchanged.

The irregular component has an erratic pattern, and its monthly values might deviate from the central value of 100 but will sum up to 1200 as the random positive and negative effects eliminate each other, and while the monthly forecasts might deviate from the actual sales, all the positive and negative deviations should compensate each other over the year. The yearly forecast, therefore, will still be consistent.

The only other important component that remains to be forecast is the cycle. This should be forecast in conjunction with economic indicators as well as the knowledge of probable events that might affect the year to be forecast. A formula cannot be produced for this—in fact, we expect 1999 to be a year rather like 1992, only slightly above trend, but with a tendency to fall away during the year. The forecast sales are 2640 units for 1999 broken down into each month as given in Table B.11.

Appraisal of Classical Decomposition Method Illustrated Above

The example given above is daunting in that so much data has been used, and there has been so much computing. It has also possibly been disappointing in two ways—the calculation of irregular factors has been ignored in the final forecast, and the cyclical component, about which the analyst has had to make guesses, turns out to be of crucial importance to the final forecast.

Three points need to be made in answer to these reproaches. First, although a long series was used in this case, the analyst should normally be able to cope with a smaller number of years. To get a good feel for the cycle (using this method) at least eight years should be employed, and the calculations are not too time-consuming in the era of portable business calculators.

Table B.11. Monthly Factory Sales of New Passenger Cars in Unteland

	Original series and its four components ($O=T×C×S×T$)—1998					Forecast of 1999 sales				
	Actual (units)	Trend (units)	Cycle (%)	Seasonal (%)	Irregular (%)	Trend (units)	Cycle (%)	Seasonal (%)	Irregular (%)	Forecast (units)
Jan.	206	206.2	119.4	76.646	109.1	213.2	110	76.646	100	179
Feb.	205	206.8	114.5	93.513	92.6	213.8	108	93.513	100	216
Mar.	306	207.4	105.8	140.094	99.5	214.4	106	140.094	100	318
Apr.	271	208.0	102.6	132.292	95.9	215.0	104	132.292	100	296
May	243	208.5	103.3	120.712	93.5	215.6	102	120.712	100	265
June	272	209.1	103.6	113.596	110.5	216.2	102	113.596	100	250
July	216	209.7	105.6	101.070	96.5	216.8	101	101.070	100	221
Aug.	153	210.3	105.8	69.830	98.4	217.4	100	69.830	100	152
Sept.	211	210.9	105.6	93.411	101.4	217.9	99	93.411	100	199
Oct.	231	211.4	106.2	103.018	99.8	218.5	97	103.018	100	218
Nov.	195	212.1	107.7	84.752	100.7	219.1	96	84.752	100	178
Dec.	155	212.7	109.4	71.066	93.7	219.7	95	71.066	100	148
Totals	2,664	2,513.1		1,200.000		2,597.6		1,200.000		2,640

Secondly, car sales *are* very cyclic, and there is no way round this fact. The analyst will spend a lot of time reading economic forecasts and looking at the performance of these calculated cyclical factors in previous upturn or downturn years in order to have a feel for which year the next year will most resemble.

Finally, calculating the irregular factors can be left out by the analyst without affecting the final forecast. All that is lost is a better understanding of the effects that strikes and other events can have on performance, and thus having a ready-prepared basis for forecast revision if something happens. Trend factors and seasonal factors will be used in a simpler forecasting model and the cyclical plus irregular components will be lumped together. It is not perfect, but it will work.

Appendix 1

Some Consultants not included in The International Research Directory of Market Research Organisations

Arthur D. Little
Berkeley Square House
London W1X 6EY
Tel. London 409–2277

McKinsey and Co. Ltd.
74 St. James's Street
London SW1A 1PS
Tel. London 839–8040

Booz, Allen and Hamilton
30 Charles II Street
London SW1Y 4AE
Tel. London 930–8144

Eurofinance
9 Avenue Hoche
Paris 8e
Tel. Paris 422–50448

This list is not intended to provide a complete catalogue of consultancy organisations.

Appendix 2

European Libraries and Sources of Information

AUSTRIA
Bundeswirtschaftskammer (Federal Economic Chamber)
Stubenring 12
1010 Vienna
Tel. Vienna 63.57.63

BELGIUM
Chambre de Commerce de Bruxelles
Avenue Louise 500
1050 Brussels
Tel. Brussels 648.50.02
(Ask for the 'Service Economique')

DENMARK
Handelsministeriet (Ministry for Trade)
Slotsholmsgade 12
1216 Copenhagen
Tel. Copenhagen 12.11.97

FRANCE
Chambre de Commerce de Paris
27 Avenue de Friedland
75382 Paris 8e
Tel. Paris 561.99.00

Many other French Chambers of Commerce possess 'Centres de Documentation et de Recherche' for the region which they serve, notably:

CCI Lyon
20 rue de la Bourse
69289 Lyon Cédex 1
Tel. Lyon 38.10.10

CCI Marseille
Palais de la Bourse
B.P. 826 bis
13222 Marseilles Cédex 1
Tel. Marseilles 91.91.51

CCI Strasbourg
10 place Gutenberg
67081 Strasbourg
Tel. Strasbourg 32.12.55

GERMANY
Deutscher Industrie-Handelstag
Adenauerallee 148
Postf. 1446
5300 Bonn
Tel. Bonn 10.41

GREECE	IOBE (Institute for Industrial Research) Mitzopoleus Street 32 Athens 1
IRELAND	Irish Export Board Merrion Hall Strand Road Dublin 4 Tel. Dublin 69.50.11
ITALY	Unione Italiana delle Camere di Commercio Piazza Sallustio 21 00187 Roma Tel. Rome 46.25.65/6/7
NETHERLANDS	Kamer van Koophandel en Fabrieken Koningin Wilhelminaplein 13 Amsterdam 1062 HH Tel. Amsterdam 17.28.82
SPAIN	Council of Spanish Official Chambers Claudio Coello 19 Madrid 1 Tel. Madrid 275.34.00
UNITED KINGDOM	London Chamber of Commerce 69 Cannon Street London EC4N 5AB Tel. London 248-4444 Statistics and Market Intelligence Library Export House Dept. of Trade and Industry 1 Victoria Street London S.W.1 Tel. London 215-5444/5 City Business Library 55 Basinghall Street London E.C.2 Tel. London 638-8215

OTHER SOURCES OF INFORMATION

GERMANY	*Verzeichnis Deutscher Informations—und Dokumentationsstellen* (Index of German Bodies for Information and Documentation), published by the Institut für Dokumentationswesen, Frankfurt, at the Reichert Press, Wiesbaden.

Verbände, Behördern, Organisationen der Wirtschaft (Trade Federations, Officials and other Economic Institutions), published by Hoppenstedt & Co., Darmstadt.

UNITED KINGDOM *Directory of European Associations, Directory of British Associations,* and *Statistics Europe* (lists addresses of Central Statistical Offices Europe-wide, libraries and other major organisations publishing statistics), all published by CBS Research Ltd., 154 High Street, Beckenham, Kent BR3 1EA. Tel. London 650-7745.

Appendix 3

Professional Marketing Research Institutions

The Industrial Marketing Research Association
11 Bird Street
Lichfield
Staffs IWS13 6PW
Tel. Lichfield 263448

The Market Research Society
15 Belgrave Square
London SW1X 9PF
Tel. London 235–4709

ESOMAR (European Society for Opinion and Marketing Research)
Central Secretariat
JJ Viottastraat 29
1071 JP
Amsterdam
Tel. Amsterdam 64–21–41

Appendix 4

Sample Size Calculator—Range of Error of Estimates of Population with One Characteristic at 95 per cent Confidence Limits (Percentage Plus or Minus)

Percentage affirmative	Sample sizes												
	25	50	100	200	300	400	500	800	1,000	2,000	5,000	25,000	50,000
98% or 2%	5.6	4.0	2.8	2.0	1.6	1.4	1.3	0.98	0.9	0.61	0.4	0.18	0.11
97% or 3%	6.8	4.9	3.4	2.4	2.0	1.7	1.5	1.2	1.1	0.75	0.49	0.22	0.14
96% or 4%	7.8	5.6	3.9	2.8	2.3	2.0	1.8	1.4	1.3	0.86	0.56	0.25	0.16
95% or 5%	8.7	6.2	4.4	3.1	2.5	2.2	2.0	1.5	1.4	0.96	0.62	0.27	0.17
94% or 6%	9.5	6.8	4.8	3.4	2.8	2.4	2.1	1.7	1.5	1.0	0.68	0.3	0.19
92% or 8%	10.8	7.7	5.4	3.8	3.1	2.7	2.4	1.9	1.7	1.2	0.77	0.34	0.22
90% or 10%	12.0	8.5	6.0	4.3	3.5	3.0	2.7	2.1	1.9	1.3	0.85	0.38	0.24
88% or 12%	13.0	9.2	6.5	4.6	3.8	3.3	2.9	2.3	2.1	1.4	0.92	0.41	0.26
85% or 15%	14.3	10.1	7.1	5.1	4.1	3.6	3.2	2.5	2.3	1.6	1.0	0.45	0.29
80% or 20%	16.0	11.4	8.0	5.7	4.6	4.0	3.6	2.8	2.5	1.8	1.1	0.5	0.32
75% or 25%	17.3	12.3	8.7	6.1	5.0	4.3	3.9	3.0	2.8	1.9	1.2	0.55	0.35
70% or 30%	18.3	13.0	9.2	6.5	5.3	4.6	4.1	3.2	2.9	2.0	1.3	0.58	0.37
65% or 35%	19.1	13.5	9.5	6.8	5.5	4.8	4.3	3.3	3.1	2.1	1.4	0.6	0.38
60% or 40%	19.6	13.9	9.8	7.0	5.7	4.9	4.4	3.4	3.1	2.2	1.4	0.62	0.39
55% or 45%	19.8	14.1	9.9	7.0	5.8	5.0	4.5	3.5	3.2	2.2	1.4	0.62	0.4
50%	20.0	14.2	10.0	7.1	5.8	5.0	4.5	3.5	3.2	2.2	1.4	0.63	0.4

SOURCE: Industrial Market Research Ltd, 'Sample Size Calculator'

Appendix 5.1

t Scores for Checking only an Upper or a Lower Limit

Level of Certainty

	90%	95%	99%	99.5%
1	3,078	6,314	31,821	63,657
2	1,886	2,920	6,965	9,925
3	1,638	2,353	4,541	5,841
4	1,533	2,132	3,747	4,604
5	1,476	2,015	3,365	4,032
6	1,440	1,943	3,143	3,707
7	1,415	1,895	2,998	3,499
8	1,397	1,860	2,896	3,355
9	1,383	1,833	2,821	3,250
10	1,372	1,812	2,764	3,169
11	1,363	1,796	2,718	3,106
12	1,356	1,782	2,681	3,055
13	1,350	1,771	2,650	3,012
14	1,345	1,761	2,624	2,977
15	1,341	1,753	2,602	2,947
16	1,337	1,746	2,583	2,921
17	1,333	1,740	2,567	2,898
18	1,330	1,734	2,552	2,878
19	1,328	1,729	2,539	2,861
20	1,325	1,725	2,528	2,845
21	1,323	1,721	2,518	2,831
22	1,321	1,717	2,508	2,819
23	1,319	1,714	2,500	2,807
24	1,318	1,711	2,492	2,797
25	1,316	1,708	2,485	2,787
26	1,315	1,706	2,479	2,779
27	1,314	1,703	2,473	2,771
28	1,313	1,701	2,467	2,763
29	1,311	1,699	2,462	2,756
30	1,310	1,697	2,457	2,750
40	1,303	1,684	2,423	2,704
60	1,296	1,671	2,390	2,660
120	1,289	1,658	2,358	2,617
∞	1,282	1,645	2,326	2,576

Appendix 5.2

t Scores for Checking Both Upper and Lower Limits

Level of Certainty

	80%	90%	95%	99%	99.9%
1	3,078	6,314	12,706	63,657	636,619
2	1,886	2,920	4,303	9,925	31,598
3	1,638	2,353	3,182	5,841	12,941
4	1,533	2,132	2,776	4,604	8,610
5	1,476	2,015	2,571	4,032	6,859
6	1,440	1,943	2,447	3,707	5,959
7	1,415	1,895	2,365	3,499	5,405
8	1,397	1,860	2,306	3,355	5,041
9	1,383	1,833	2,262	3,250	4,781
10	1,372	1,812	2,228	3,169	4,587
11	1,363	1,796	2,201	3,106	4,437
12	1,356	1,782	2,179	3,055	4,318
13	1,350	1,771	2,160	3,012	4,221
14	1,345	1,761	2,145	2,977	4,140
15	1,341	1,753	2,131	2,947	4,073
16	1,337	1,746	2,120	2,921	4,015
17	1,333	1,740	2,110	2,898	3,965
18	1,330	1,734	2,101	2,878	3,922
19	1,328	1,729	2,093	2,861	3,883
20	1,325	1,725	2,086	2,845	3,850
21	1,323	1,721	2,080	2,831	3,819
22	1,321	1,717	2,074	2,819	3,792
23	1,319	1,714	2,069	2,807	3,767
24	1,318	1,711	2,064	2,797	3,745
25	1,316	1,708	2,060	2,787	3,725
26	1,315	1,706	2,056	2,779	3,707
27	1,314	1,703	2,052	2,771	3,690
28	1,313	1,701	2,048	2,763	3,674
29	1,311	1,699	2,045	2,756	3,659
30	1,310	1,697	2,042	2,750	3,646
40	1,303	1,684	2,021	2,704	3,551
60	1,296	1,671	2,000	2,660	3,460
120	1,289	1,658	1,980	2,617	3,373
∞7	1,282	1,645	1,960	2,576	3,291

By permission of Texas Instruments

Appendix 6

The Normal Distribution Tables

			Area of the Standard Normal Distribution				
z	A(z)	z	A(z)	z	A(z)	z	A(z)
0.00	0.00000	0.50	0.19146	1.00	0.34134	1.50	0.43319
0.01	0.00399	0.51	0.19497	1.01	0.34375	1.51	0.43448
0.02	0.00798	0.52	0.19847	1.02	0.34614	1.52	0.43574
0.03	0.01197	0.53	0.20194	1.03	0.34849	1.53	0.43699
0.04	0.01595	0.54	0.20540	1.04	0.35083	1.54	0.43822
0.05	0.01994	0.55	0.20884	1.05	0.35314	1.55	0.43943
0.06	0.02392	0.56	0.21226	1.06	0.35543	1.56	0.44062
0.07	0.02790	0.57	0.21566	1.07	0.35769	1.57	0.44179
0.08	0.03188	0.58	0.21904	1.08	0.35993	1.58	0.44295
0.09	0.03586	0.59	0.22240	1.09	0.36214	1.59	0.44408
0.10	0.03983	0.60	0.22575	1.10	0.36433	1.60	0.44520
0.11	0.04380	0.61	0.22907	1.11	0.36650	1.61	0.44630
0.12	0.04776	0.62	0.23237	1.12	0.36864	1.62	0.44738
0.13	0.05172	0.63	0.23565	1.13	0.37076	1.63	0.44845
0.14	0.05567	0.64	0.23891	1.14	0.37286	1.64	0.44950
0.15	0.05962	0.65	0.24215	1.15	0.37493	1.65	0.45053
0.16	0.06356	0.66	0.24537	1.16	0.37698	1.66	0.45154
0.17	0.06750	0.67	0.24857	1.17	0.37900	1.67	0.45254
0.18	0.07142	0.68	0.25175	1.18	0.38100	1.68	0.45352
0.19	0.07535	0.69	0.25490	1.19	0.38298	1.69	0.45449
0.20	0.07926	0.70	0.25804	1.20	0.38493	1.70	0.45543
0.21	0.08317	0.71	0.26115	1.21	0.38686	1.71	0.45637
0.22	0.08706	0.72	0.26424	1.22	0.38877	1.72	0.45728
0.23	0.09095	0.73	0.26730	1.23	0.39065	1.73	0.45818
0.24	0.09483	0.74	0.27035	1.24	0.39251	1.74	0.45907
0.25	0.09871	0.75	0.27337	1.25	0.39435	1.75	0.45994
0.26	0.10257	0.76	0.27637	1.26	0.39617	1.76	0.46080
0.27	0.10642	0.77	0.27935	1.27	0.39796	1.77	0.46164
0.28	0.11026	0.78	0.28230	1.28	0.39973	1.78	0.46246
0.29	0.11409	0.79	0.28524	1.29	0.40147	1.79	0.46327
0.30	0.11791	0.80	0.28814	1.30	0.40320	1.80	0.46407
0.31	0.12172	0.81	0.29103	1.31	0.40490	1.81	0.46485
0.32	0.12552	0.82	0.29389	1.32	0.40658	1.82	0.46562
0.33	0.12930	0.83	0.29673	1.33	0.40824	1.83	0.46638
0.34	0.13307	0.84	0.29955	1.34	0.40988	1.84	0.46712
0.35	0.13683	0.85	0.30234	1.35	0.41149	1.85	0.46784
0.36	0.14058	0.86	0.30511	1.36	0.41309	1.86	0.46856
0.37	0.14431	0.87	0.30785	1.37	0.41466	1.87	0.46926
0.38	0.14803	0.88	0.31057	1.38	0.41621	1.88	0.46995
0.39	0.15173	0.89	0.31327	1.39	0.41774	1.89	0.47062
0.40	0.15542	0.90	0.31594	1.40	0.41924	1.90	0.47128
0.41	0.15910	0.91	0.31859	1.41	0.42073	1.91	0.47193
0.42	0.16276	0.92	0.32121	1.42	0.42220	1.92	0.47257
0.43	0.16640	0.93	0.32381	1.43	0.42364	1.93	0.47320
0.44	0.17003	0.94	0.32639	1.44	0.42507	1.94	0.47381
0.45	0.17364	0.95	0.32894	1.45	0.42647	1.95	0.47441
0.46	0.17724	0.96	0.33147	1.46	0.42785	1.96	0.47500
0.47	0.18082	0.97	0.33398	1.47	0.42922	1.97	0.47558
0.48	0.18439	0.98	0.33646	1.48	0.43056	1.98	0.47615
0.49	0.18793	0.99	0.33891	1.49	0.43189	1.99	0.47670

		Area of the Standard Normal Distribution					
z	A(z)	z	A(z)	z	A(z)	z	A(z)
2.00	0.47725	2.50	0.49379	3.00	0.49865	3.50	0.49977
2.01	0.47778	2.51	0.49396	3.01	0.49869	3.51	0.49978
2.02	0.47831	2.52	0.49413	3.02	0.49874	3.52	0.49978
2.03	0.47882	2.53	0.49430	3.03	0.49878	3.53	0.49979
2.04	0.47932	2.54	0.49446	3.04	0.49882	3.54	0.49980
2.05	0.47982	2.55	0.49461	3.05	0.49886	3.55	0.49981
2.06	0.48030	2.56	0.49477	3.06	0.49889	3.56	0.49981
2.07	0.48077	2.57	0.49492	3.07	0.49893	3.57	0.49982
2.08	0.48124	2.58	0.49506	3.08	0.49896	3.58	0.49983
2.09	0.48169	2.59	0.49520	3.09	0.49900	3.59	0.49983
2.10	0.48214	2.60	0.49534	3.10	0.49903	3.60	0.49984
2.11	0.48257	2.61	0.49547	3.11	0.49906	3.61	0.49985
2.12	0.48300	2.62	0.49560	3.12	0.49910	3.62	0.49985
2.13	0.48341	2.63	0.49573	3.13	0.49913	3.63	0.49986
2.14	0.48382	2.64	0.49585	3.14	0.49916	3.64	0.49986
2.15	0.48422	2.65	0.49598	3.15	0.49918	3.65	0.49987
2.16	0.48461	2.66	0.49609	3.16	0.49921	3.66	0.49987
2.17	0.48500	2.67	0.49621	3.17	0.49924	3.67	0.49988
2.18	0.48537	2.68	0.49632	3.18	0.49926	3.68	0.49988
2.19	0.48574	2.69	0.49643	3.19	0.49929	3.69	0.49989
2.20	0.48610	2.70	0.49653	3.20	0.49931	3.70	0.49989
2.21	0.48645	2.71	0.49664	3.21	0.49934	3.71	0.49990
2.22	0.48679	2.72	0.49674	3.22	0.49936	3.72	0.49990
2.23	0.48713	2.73	0.49683	3.23	0.49938	3.73	0.49990
2.24	0.48745	2.74	0.49693	3.24	0.49940	3.74	0.49991
2.25	0.48778	2.75	0.49702	3.25	0.49942	3.75	0.49991
2.26	0.48809	2.76	0.49711	3.26	0.49944	3.76	0.49992
2.27	0.48840	2.77	0.49720	3.27	0.49946	3.77	0.49992
2.28	0.48870	2.78	0.49728	3.28	0.49948	3.78	0.49992
2.29	0.48899	2.79	0.49736	3.29	0.49950	3.79	0.49992
2.30	0.48928	2.80	0.49744	3.30	0.49952	3.80	0.49993
2.31	0.48956	2.81	0.49752	3.31	0.49953	3.81	0.49993
2.32	0.48983	2.82	0.49760	3.32	0.49955	3.82	0.49993
2.33	0.49010	2.83	0.49767	3.33	0.49957	3.83	0.49994
2.34	0.49036	2.84	0.49774	3.34	0.49958	3.84	0.49994
2.35	0.49061	2.85	0.49781	3.35	0.49960	3.85	0.49994
2.36	0.49086	2.86	0.49788	3.36	0.49961	3.86	0.49994
2.37	0.49111	2.87	0.49795	3.37	0.49962	3.87	0.49995
2.38	0.49134	2.88	0.49801	3.38	0.49964	3.88	0.49995
2.39	0.49158	2.89	0.49807	3.39	0.49965	3.89	0.49995
2.40	0.49180	2.90	0.49813	3.40	0.49966	3.90	0.49995
2.41	0.49202	2.91	0.49819	3.41	0.49968	3.91	0.49995
2.42	0.49224	2.92	0.49825	3.42	0.49969	3.92	0.49996
2.43	0.49245	2.93	0.49831	3.43	0.49970	3.93	0.49996
2.44	0.49266	2.94	0.49836	3.44	0.49971	3.94	0.49996
2.45	0.49286	2.95	0.49841	3.45	0.49972	3.95	0.49996
2.46	0.49305	2.96	0.49846	3.46	0.49973	3.96	0.49996
2.47	0.49324	2.97	0.49851	3.47	0.49974	3.97	0.49996
2.48	0.49343	2.98	0.49856	3.48	0.49975	3.98	0.49997
2.49	0.49361	2.99	0.49861	3.49	0.49976	3.99	0.49997
						4.00	0.49997

Appendix 7

Bross Plan B Sequential Analysis Chart

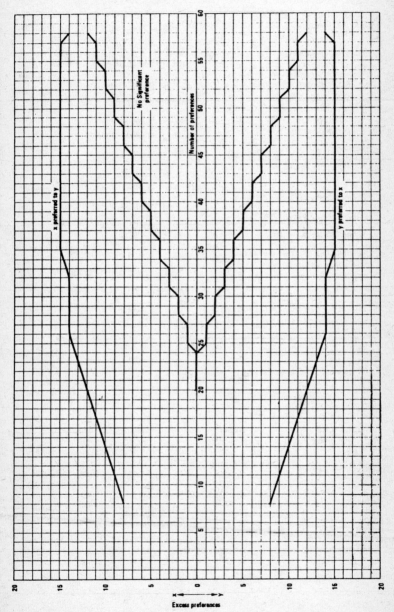

Appendix 8

Simple Checklist for Industrial Interviewing

Demand factors	*Supply factors*

Demand factors

1. What are you buying?

   (*a*) Technical characteristics, size of order, frequency, specification.
   (*b*) Competing products, trends in competition with regard to the product.

2. Are there any factors which will change what you buy?

   (*a*) Government standards.
   (*b*) Other changes.

3. How much are you buying?

4. What affects growth?

5. What is happening and will happen in the market in which you compete, for which our product is a raw material/component?

6. Where do you buy your product?

(*a*) Direct.
(*b*) From a wholesaler.
(*c*) By some other route?

7. Will you continue to do so?

Supply factors

1. Will the way that the product reaches the market change in the years ahead?

2. Who are the major suppliers?

3. What is their share of

(*a*) your orders?
(*b*) the market in total?

4. How do they compete?

(*a*) Special characteristics.
(*b*) Normal parameters of competition:

   (*i*) price,
   (*ii*) quality,
   (*iii*) delivery,
   (*iv*) advertising,
   (*v*) sales representatives

5. What are the suppliers like?

(*a*) Innovative, growing, declining.
(*b*) Aggressive, cheap, high quality, other.

Personal

Business cards	Traveller's cheques	Driving licence
Hotel list, bookings	Travel tickets	Pocket calculator
Contact list	Timetables	Questionnaires/aides-
Cheque book	Car hire data	memoire
Passport	Road maps	Writing paper
Credit cards	Dictionaries	

Appendix 9

Recommended Reading

Armstrong, J. Scott, *Long Range Forecasting,* Wiley Interscience, New York, 1978.

Belson, William A. *The Design and Understanding of Survey Questions,* Gower, Aldershot, 1981.

Foxall, G. R. *Consumer Behaviour: A Practical Guide,* Croom Helm, London, 1984.

Harris, Paul, 'The Effect of Clustering on Costs and Sampling Errors of Random Samples'. *Journal of the Market Research Society, July 1977.*

Kotler, Philip, *Marketing Management—Analysis, Planning and Control,* Prentice-Hall International, Englewood Cliffs, 1984.

Maclean, Ian, *Handbook of Industrial Marketing and Research,* Duncan Publishing, London, 1985.

McGowan, K. L. *Marketing Research—Text and Cases,* Winthrop Publishers Inc., Boston, 1979.

McIntosh, Andrew R. 'Improving the Efficiency of Sample Surveys in Industrial Markets', *Journal of the Market Research Society,* October 1975.

Montagnon, P. *Foundations of Statistics—A Survey for Managers*, Stanley Thornes, 1980.

Oppenheim, A. N. *Questionnaire Design and Attitude Measurement,* Heinemann Educational Books, London, 1966.

Pickering, J. F. and Isherwood, B. C. 'Purchase Probabilities and Consumer Durable Buying Behaviour', *Journal of the Market Research Society*, July, 1974.

Worcester R. and Downham J. S. *Consumer Market Research Handbook* (3rd Edition) North-Holland Elsevier, 1986.

Worcester R. M. and Burns T. R. A Statistical Examination of the Relative Precision of Verbal Scales, *Journal of the Market Research Society,* July 1975.

Wilmshurst, John, *The Fundamentals and Practice of Marketing,* Heinemann, London, 1984.

Wilson, R. M. S. *Management Controls and Marketing Planning,* Heinemann, London, 1982.

Index

Advertising, 9–11, 124, 139
Agency presentation exercise, 219
Agency research, 213–19, 234–7
Aide-memoires, 94–5
Analysis
  actionable, 81, 197–211, 225
  comparative product, 12
  defined, 2
  sheet, 100
Analyst, 211, 239
Automotive forecasting, 187, 250–68
Awareness, 9–11, 12, 110–11, 124

Box-Jenkins, 181
Brand awareness, 110–11, 124
Brevity, needed in reports, 205–8
British Overseas Trade Board, 55
Bross chart, 75–6, 279
Buyer's inertia, 64
Buying intentions, 120–2

Certainty needed, 63–4, 81
Competition, 11–12, 37, 56, 229
Competitive products, 7, 19, 25–6,
  29, 229
Computerised forecast monitoring,
  181
Confidence limits, 71, 72, 79–80, 82
Construction, 50–1
Consultants, to find, 215, 269
Consumer
  questionnaire, 112–20
  research, 107–25
Consumption statistics, 52
Correlation analysis, 139, 140
Cost of research, 60, 215
Customer, 6–7
  needs, 4, 15–19, 24–6
  satisfaction, 7–8
Cyclical effects on sales, 47–50, 139
Cycle, see *Trend cycle*

Data-banks, 55
Deflated statistics, 51
Desk research, 37, 61, 127–30; see
  also *Statistics*
Discussions, 112–13, 124
Distribution, 11, 202, 208

Eighty-twenty rule, 73, 82
End-user research, 229–31; see also
  Consumer
Entrepreneur, 11, 81, 239
Exports
  espirit de conquete, 131
  success, 131, 132
  market research, 127–37
  need for language skills, 131
Extrapolation in forecasting, 140–53

Field research, 34, 55–61
  in export markets, 133–5
FMCG, 64, 124
Forecasting, 32–3
  and seasonal adjustment, 159–65
  by classical decomposition, 250–
    68
  by trend-line, 140–3
  extrapolation, 140–53
  for a new product, 14–29, 111–22
  methods employed in business,
    178–81
  monitoring a forecast, 162–6,
    188–94
  quantitative techniques, 138–66
  statistical methods generally,
    180–1
  using exponential trend curve,
    144–8
  using growth rates, 143–53
  using market share, 183–8
  using models, 181

Geneen, 206
Gompertz curve, 151
Gross domestic product, 47–50
Gross national product, 47–50
Groups, see *Discussions*
Growth rates, 53

Hands-on product, 36–41, 43–5
Heald, Gordon, 120
Heller, Joseph, 225

Image study, 219
IMRA, 273
Indicators, 128–30
Industrial Market Research Association, 273
Industrial marketing research
  check-list, 280
  generally, 84–106, 231
  organising fieldwork, 92–4
Inertia, 15, 33, 81
Information
  actionable, 81
Intentions to buy, 120–2
International market research, 55
Interviewees, 84–8
Interviewing, 94–100
Interviews
  getting, 88–92
  postal, 102–6
  telephone, 101–2
  unstructured, 95–100, 106

Language, need for knowledge in export research, 131
Leading market, 5
Least-squares calculation, 142–3
Libraries, 270–2
Literature search, 54–5
Logarithmic transformation, 143–5

Managing director's wife's syndrome, 204
Market
  available, 12
  leading, 5
  non-served, 12
  penetration, see *Penetration*
  saturation see *Saturation*
  segmentation, see *Segmentation*
  served, 12
  ultimate, 23, 28
  window, 22, 30

Market research agencies, 10, 213–19
  to find, 215, 269, 273
Market research agency exercise, 219–24
Market Research Professional Associations, UK, 273
Market Research Society, 273
Market share, 183–8
  dynamism, 195
  inertia, 195
  platform, 195
Marketing
  analysis, 2
  defined, 1, 4–12
  hypothesis, 37
  myopia, 229
  research, see *Research; Industrial marketing research*
  strategy, 225–39
Maslow, 16
Mathematical symbols explained, 252
Mature markets, 165
Merchandising, 10, 12
Moving averages, 153–9, 166
MRS, 273
Multi-client surveys, 218–19

Needs, 4, 15–19, 24–6
Net acquisition of financial assets, 53
New products, 14–29, 111–22
Normal distribution, 72, 277–8

Omnibus survey, 76

Packaging, 226–38
Paralysis by analysis, 63
Park, 6, 142, 166, 176
Partial census, 74
Penetration, 8, 22–3, 30, 148–53, 166
  typical household, 177
Permut, 225
Personal computer, 17, 20–1
Postal questionnaires, 102–5
Presentations, 197–205
Price, 8–9, 139
  competition, 8
  evolution, 23
  threshold, 9, 12, 21–2, 27–8, 30

Product
  familiarisation, 36–41, 43–5
  life-cycle, 175–6
  mature, 165
  mix, 8, 12
  strategy, 238
Products, see *Competitive products; Similar products*
Profit, 10–12
Promotion, 9, 12, 139
Prompt card, 124
Proposal, 37–40; see also *Terms of reference*
Purchasing intentions, 120–2

Questionnaires
  consumer, 112–20
  design of, 112–20
  postal, 102–6
  telephone, 67–8, 94–6
  testing, 112–20, 124
Quick-and-cheap, 60, 61

Randomness, 82
Reading list, 281
Recommendations, need for, 211
Reports, how to write, 205–11
Research
  briefing, 35–7
  consumer, 107–25
  continuous, 108–11
  desk, 37, 61, 127–30
  export, 127–37
  industrial, see *Industrial marketing research*
  proposal, 37–40
Retail outlets, 122–3

Sales forecasts, 28–9; see also *Forecasting*
Sales persons as analysts and researchers, 132–3
Sample
  method used in deciding size, 80–1
  size calculator, 274
  size required, 64–75
Sampling, 64–79
  cluster, 77
  for consumer goods, 76–7
  for industrial goods, 77, 78, 84–7
  list, 76
  of segments, 78–9
  problems of grossing up, 39
  quota, 77
  stratified random, 77
Saturation, 24
Seasonal adjustment, 159–65, 241–9
Seasonality, 139, 159, 166, 171
Sectors, 5–6
Segmentation, 5–6, 12
Semi-log paper, 145
Sequential analysis, 279
Service industry statistics, 51
Shoe salesman story, 66
Significance, 110–11
Similar products, 20–1, 26, 30
Speak and Spell, 32
Standard deviation, 69, 72, 82
Statistics
  construction, 50
  deflated, 51, 61
  industrial investment, 50
  industry, 51
  providing market background, 45–54
  retail, 52
  service industry, 51
Straight-line projection, 140–3
Strategy, 225–39
Summary, need for in actionable reports, 206–7
Symbols, mathematical, explained, 252

Tables, 6
Telephone, 17–19, 22
  demand forecast, 140–3
  questionnaire, 67–8
  in research, 88–92, 101–2
Televisions, colour, forecasting for, 148–55
Terms of reference, 37–41, 231
Test market, 5
Threshold price, 9, 12, 21–2, 27–8, 30
Time-series analysis, 170–5, 250–68
Trend-cycle, 171–5, 250–7
t-value, 69–72, 275–6

Videotex, 5, 14, 24–9

Walpole, Colin, 219
Wilmshurst, John, 1
Work in person-hours, 60

X11 seasonal adjustment, 139

Z-charts, 188–95